ARE YOU READY FOR LOVE?

—Do you want an exciting sex life?
—Do you want to make love more frequently?
—Are you prepared to show your lover what you want?
—Is there any limit to what you would do in bed?
—Is there something you've always wanted to do, but have been embarrassed to reveal to your lover?

If you've answered "yes" to any of these questions, this is the book you've been waiting for . . .

HOW TO DRIVE YOUR MAN EVEN *WILDER* IN BED

HOW TO DRIVE YOUR MAN EVEN *WILDER* IN BED

Graham Masterton

A SIGNET BOOK

SIGNET
Published by the Penguin Group
Penguin Books USA Inc., 375 Hudson Street,
New York, New York 10014, U.S.A.
Penguin Books Ltd, 27 Wrights Lane,
London W8 5TZ, England
Penguin Books Australia Ltd, Ringwood,
Victoria, Australia
Penguin Books Canada Ltd, 10 Alcorn Avenue,
Toronto, Ontario, Canada M4V 3B2
Penguin Books (N.Z.) Ltd, 182–190 Wairau Road,
Auckland 10, New Zealand

Penguin Books Ltd, Registered Offices:
Harmondsworth, Middlesex, England

First published by Signet, an imprint of Dutton Signet,
a division of Penguin Books USA Inc.

First Printing, June, 1995
10 9 8 7 6 5 4 3 2 1

Portions of this book first appeared in *Complete Woman* and *Woman's Own*.

Contents

Prologue

10 Things You Should Ask Yourself Before You Go to Bed Tonight

One: Do I want a more exciting sex life?
Two: Do I want to make love more frequently?
Three: Do I want to make love in different ways, in different positions?
Four: Am I prepared to show my lover what I want?
Five: Am I prepared to be bolder, more adventurous, and show myself off?
Six: Is there any limit to what I would do in bed?
Seven: Is there something I've always wanted to do, but I've been embarrassed to tell my lover about?
Eight: Is there any way in which I can make myself more sexually attractive tonight?
Nine: Is there anything I can do to turn my lover on tonight? And tomorrow night? And the night after?
Ten: How can I be even wilder in bed?

ONE

Women Who Say "Yes!"

Just before I started my research for this book, I received in the mail a copy of my very first "how-to" book—*How to Drive Your Man Wild in Bed.* Along with it came a letter on pink, very feminine notepaper—a letter from Annette, a 47 year-old homemaker from Seattle, Washington. Annette said, "Please will you sign this book for my daughter Lorraine, who is 22 and just about to get married. I first read this book 20 years ago, and it opened my eyes to a whole new world of sexual excitement that, up until then, I had never even realized existed. It's partly thanks to you that Lorraine was conceived at all!

"You taught me to be proud of myself and my body, and to explore my sexual potential to the full. I have had a wonderful, wonderful sex life, doing everything and anything I wanted, and enjoying it without feeling frightened or guilty. For instance my husband Rick says that he would never leave me because he could never find another woman who could give him oral sex the way I do!

"I want Lorraine to have the same advantage in life, and to enjoy sex without ever thinking that 'nice girls aren't really supposed to have a great time in bed.'"

Of course it's always a pleasure to receive letters of

thanks. But when I sent back Annette's signed copy, it occurred to me that the kind of sexual fulfillment that her daughter Lorraine will be able to enjoy will be greatly enhanced by the dramatic social changes that have taken place in the past two decades. Not the least of these social changes is the fact that her mother can actually give her a book like *How to Drive Your Man Wild in Bed* without any embarrassment.

These days, sex is freely and openly discussed in newspapers, in women's magazines, and even on prime-time television. Even before she first becomes involved in any kind of intimate relationship with a man, the woman of today is far more knowledgeable about sex than her sister of 20 years ago. She knows more about her body, she knows more about her sexual responses. She is familiar with most of the various methods of contraception (who couldn't be, with Dr. Ruth shouting "Wear a condom!" from the rooftops!).

Usually, she is aware of sexual variations such as oral and anal sex. She's heard of vibrators, even if she doesn't actually own one. She knows about self-pleasuring, which is what I prefer to call masturbation these days, and she knows about erotic fantasies—both her own, and those of the men she is likely to meet.

She knows about the importance of orgasms, but she also knows that making love isn't a contest to see who can reach a climax first.

More than anything else, she is conscious that she can take control of her own sex life to a remarkable degree—so that *she* can enjoy just as much physical and emotional pleasure as her partner—so that *she* can be fully satisfied too.

Up until comparatively recently, men expected to set the pace, style, timing, and frequency of lovemaking—and women expected them to do it, too. But those days are gone—whether some men are aware of it or not! If a woman is skillful, knowledgeable, and daring, she has the power not only to initiate exciting new sexual encounters, but to transform a humdrum marriage or long-term liaison so that every night is both sexually thrilling and sexually fulfilling.

Today's woman knows what she wants out of her sex

life and is prepared to say "*Yes*—I want it, and I don't see any reason why I shouldn't have it." She can have sex when she wants, how she wants, for as long as she wants it, and as often as she wants it.

This doesn't make her any less of a woman. Just because she knows what she expects out of her relationships, and just because she's capable of achieving it, she hasn't forfeited any of her femininity. Quite the opposite, in fact—because the way in which she can achieve a more exciting sex life is by enhancing her femininity and enhancing her lover's masculinity.

Being more of a woman and helping your man to be more of a man; these are the two keys that open the door to really pleasurable sex, and this book is intended to show you how you can have both of them, *even if your partner is reluctant to cooperate.*

First off, you shouldn't be afraid in any way of taking control of your sex life. I talked to several groups of women about the idea that they should exert a greater influence over their lovemaking. Many of them said, "That's all very well . . . but part of the pleasure I get out of sex is that I *like* my lover to dominate me—it turns me on to be dominated in bed. I simply don't *want* to have more control. I like to be *taken*."

Tricia, a 28-year-old accountant from Boston, Massachusetts, said, "What really excites me is when Bryan comes home from work, picks me up, carries me into the bedroom, pushes me facedown on the bed, lifts up my skirt, pulls my panties to one side, climbs on top of me, and fucks me real hard. He doesn't hurt me. He's strong rather than rough. But it makes me feel helpless and I have to admit that it excites me, feeling helpless. I think you'll find that a whole lot of women are excited by it."

Lilian, a 31-year-old hairstylist from Baltimore, Maryland, said, "Whenever we have sex, it's always my husband who initiates it, very rarely me, if ever. Sometimes I wake up in the morning and he's licking me between my legs. I really enjoy that. I'll be having a dream and suddenly this beautiful sexy feeling comes into it, and I'll open by eyes and there he is, licking my clitoris. There are times when I feel like making love when he obviously doesn't, but I don't think I could initiate anything. He likes to feel that he's in charge . . . and *I* like to feel that he's in charge, too . . . even though there are times when I feel frustrated."

Kirsty, a 25-year-old public relations assistant from Pittsburgh, Pennsylvania, said, "I wouldn't be happy having a sexual relationship with a guy who wasn't obviously the dominant partner. I'm not exactly talking about a me-Tarzan you-Jane situation, but I wouldn't like to feel that I was always the one who was setting the sexual agenda. I want a man who really is a man. That's what makes a man sexy."

Too often, however, there is another side to the sexual personality of "men who are really men." At best, they can be well-meaning but simply lacking in sexual knowledge, especially about the physical and emotional needs of women. This is the single most common problem of all, and in some ways the most difficult to deal with—because how *do* you say to your handsome, sexy, and well-intentioned lover that his lovemaking leaves so much to be desired?

You don't want to hurt his feelings, after all. You may be frightened of breaking up your relationship. Yet if you have to suffer just one more unsatisfying night in which he fails again to give you the pleasure and fulfillment you really need—that deep-down, all-over stimulation, that orgasm that could bring you so close together and release all of that pent-up sexual tension in you—well, you think you'll probably scream.

But you don't scream because you have so much to lose if you do. Literally millions of women tolerate unsatisfactory sex lives for years and years because they don't want to lose their home and their security and the man they still love, and yet they can't find a way to tell him, "Darling . . . you're not particularly good in bed."

If this is your problem, then I believe this book will show you how you can change your love life forever, *without risking your relationship* in any way.

The problem for the well-meaning-but-not-very-knowledgeable lover is that there are very few ways in which he can acquire the information he needs (apart from reading books like this). And the worst part of it is that he will never read a book like this, because he isn't aware that anything's wrong.

As far as *he's* concerned, his occasional exhibitions of staglike rutting are all that any woman could possibly want.

Here's Shelagh, 31, an attractive brunette from San Diego, California: "I've been married to Steve for six years and he's the best husband that any woman could ask for. He provides for everything, he's always buying me gifts, and we go out dancing and dining two or three times a month. He's good-looking, he's funny, he's terrific. But he never satisfies me in bed. He's very *animal*, for sure. But when he makes love, he's so fierce and quick that it's all finished before I'm even in the mood for it. For instance, I was cooking supper for us last week, and he came into the kitchen and he started nuzzling me. I don't mind that . . . I liked it. But then, when I was washing the lettuce over the sink, he lifted up my skirt at the back, and pulled my panties halfway down my thighs, and rammed himself into me. He's very big, and he was very hard, and it was quite exciting. But then he grunted a lot, and came, and that was it—all over. I was standing over the sink with a lettuce in my hand and my panties filled with sperm, and can you imagine what I felt like? I felt like nothing. I felt like this big—" indicating a tiny space between finger and thumb.

This is Katya, 29, a grade-school teacher from Hartford, Connecticut: "John is very loving and attentive, there's no question about it. But he does believe that men are men and women are women . . . in other words, I ought to know my place. He makes love to me every Saturday morning before seven o'clock and then he gets up and takes a shower. Every Saturday, same time, like a ritual, like a habit, like something he has to do before he goes to play golf. Like, What do you do, Saturdays, John?' 'Well, I have sex with my wife, I understand that wives have to have sex on a regular weekly basis, then I play golf, then I go drink with my friends.'

"I'm quite sure that John genuinely believes that he's a good lover, and that he gives me all the sexual satisfaction I need. He doesn't seem to understand that I feel like making love a whole lot more often than once a week, when there's a window in his diary, and that I'm *aching* for some spontaneity."

This is a typical example of a well-intentioned but fundamentally ignorant husband. He loves his wife, there's no doubt about it. He would probably die for her. But, sexually, he doesn't understand her at all—neither her physical appetite nor her emotional needs.

I had the opportunity to talk with John about Katya, and here's what he said: "I adore Katya and we're very happy together. In fact I would say that we have an exceptional marriage, the kind of marriage that has depth and substance and which is really going to last. Katya is a very understanding and appreciative person—and, yes, I think she's very sexy. We have sex regularly every week, at least once, sometimes more often. It's very satisfying sex, yes. I don't know about spontaneous. What do you mean by spontaneous? You don't play golf spontaneously, you make time for it, just like you make time for sex . . . it's a routine part of any relationship, a very pleasurable routine, for sure, but I think that Katya likes it that way. It's something that she can look forward to."

Again and again, women have told me about sexual relationships that aren't exactly disastrous, *but.* They're routine, they're unexciting, they never take wings, not even once. But these women still love their husbands or lovers, they're afraid of losing their security, and quite often there are children involved, too, so they're not at all free to pack their bag and go out looking for that perfect lover. And, who knows, even that perfect lover could turn out, in time to be just as dull in bed as their previous lovers were.

Subsequently, they elect to stay where they are, and live out a life that never brings them the sexual ecstasy which even moderately good lovemaking could bring them, and which they *deserve.*

Does that sound like you? If it does, read on. Because there *is* hope. You, too, can have an exciting time in bed, without having to give up everything and search for another partner. Even the *worst* sexual relationship can be transformed within a very short space of time . . .

provided you're ready to be wilder than you ever were before.

This is Anne-Marie, a 32-year-old physics graduate from Houston, Texas: "Chet and I had been married for three years before I took stock of myself and realized how discontented I was. Chet's a very good man, as men go, he never cheated on me, not so far as I know, and although we had a spat from time to time the same way that every couple does, he never once laid a finger on me or swore at me. The plain trouble was that he never satisfied me in bed. He woke up every morning at six o'clock so that he could jog before work, then he worked all day, then he went to the gym almost every evening, and when he didn't go to the gym he came home and fell asleep in front of the TV.

"We went through weeks and weeks without making love at all. I was beginning to believe that Chet had fallen out of love with me; that he was coasting through our marriage until he could find somebody else. When we did make love, he always did it in total silence, except for a grunt or two, and I never knew whether he liked it or not. He never tried oral sex on me, he never tried anything. I don't like anal sex very much, I usually find it painful, but I wouldn't have minded *anything* so long as he showed me he loved me.

"I was so frustrated that I regularly masturbated, almost every day. At first I didn't use anything else except my finger, but then I confessed what I was doing to a close girlfriend of mine, Lydia, and she recommended a vibrator. She said that men had to have their natural instincts aroused, now and again, and that what *she* always did was openly use a vibrator in front of her husband. He couldn't be jealous—because who could be jealous of a piece of plastic and two batteries?

"As it turned out, I bought a double vibrator, which has twin penises . . . one really thick one and one thinner one, so that you can masturbate yourself vaginally and anally both at the same time. It was over a week before I first dared to use it, and then I waited until Chet was at the gym. I knelt down in front of my full-length dressing-room mirror, and pulled up my skirt.

"I smothered the vibrator with lubricating jelly, so that

it was all shiny and slippery, and then I switched it on. I was very cautious with it to begin with, and I remember that my hand was shaking. I smoothed the head of the big penis all around my public hair and my pussy lips, and I really liked the feeling of that. It was so—I don't know, *buzzy*. It made all my nerve ends tingle, and I started to get very juicy and wet.

"I gently pressed the head of it against my clitoris, and then rubbed it slowly up and down, and that was unbelievable. I had never had a sensation like that in my whole life. I always had an orgasm then and there, and the juice was literally dripping out of my pussy and down the side of my thigh. I had never felt so sexually excited in my life. My cheeks were flushed, I was panting, and you would have thought that I had been jogging for about ten miles.

"I was becoming so aroused that I slid my hand inside my blouse and into my bra, and started to twist and tug my nipple.

"I leaned back a little, and placed the head of the large penis right up against my pussy, in between my lips. It was bright pink, but it looked exactly like a real penis, only bigger, with a huge head and bulging veins. It was a pity there was no man attached to it!

"Next I had to take my hand out of my bra, and reach behind me so that I could spread my bottom cheeks. I had never inserted anything into my bottom before, and I was a bit tense about it. But I slipped my finger into my bottom first so that it was really lubricated and slippery, and the thinner penis was so much thinner than a real penis that it slid in easily. I was able to push the vibrator right up inside me, as far as it would go, so that I had two plastic penises buzzing away, both at once, and the sensation was indescribable. As I say, I had never had anything up inside my bottom before, and I had never realized how exciting it could feel. I thought, what have I been missing?

"I stretched open my pussy lips with my fingers so that I could see the vibrator right up inside me, and I could stroke my clitoris, too. I like a strong, slow, downward stroking, that really turns me on. There was a moment when I hardly knew who I was . . . then I had the most earth-shattering orgasm I've ever had in my life. I was kneeling forward with my forehead pressed against the floor, shuddering and shaking and churning that vibrator around and around inside my pussy and my bottom. I wouldn't let myself stop. I didn't *want* to stop.

"That night, when Chet had come back from the gym, and we had eaten supper and everything, I poured Chet a glass of wine and we sat on the couch together. He told me all about this great new equipment they had at the gym, something for developing his stomach muscles—his "six-pack," he always calls them. I said that I had some great new equipment, too, and I took the vibrator out from under the cushions.

"I didn't expect him to react the way he did. He was actually very embarrassed, and he went all red. I said, you don't have to blush, it's only a piece of plastic, and it's terrific. He said, do you mean to say you've actually tried it? and I said sure, it's terrific, it really gets me in the mood. I didn't tell him that it had also given me the best orgasm I'd ever experienced.

"I pulled up my skirt, and it was then that Chet saw that I wasn't wearing panties. I opened my legs and switched on the vibrator and started to rub the head of it up and down my pussy. He couldn't believe it. I didn't know whether he was going to be angry or not, but I didn't give him the chance. I said, here, *you* do it, and I took hold of his hand and let him hold the vibrator.

"He was cautious at first, but when I held open my pussy with my fingers, and said, go on, push it inside, there was no stopping him. I said, up my bottom, too, and I put two fingertips in my bottom and stretched it open so that he could slide the thin penis into it. I closed my eyes and said, you can kiss me if you like.

"He leaned over me and kissed me. At the same time he kept on thrusting the vibrator in and out of me, deep and slow, which is something he never used to do with his real cock! He massaged my pussy lips and my clitoris with his fingers, and all around my bottom, too.

"I was building up toward another orgasm, but I didn't want to have it until Chet was inside me. I reached down and unbuckled his belt, and pulled down his pants a little way. His cock was so hard that it could hardly fit inside his shorts! I reached inside his shorts and took hold of his cock. It felt enormous, and the head of it was so slippery that I thought he might have climaxed already, although he hadn't. I rubbed it slowly up and down, digging my fingernails into it just a little, and lightly scratching his balls, too. He moaned ... I mean, you read about it in stories about people moaning when they make love, but Chet actually *moaned.*

"I was rubbing his cock up and down in the same rhythm that he was pushing the vibrator in and out of me, so for the first time ever we were making love to the same beat. It didn't matter that we weren't having ordinary intercourse. What mattered was that we were both so close, both so excited. We were kissing so furiously that we were almost eating each other alive, and Chet was shoving that vibrator in and out so hard that my bottom began to hurt, but it was a good hurt, it was such a good hurt, and it turned me on even more.

"In the end, I didn't want him to stop, even though I wanted his cock, too. I said, turn around, and he pulled off his pants and turned around so that he was kneeling over my face.

"He kept on pushing that vibrator in and out of me, but now he could lean forward and lick my clitoris and my pussy and all around my bottom at the same time. I can tell you—what with those two plastic penises buzzing up inside me, and Chet's tongue licking all around them, I think I understood what seventh heaven was!

"His big stiff cock was bobbing right over my face, so I stuck out my tongue and give it six or seven quick licks. He was so turned on that he was dripping his juice all over my face. I took hold of is cock in my hand, and rubbed it up and down a few times, then I opened my mouth wide and sucked it. That was good for another moan! My whole mouth was filled up with cock, and I ran my tongue around it and around it, and then I took it out and licked him all the way up the shaft of his cock. I was doing things that I had never done before, because I had never been excited enough to do them before. There's no question about it, when you're really turned on, you lose all of your inhibitions ... all you want to do is give your partner everything you possibly can.

"I licked his balls, I gave him such a thorough licking, and then I licked all the way back down to the head of his cock again. Because of the way he was kneeling over me, with his head between his legs, his cock was 'upside-down,' if you understand what I mean, so I could take hold of the head of his cock in both hands like I was holding a plum, and stretch open the hole in it, and stick the tip of my tongue right into his cock hole and lick that juice as it came out.

"When he climaxed, it was amazing. I had stretched his cock hole open as far as it would go, and suddenly this thick warm sperm squirted out, all over my tongue, all over my lips, halfway up my cheek. I could actually feel his cock throbbing as it came out. He squirted again, and again, and my face was smothered in sperm. It was clinging to my eyelashes and running down my chin. I licked and sucked his cock, and at the same time he was still pushing that vibrator in and out of me, but then he took it out of me, and buried his face right between my legs and sucked my pussy, and pushed his finger up my bottom.

"I had an orgasm that hit me like a tidal wave. I was washed away. It was even better than the orgasm that I had had before, with the vibrator. Afterward we both lay on the couch arm in arm, sweating and panting, and we didn't speak for almost five minutes. What can you say after something like that?

"That evening didn't turn our whole sex life around in a matter of minutes. But Chet had learned that I was very interested in sex, that I really needed it, and that together we could have the kind of wild sex that you think only exists in porno movies . . . not that I've ever seen a porno movie! I think both of us learned not to be afraid of sex, not to be embarrassed about it. Chet found it exciting, pushing a vibrator up my pussy and my bottom, *I* found it exciting, so where's the harm in it? It got us jump-started sexually, and things have been better and better ever since.

"Before this happened, I used to hate the idea of oral sex. Ugh! you know—the thought of a man putting his cock into your *mouth,* and sucking it, not to mention *sperm.* But now I think that once you get used to it, it's one of the greatest ways in the world to turn a man on, especially if he's tired or stressed, and you don't have to drink his sperm if you really don't want to . . . just squirt it around and he'll be just as happy.

"I think what we both learned was that sex is nothing to be afraid of. It can't harm you, no matter what you do. All you have to do is to forget about being afraid and try it."

You might think from the way she described her experience with Chet that Anne-Marie is a very outspoken woman. In fact, she is very soft-spoken, very reserved, and it took her a long time to find the words to describe in detail how she had found a way to revolutionize her sex life. If you saw her, you certainly wouldn't think that she was a flag-waver for double-vibrators and oral sex, but what you would think is that you were talking to a happy, well-balanced, well-fulfilled woman who was very much in love with her husband and very much at peace with her own emotions and her own femininity.

Her friend Suzie (who first suggested she use a vibrator) was much more sexually outspoken, but all the same she was perfectly ordinary, smart without being voguish, attractive without being devastatingly beautiful. What she did have was tremendous personal warmth, and an almost palpable sexiness which came not from a stunning appearance or a seductive approach to men, but from a lack of fear about her own desires, and the confidence that she could do anything she wanted, without embarrassment.

Suzie was an insurance broker, twice-married. After the failure of her first marriage because of her husband's adultery with another (older) woman, she decided that she was going to teach herself how to make love in a way that would not only drive her subsequent husband wild in bed, but which would ensure that she never had to suffer the pain of a second rejection.

She read as many sex manuals as she could, including several of mine, and tried many different kinds of sex toys and erotic clothes. "After the initial shock," she said, "I began to feel comfortable about sex and about my own sexuality. I began to understand that what had seemed lurid when I first saw it was exciting and liberating. I tried looking at 'tasteful' pornography, but that didn't turn me on. Really exciting sex has nothing to do with taste. It's all to do with being as dirty as you like, and enjoying it. It's about fucking and sucking to your heart's content, and not feeling guilty about it."

"After all, if you're doing it with somebody you love, to give them pleasure, how can it possibly be wrong?"

Suzie's opinions were daring and mature, but these days, more and more women *are* daring, and they *are* mature. And, as she said, *how can it be wrong?*

Her suggestion to Anne-Marie to try using a vibrator to arouse Chet was especially shrewd. If Anne-Marie had tried to arouse Chet's attention in the traditional way, by flirting with other men, then she ran the risk of alienating him and losing his affections. She was trying to intensify his interest in her sexuality—not make him feel jealous. Jealousy is dangerous and destructive enough without it being whipped up artificially.

As Anne-Marie said, Chet could hardly feel cuckolded by a piece of plastic and a couple of batteries. He might have been miffed that she seemed to prefer a pretend penis to the real thing, but she very quickly encouraged his participation in her self-pleasuring, and handed over control of the vibrator to him, so that he then felt that he was in charge of the situation.

Involving a vibrator in a sexual relationship can be beneficial, especially when the man feels that he is in charge of it. It enables him to penetrate his partner after he has lost his erection (or when he has failed to achieve an erection). It also allows *her* to penetrate him when she feels like it (although more about that later.)

Of course, it *does* take nerve. You may find it easier to introduce it to your lover if you wait until it arrives in the mail, and then say, "I heard they were amazing ... I thought we could try one." Then let *him* open the package and let *him* immediately take control of it.

Even if the idea of a vibrator isn't to your liking at all, you can still encourage a similar response from your lover by using nothing more than ... your own fingers. But more about that later.

Let's now turn from the well-meaning but unsatisfying lover to the selfish lover. The *really* selfish lover, and haven't we all known them? They make the minimum effort in bed, except when you're doing something that excites *them,* and they seem to have forgotten all about romancing and teasing and tickling and licking. When they want a fuck, they have a fuck. Then they go to sleep, or bounce straight out of bed and go to the fridge in search of a sandwich.

Their selfishness isn't confined to the bedroom, either. They always seem to have something more important to do than kiss you, or pay you a compliment, or touch you and caress you and let you know just how sexy you are. They're so selfish, in fact, that they're not even *aware* that they're acting so selfish. If they were accused of ignoring you sexually, they would be amazed. They would probably even be insulted. But their behavior is one of the most common causes of sexual and marital unhappiness.

To be totally fair, men are not always at fault for being sexually selfish. When they were growing up, their father may have treated their mother and other women in a selfish manner. They may have had no male role model, and boys who have been brought exclusively in female company often tend to be self-centered and domineering in their sexual relationships.

At school, these men may have been told how to dismantle an automobile engine. They may have learned all about history and math and how to play football. But too many of them are brought up without ever being made aware that they have an obligation to give the women in their lives the very best sexual care and attention of which they are capable—and then some.

These days, however, my patience with sexually selfish men is extremely limited, especially since they cause so much frustration and discontent. So what if they didn't learn about generous, affectionate hearted lovemaking at their daddy's knee? In criminal court cases, ignorance of the law is not accepted as a mitigating circumstance—"Nobody told *me* that it was wrong to hold up 7-Eleven's, y'r honor!")—and in today's outspoken society, where anybody can lay their hands on explicit and wide-ranging information about sex and loving, there is no excuse whatsoever for any man to behave like a sexual Bigfoot.

There is an added problem in sorting out a man's sexual selfishness, and that is that many women *allow* their husbands or lovers to behave this way. They'll complain about them to their friends, but when it actually comes down to taking a stand—well, they won't, they just won't, and we can all understand why.

This is Harriet, a 26-year-old junior banking executive from Detroit, Michigan. Harriet is black, well-educated, with a passionate interest in improving the social status of low-income black families. It was while she was pursuing this interest that she met Carlton, now 24, and helped him to find work customizing automobiles. "At first, I thought it was going to be all fireworks between us—a sexual Fourth of July, the whole year round. We met at a social function—a dance that I had helped to arrange for younger people in one of the worst sections of Dearborn. He was out of work at that time, but he seemed very positive, almost arrogant, I'd call it, and he had such a strong belief in himself that it really radiated out of him, like the sun's rays, almost. He's tall, he's *very* handsome, he dresses tasteful but not sharp. He's streetwise and fairly knowledgeable, but he's not well-educated, and I think one of the bones of contention between us is that I'll say something like, 'you're quite a Renaissance man,' and Carlton will get angry because he doesn't know whether I'm paying him a compliment or putting him down.

"The first time we made love, though, it was fabulous between us. It was sheer excitement. When he met me at the dance, he asked if we could meet again so that he could tell me more about the area, and what was going down there, and who was who. I met him after work at a restaurant and bar not far away from my bank. He was talkative and funny and sexy and interesting. In two hours with Carlton, I learned more about the social problems in Detroit than I ever learned in two years talking to social workers and cops and all those well-meaning people from city hall. I didn't only learn what the problems were, but why.

"Anyhow, one thing kind of led to another. We had

some fried chicken and a bottle of wine, and then I invited Carlton back to my apartment, so that we could talk some more. As we climbed into the car, he leaned over and kissed me. No 'may I?' No nothing. Very non-PC! But all the same, a woman wants a man to behave like a man, doesn't she, and he sent a tingle right through me. I thought: here's a man I could really go for.

"We bought another bottle of wine on the way home. We went up to my apartment. Usually I share with two other girls but both of them were away on a study course. We talked for a while and drank some more wine, and then Carlton said to me, 'I have to tell you, Harriet . . . there's no use my pretending. You really set me on fire.' "

"Well, no man had *ever* said anything like that to me before. And, to tell you the truth, he set me on fire, too. We kissed again and again, and started getting really turned-on. Physically, Carlton was superb. He was fit, he was handsome, he had such muscles! We were sitting on the couch and he was rousing me so much that I was gasping for air, and I knew that he had made me wet between my legs.

"He unbuttoned my blouse, and opened it. I think that really did it for him. I have very big breasts and Carlton was definitely a breast man. He knelt on the floor in front of me, kissed my lips and kissed my neck, like he wanted to eat me or something. He was going at me like a wild beast, and it was exciting and frightening at the same time. But he was expert. He managed to unfasten my bra with just one slide of his thumb, and considering its a 42DD with four hooks-'n-eyes that takes some doing.

"He said, 'Oh man, you're beautiful, I'm burning up!' He held my right breast in both hands, and kissed and licked my nipple until it stood up all stiff. Then he kissed my mouth again, and believe me, Carlton could kiss. Then he did the same with my left breast, tugging my nipple between his teeth until it stood up harder than I ever saw it stand up before.

"He was fierce, but he really loved my breasts. He kissed them and massaged them and pulled at my nipples until I was thinking, *please,* take me further, I really need you now. I opened his shirt and caressed his back and his hips, and I could feel how hard he was inside of his jeans.

"I unbuckled his belt, and pulled open his fly buttons one by one. He wasn't wearing any shorts, and what came out of that open fly was a huge, hard naked cock, I mean it was so big I could hardly get my hand around it. I rubbed his cock up and down with one hand, and with my other hand I reached inside his jeans and played with his balls. They were so tight and hard you would have thought they were giant walnuts.

"He stood up in front of me, and stripped off his shirt and climbed out of his jeans, so that he was totally naked. That was something else I hadn't had before, with any other man. Usually they undress *you* first, and then undress themselves. Somehow it made Carlton seem kind of vulnerable but sexy at the same time. And he has such a body! His cock was sticking up so hard that it had an upward curve on it, and the head of it was a beautiful dark shiny purple, the same color as an eggplant. The veins in his cock were like the sculpture of a tree. He had no pubic hair at all, his cock was completely bare. He told me afterward that he did body-building and they had to wear those little pouches when they showed off their muscles, so all of them shaved. But right then I thought it was the sexiest thing that I'd ever seen.

"He took hold of his cock and he massaged my breasts, thrusting it into my cleavage and rubbing the head of it around and around my nipples. My nipples were all shiny with cock juice, and I lifted each of my breasts in my hand, one after the other, and licked my own nipples. He said, 'I can't believe my *eyes!*'"

"After that, things got really wild. He lifted me onto the floor, and unzipped my skirt, and pulled off my skirt and my pantyhose all in one. There was no stopping him now: he really wanted me and I really wanted him. He climbed on top of me with his cock in his hand, but I said 'condom . . . you have to use a condom.' He said, 'I just want you . . . I hate fucking with condoms.' He tried to push his cock into me, but I held my hand between my legs and I wouldn't let him.

"He said, 'What the hell do you think, Harriet? You think I'm HIV? Just because you know what Picasso used to eat for lunch, and all of those fancy words. You think that your education makes you superior to me?' I said, 'Of course it doesn't, but I don't know whether you're HIV or not . . . even *you* may not know whether you're HIV or not. Besides that, it makes sense for both of us. Supposing *I'm* HIV? Suppose I have some kind of infection? More than anything else, we don't want to have a baby, do we?"

"Well, he went crazy at that. He said, 'Come on, Harriet,' and he tried again. He even tried to force my hand away from my cunt but every time he did that I just changed hands. I said, 'It's no use, lover, you have to wear protection, otherwise I'm not going to play.'

"Let me tell you something, in case you misunderstand me. I wanted Carlton to make love to me just as much as Carlton did . . . maybe more so. But unprotected sex with somebody you've only just met makes no sense at all. I didn't work my way up through high school and college and pass all of my exams just to wind up as a single mother on welfare. Or, worse than that, HIV positive.

"Carlton was very angry and sulky. I told him I had some condoms in the bedroom but he said he wasn't in the mood any longer, and he left. He didn't like to be defied, that was Carlton's problem. It wasn't a class problem and it wasn't an education problem. It was a personality problem. Carlton had been brought up to believe that women were an underclass, no matter how ritzy and educated they were. Underneath those nice clothes and that nice smile was a man who thought that all women were 'hoes' for his own use and convenience, and that if he wanted to make love to a woman without wearing a condom—well then, that was exactly what he was going to do.

"I thought I'd seen the last of him, but he called me the next afternoon and said he was sorry and could he see me again—he wanted to talk. I met him again that evening and he was all goofy and apologetic, he didn't know what had gotten into him. I set him on fire, et cetera, et cetera, and he really wanted to make love to me. Right then and there he took a pack of Trojans out of his pocket and said, 'How about you and me getting it on again?'

"Of course what I later discovered was that his regular girlfriend had found out that he was dating somebody new, and that they had argued. The only way he was going to score that evening was by going out with me.

"But at the time, he still charmed me, and I still had the hots for him, I have to admit. We drove back to my apartment and this time we took it a little easier, a little slower. We drank some wine and listened to some music, and then Carlton asked if he could take a shower. I said for sure, and so he did. But while he was still showering, I turned the lights low, and plumped up the cushions. then I took off all my clothes and went to join him in the bathroom. He was was washing his hair when I stepped into the shower with him, and took hold of him from behind, so that my breasts were pressed against his back. I reached up and touched his face and he kissed my fingers. Then I ran my hands down that beautiful hard chest of his, and around his stomach, and he shivered because I had touched a nerve. I kissed his neck, between his shoulder blades. He didn't have a spare ounce of fat on him at all. Physically, he was the best-looking man I've ever known.

"I reached down and took hold of his cock. It was totally hard. I cupped his balls in one hand and slowly rubbed his cock with the other. He tilted his head back and said, 'That's heaven . . . that is heaven.' I caressed him all around his cock and his balls and they were smooth and hairless and so darn hard. His cock was so stiff it felt like it had a bone in it.

"We climbed out of the shower stall and we didn't even bother to dry ourselves. We were kissing like crazy and we couldn't keep our hands off each other. I lay down on the living-room rug, and would you believe it? Carlton was going to try it again, without a condom. But I'd laid them out already, and I said, 'Here . . . I'll do it for you.' I opened the wrapper and took out the condom. I fitted it over the head of his cock, and then sl-o-w-ly rolled it down, rubbing his cock with this downward motion all the time, so that it was pulled on real tight.

When I was sure it was all the way down, and properly fitted, I lay back on the floor and held up my arms to him.

" 'You're the only woman who ever made me do that,' he said. He didn't seem to understand that I don't care for condoms, either . . . even when you make them a part of your foreplay they interrupt what you're doing . . . but what could happen to me if I didn't wear a condom could be so much worse.

"I wanted him real bad right then, I needed his cock inside me. I opened my legs, and I reached down with my fingers and stretched my cunt wide open. I couldn't resist looking down and watching while Carlton's huge black rubber-covered cock slid right inside of me. It was big, maybe nine inches, but it felt like it was three feet long. I could feel it rising up inside me, huge and hard, and my cunt muscles gripped it and twitched and gripped it again.

"He went inside me right up to the balls. I reached down and my cunt was already juicy. I smothered my fingers in juice and squeezed and massaged his balls with it. He kissed me, a really deep kiss, and then he started to fuck me. Actually, to tell the truth, 'fucking' is the wrong word. He used me to get his rocks off, more like. I hadn't had much experience before Carlton, but none of my boyfriends had been quite so violent. He shoved himself in and out of my cunt like a huge black locomotive piston. He was so fast and so hard that I couldn't even catch my breath.

"I'm not saying it wasn't exciting. It was. But I felt like Carlton was doing high-speed push-ups and I just happened to be lying in the way.

"He rolled me over so that I was facedown on the floor. He opened up my thighs and pushed himself into my cunt from behind. Then he lifted me up so that I was on my hands and knees, and he was fucking me doggy-fashion. He was going crazy. My breasts were swinging and he grabbed hold of them and squeezed them hard, so hard that he hurt me. He fucked me faster and faster, forcing himself deeper and deeper into me, and pushing me so strongly that my arms gave way and my head was pressed against the floor while he shoved himself into me. I was turned on, yes. I think every woman has some kind of fantasy about a man taking her so violently. But I can remember thinking that he didn't care about me at all. There I was with my face squashed into a cushion, with my nipples being pinched and pulled, while this man kept pounding and pounding at my cunt as if he had a grudge against it.

"As he came close to his climax, he gripped my hips real tight, and slowed down to this real slow, sexy rhythm. I was just beginning to enjoy myself when I felt his cock shudder. I squeezed my cunt muscles tight, and I actually felt the bulb of the condom fill up inside me.

"I thought, '*now* he's going to do something for me . . .' but did he even think about it. As soon as he'd finished climaxing, he took himself out of me, and pulled off his condom. I turned over and lay on my back and looked up at him. I really expected him to *do* something for me, go down on me maybe, or rub me with his finger or anything. I felt like I'd been lifted right up to the brink, right up to the very edge, and then left hanging. He knelt astride me, and emptied his condom all over my breasts, and started to massage his sperm into them. It was incredibly sexy to begin with, and I joined in, so that we were both smearing his sperm around my breasts and my nipples. Warm black breasts, warm white sperm, it was such a turn-on, and I love the smell of it.

"But then it began to dry, and Carlton got bored, and he got up and said, 'Let's have some more wine, huh?' and left me lying there.

"Carlton and I stayed together for more than two years. You would think that I was nuts just to see him again, after that, but I had this strong reforming instinct in me, as you know, and I suppose I deluded myself into thinking that I could change him. The trouble was, the nicer I was to him, the more eager I was to please him, the less he cared about me. He made love to me only when *he* felt like it . . . he went out with other girls. Every time I tried to assert myself he accused me of shoving my class and my education down his throat.

"Our lovemaking became less and less frequent, and less and less exciting. After a year of it, I began to feel that I was no more sexually important to him than one of those inflatable women.

"The reason I didn't break up with him sooner, though, was because outside of the bedroom he was funny and friendly and very protective. I *liked* him. At times I almost loved him . . . and when he wasn't there I missed him, I admit. I even missed his wham-bam love-making. But I couldn't find a way of telling him that I needed so much more, and even if I had, I'm not at all sure how he would have reacted. Badly, I expect."

Telling the man in your life that his lovemaking leaves a lot to be desired is not easy. Even the most selfish of men is touchy about his virility. But if you're living with a chronically inconsiderate lover, it is critically important that you do something positive to improve the sexual side of your relationship.

How often do I hear women saying, "I'm afraid to—he'll go ape if I tell him." Or, "He doesn't like to talk about sex . . . it embarrasses him." Or, "He doesn't think that sex is all that important." Or, "He wouldn't understand what I'm talking about."

But the problem is that sexual dissatisfaction has an insidious effect on many other aspects of your relationship. It is a major cause of physical and emotional stress. It can lead to alienation from your partner, and sometimes from your whole lifestyle. It can give you a feeling of lonesomeness, emotional isolation, and can lower your self-esteem. Couples who have unsatisfactory sex lives almost invariably argue more, and there is a direct correlation between the number of times that a couple make love to their feelings of contentment not just about sex but about life in general.

When I say "make love" I don't necessarily mean full intercourse but any sexual act intended to display mutual affection, even if it's just a cuddle.

Sex is good for you. Good sex is better for you. Wild sex is positively self-improving. *Wilder* sex can reward you with more well-being than you thought possible. Don't you think it's time you woke up in the morning with a broad grin on your face, because of what you and your partner got up to, the night before?

You don't have to be afraid to take whatever steps

are necessary to improve your love life. In this book, we're going to be looking at ways in which you can educate your lover in the skills of lovemaking without him feeling that you're being at all disparaging. Even though you feel that your lover may be failing you, it's vitally important not to dent his sexual pride—for your sake, as much as his. Even if you have the nerve (which not many women do), all you will ever achieve by telling him that he makes love like Fred Flintstone is resentment and annoyance—and even, possibly, impotence. You can let out a long patronizing "aaaaaahhhh," if you like, but even the most macho men entertain doubts about their sexual ability and their sexual performance, and while your lover may become angry at you for criticizing his performance, he will go away afterward and dwell on what you've just told him, and feel very anxious about it indeed. Anxiety is one of the major causes of impotence: the more he worries, the less capable he becomes. Anxiety = no hard-on = more anxiety = even fewer hard-ons. Result = him humiliated, you even more frustrated. So where's the sense in that?

You don't ever have to risk a face-to-face confrontation about your partner's sexual inadequacies. In fact, you shouldn't, for your own good, as well as the good of their relationship. I have never known any angry confrontation about sex to be helpful. Because what are you actually going to say, 'You're no good in bed? You never give me climaxes? You're too quick? You're too slow? You always rub my clitoris too hard? I don't think I turn you on any longer?'

Sexual arguments by their very nature are deeply hurtful and destructive. So much of our sexual relationships are conducted by touch and by suggestion and by implication that—if and when they go wrong—we have a very limited vocabulary when it comes to arguing about our problems in words. I remember sitting in at one discussion between two arguing lovers of 10 years' standing, and after 10 minutes the man screamed out, "Every time I climax, you always squeeze my balls so hard that you made my eyes water! What in hell did you think you were doing, milking a cow?"

Immediately, she retaliated, "Well, you keep sticking two fingers up my bottom, and that *hurts.*"

They continued to tear each other apart until there was nothing left of 10 years of loving but hatred and resentment. And yet there needn't have been. If you have any difficulty in driving your man that little bit wilder in bed, you don't need to demolish your relationship, either. Neither should you be tempted to turn your back on it—not until you're absolutely cross-your-heart sure that there's nothing left to salvage. Just remember that people are odd creatures, and that both women and men need affection and flattery and tickles where it matters.

To solve any sexual problem, it's far better to build on what you've got, no matter how unsatisfactory it may be, than try to rip your relationship apart like a broken clock, trying to get "to the bottom of it." Unless you're a sexologist or a qualified clinical psychiatrist, you can never hope "to get to the bottom of it," and even if you could, it wouldn't help your relationship.

So your husband was brought up by a sexually repressed father? So he was seduced by his geography teacher at the age of 14? When it comes to sex, what *was* makes very little difference. What *is* is what counts, and what *is about to be* is even better.

You should ask yourself, 'My partner is sexually selfish . . . I want better loving, more considerate sex, more exciting sex, how can I go about getting it?"

Then you should answer yourself, 'I'll accept that he's sexually selfish . . . I won't work on him, I'll work on me. I'll learn so much about sex that he won't find it *possible* to be sexually selfish. I won't just drive him wild in bed. I'll drive him even wilder in bed."

You're one of today's women, and you have every right to say Yes! to wilder sex.

TWO

Why You'd Better Get Better in Bed

Of course, you may be one of those lucky women who is having no trouble at all in her love life. You may have the most sensitive, skilled, selfless of sexual partners. All the same, I hope you will find in these pages some arousing new ways of enhancing the sex that you are already enjoying so much. There is never any harm in trying something wilder—and, who knows, you may open the door to a whole new dimension of erotic pleasure that you never thought possible.

Even when couples have been carrying on a satisfactory sexual relationship for many years, they can transform their love life almost overnight by trying a new sexual variation which they never considered before, or which they shied away from because they were too embarrassed or too cautious or because they had a feeling that it was "wrong."

There is no doubt that even the happiest and most satisfied of lovers can get into a sexual rut. The man has discovered exactly how to stimulate his woman physically so that she is almost guaranteed an orgasm—the woman is content to let him do it. They both enjoy their lovemaking, and on the whole they feel satisfied when it's over. But it's very easy to allow familiarity and routine to take over your sex life—so that while you may *think* you have a fulfilling sexual relationship, you're no longer feeling that wild, erotic passion that you used to enjoy before.

It's at times like these that marriages and long-term sexual relationships are at their most vulnerable. If a woman happens to meet another man who is charming and attentive and turns her on, she is very likely to be tempted, at the very least, to fantasize about an extramarital affair. His interest in her will hugely stimulate her sexual ego, and that's simply because he's different, he's something new.

There's no harm at all in responding to sexual flattery—so long as you don't allow your responding to get out of control. Sexual flattery is good for us. It renews our sense of our own attractiveness, which is a critically important ingredient in any sexual relationship. Men and women who have doubts about their own sexiness don't make for very sexy lovers. They're always so concerned that they're not arousing their partners enough that they don't give themselves 100 percent, and there are few acts so discouraging as sex that isn't 100 percent wholehearted.

For example: man doesn't achieve a full erection during foreplay. Woman thinks: I'm not turning him on. She tries halfheartedly to arouse him with her hand; man senses her halfheartedness and his penis subsides even more. Woman tells him to stop caressing her and turns her back. Result, from a few moments' self-doubt: no lovemaking, frustration, and resentment. It's easily done, and it happens very often, even to the closest and sexiest of couples.

What's more, once this kind of self-doubt gets into a sexual relationship, it's like a virus, and it's extremely difficult to get rid of.

I have had dozens of letters from women who have told me, "I'm in love with my husband, and our sex life is very good . . . but I met this younger man at a party/office/country club and I can't get him out of my mind. I keep having fantasies about him making love to me, and I'm beginning to believe that if he asked me, I would. In fact, I've started to encourage him a little, by making a special point of talking to him, and always wearing my sexiest dresses when he's around. I don't want to betray my husband, but this young man really excites me in a way that my husband hasn't excited me for years. What should I do?"

The question "What should I do?" is a coded request for permission to have an extramarital fling. After all, I'm the fellow who says that you should never turn your back on exciting sex. How can I possibly say that these women should forget about this arousing new opportunity and return home to the pleasant but dull routine of making love to their husbands?

The answer to that is, don't have that affair. Go back home, but *don't go back home to routine sex.* Learn how to turn your sex life around, learn how to drive your husband or lover even wilder in bed. Don't risk losing somebody you love and like—somebody in whom you've invested so much of your affection and so much of your time—simply for the sake of a problem which—once you know how—you yourself are capable of sorting out.

You should be having exciting sex, for sure. But exciting sex is not an automatic entitlement. It doesn't appear in the Bill of Rights. Exciting sex is a reward you have to work for—just the same as your husband or long-term lover should be working for it, too. You see, the chances are that if you have an extramarital affair simply because your home sex life has become boring, *any* sexual relationship that you ever have will eventually turn out to be boring. The responsibility for achieving wilder sex lies with you, just as much as the man in your life.

Time and time again, women say to me, "My husband is so unexciting in bed. He always makes love the same way. I don't get turned-on anymore, the way I used to."

So I say to them, "What have *you* done about it? Have you tried talking to him? Have you tried changing your position during lovemaking? Have you tried dressing sexily? Have you tried oral sex on him? Have you encouraged him to try oral sex on you?" And so on, and so on.

And most of them look at me blankly, and say, "No." They were brought up to think that exciting sex was something that a man did to you. It never once occurred to them that they could actually do something to improve their husband's lovemaking—that, in a single night, they could stand their sex life on its head, and never, ever have to be bored with sex again.

Don't let's be *too* starry-eyed about it. There may be other problems with your marriage or long-term sexual relationship—age, money, conflicting leisure interests, even politics. Couples who live together for a number of years can grow widely apart in their interests and their outlook. After all, you can't expect a woman of 45 to look or behave like a woman of 25, and it would be absurd if she did.

I'm not in favor of incompatible couples staying together simply out of habit or guilt or "it's best for the children." But when the principal problem isn't a fundamental clash of personalities, but nothing worse than a sex life that has run out of energy, I strongly believe that couples should do their best to try new and wilder lovemaking. They should explore every erotic possibility they can think of before they consider separation or extramarital affairs. And why? Because couples who try raunchy new sexual variations with familiar partners almost always find the formula to be hugely explosive.

This is Joy, a 25-year-old furniture restorer from Charleston, South Carolina. Joy is blonde, always perfectly groomed. She says that her friends call her "Marilyn Monroe." Joy has been living with Dean for two-and-a-half years. Dean is 31 and an architect. He was married, briefly, and left his first wife so that he and Joy could live together.

"I don't quite know when I started to grow bored with our sex life. It kind of crept up on me. Last spring I found that I was going to bed first and then pretending to be asleep when Dean came up to bed, so that I wouldn't have to do it. Dean had turned me on so much when we first met. The first six months we were doing it all the time, everywhere. We couldn't even go for an afternoon walk in the woods without fucking up against a tree. It seemed like my panties were always wet, and I used to be worried when I met my girlfriends that I smelled of sex.

"Dean was a good lover. He plays a lot of tennis so he's always very fit. The trouble was, he didn't have much imagination. When he wanted to make love to me he would always start by kissing me the same way, then by touching my breasts the same way, then by taking off my bra the same way. He would always pick me up and carry me over to the bed or the sofa or wherever we were going to make love, and then he would always slip his hand inside my panties the same way, and slip his middle finger into my cunt, and diddle me, and then he would undress and climb on top of me and that was how we *always* did it . . . oh, except I managed to roll him over once, so that I was sitting on top of him, and I *loved* that position, I loved sitting on top of him. His cock seemed to be buried so deep inside me that I thought it was going to come out of my mouth, and his balls were all squashed up in the crack in my bottom. I could reach behind me and tickle them. I *loved* it, but Dean didn't seem very happy about it—it seemed to throw him off his rhythm—and after a while he rolled me back over again.

"He was good, that's all I can say. But he started to bore me, and I felt that I couldn't talk to him about it, because he seemed to think that everything was fine. I didn't want to hurt him, either. That was the very last thing I wanted to do. But I was beginning to feel trapped. I kept thinking to myself: is this all there's ever going to be?

"It was then that I went shopping during my lunch hour with a friend of mine from work. She went to the drugstore to buy some nail-polish remover and also some depilatory cream. She asked me how I depilated because sometimes this particular cream gave her a mild rash. I said I used a razor. She said, not for your bikini area, surely? I told her I didn't depilate my bikini area. She was amazed. She said, you don't even *trim* it? You should, it drives my husband absolutely wild. He loves it. She said that she shaved herself lightly first, then used a cream, then a moisturizer . . . 'it ends up bare as a baby's bottom.'

"She said she wore a tight satin basque that left her breasts bare, and black stockings, and black stiletto heels, and when he came home from the office in the evening that was all she had on.

"She said, 'Sometimes he can't wait, and he starts fucking me in the hallway, still holding his briefcase.' I asked her how long she had been married and she said eight-and-a-half years. I'm telling you, eight-and-a-half years and they're still fucking in the hallway when he gets home?

"I thought about what she had told me all afternoon. It excited me, but it embarrassed me and frightened me a little, too—I don't know why. I wasn't sure what Dean thought about basques and stockings and that kind of thing, so I decided to be cautious, and not dress up like Madame Whiplash—not on the first night, anyhow. I think it might have put him off. I wanted to turn him on, not brighten him half to death. Besides, I didn't want him to think that I was a secret S&M enthusiast or something like that.

"Anyhow, I left the office early, and stopped off at the drugstore to buy some depilatory cream. Back home, I ran myself a bath, and lightly shaved off my pubic hair. Then I applied some depilatory cream, and waited while it took effect. It stung very slightly, and there was a smell like burning hair, but when I came to wash it off, my cunt was completely hairless. I really liked the look of it, and I wished that I'd tried it before.

"I put on makeup, and plenty of perfume. All I wore were my black patent high-heeled shoes and a wide black patent-leather belt, buckled up really tight. Apart from that I was completely naked. I walked around the apartment, admiring myself in the mirror, and I must say that I looked pretty damned sexy. In fact I looked so sexy I started feeling real excited, and I kept touching myself and stroking myself.

"I couldn't say that I wasn't nervous about Dean coming home and seeing me naked like that. I wasn't at all sure how he was going to react. But I needn't have worried. When I heard his key in the door I went into the halfway to welcome him. I gave him a kiss and put my arms around him and said, 'Welcome home, darling,' and his eyes almost popped right out of his head.

"He said, 'What's *this* for? Look at you—you shaved

yourself!' I kissed him some more and said, 'It's for you, special surprise.'

"He dropped his briefcase and I took hold of his hand and pulled him into the living room. Then I fell right back on the couch with my legs apart and my arms held up for him, and said, 'Come and get it!'

"He sure didn't need telling twice. He stripped off his shirt and his pants faster than any man I ever saw. Mind you, he could hardly manage to take off his shorts because his cock was so hard.

"I reached down between my legs and I pulled open my cunt lips with my fingers. Dean climbed on top of me, and buried his cock in my cunt. He slid right up inside me and I could feel every inch of him. I don't know whether it was imagination or not, but I'd never felt him so big. Because my cunt was shaved, I could feel his pubic hair tickling against me, too, and *that* was a terrific turn-on.

"He buried his fingers in my hair and kissed me like he hadn't kissed me in months . . . like I really excited him, like he really wanted me. I spread my legs as wide as I could and lifted them right up, so that he could lie down and see his cock sliding in and out of my hairless cunt. I kept my cunt lips pulled open as wide as possible, so that both of us could watch that big fat purple cock head of his plunging into my pinky juicy hole. I had never actually *watched* myself making love, never actually seen it like that. I found it tremendously exciting, seeing that huge slippery cock actually disappearing inside me. It kind of brought the whole meaning of sex alive to me. Like, he wanted to put himself right into my body, and I wanted him in there .. and there he was, actually doing it.

"He was starting to fuck me with the same rhythm as he always does, but I thought, I'm not letting this happen, not again. I took his cock out of my cunt, and I wriggled down between his legs, and took his cock into my mouth. It was so big and juicy that I almost choked on it. But I sucked it up against the roof of my mouth, and stuck the tip of my tongue into the little hole in it, and then I gently ran my teeth all the way down the length of it, until I reached his balls, I pinched a little bit of skin of his balls in between my teeth and tugged at them, and at the same time I rolled his cock against my face, and into my hair.

"The good thing about it was, he still felt like he was in charge, even though it was me who was setting the pace. I kept saying things like 'I love your cock, I want to suck it all night,' and 'I want to taste your come'—which weren't fake or hypocritical or anything, because I *did* love his cock and I *did* want to suck it all night. I wanted to taste his come, too.

"I wriggled right out from under him, and then I stood up beside him and gently pushed him onto his back. Then I climbed on top of him—I actually hunkered down on top of him—and I pulled open my cunt lips again, so that he could slide his cock right up inside me.

"I'd never felt anything like it. It went up so *deep*—even deeper than it had the first time I'd done it with him. The head of his cock actually touched the neck of my womb and made me jump, but it was a nice jump, the kind of sensation that shocks and tingles you both at the same time. I sat down on his cock even harder, so that I could feel his cock touching my womb again and again. If a man does it to you and you're not expecting it, it can be quite unpleasant ... but if you're doing it yourself, the way I was, then it can be fantastic. I did it again and again, and I could feel my whole womb move.

"I didn't expect to have an orgasm so quickly. But suddenly this feeling gripped the back of my legs and up in between them, too—and the next thing I knew I was crouched on top of Dean, trembling and shaking. I thought I was going to black out for a moment.

"Dean held me tight while I climaxed. It was one of the most beautiful things he'd ever done, to hold me like that. His cock was still right up inside me, and every time my cunt muscles tried to relax, I'd feel his cock again, and I'd started off trembling and shaking all over again.

"Afterward, he gently rolled me over onto my back, and he started to fuck me very, very slowly. It was amazing ... I could feel another orgasm building inside of me, it was like my whole body was gradually tightening up, every nerve and every muscle. Dean pushed, and pushed, and pushed . . . and then he took his cock right out of me, and said, 'look. . . ,' and I looked down between my legs and he was shooting all of his come all over my cunt, great warm blobs of it.

"Then he slid down in between my thighs, and started to lick my cunt, even though it was covered in his own come. There was thick white come on his tongue, and all he did was swallow it, which excited me even more . . . a man swallowing his own come. I closed my eyes. The feeling was so good that I could hardly bear it. He was licking all around my cunt lips . . . he was even sucking my cunt into his mouth, which he'd never ever done before I shaved it. His tongue was playing with my clitoris and wriggling right inside my vagina, and I knew for an absolute fact that I couldn't stop myself from having another orgasm. When it came, it was so intense that I was rocking backward and forward on the sofa like a rocking horse.

"That evening, our sex life took an incredible step forward, no question about it. Dean still gets back into his old routine, now and again, especially if he's tired, but I don't mind that. It's better to have routine sex than no sex at all. But we still have plenty of good, varied sex . . . in the living room, listening to music and drinking wine . . . in the shower, under a stream of warm water, with plenty of soap. In the yard once, at night, when the neighbors couldn't see what we were doing.

"We think about sex more and we talk about sex more, and these days we're willing to try anything."

Most sexual relationships need some kind of "detonator" to blow them out of a rut. It's no use carrying on as usual and expecting things to get better by themselves. They won't. In most cases, they'll gradually get worse. Joy provided the detonator: a clear and unmistakable demonstration that she liked having sex with Dean, but that she wanted it to be more varied, and more exciting, and that she wanted to have some control over the way they made love.

In the same way that Anne-Marie introduced a non-threatening sexual object like a vibrator into her relationship, Joy did something that might have appeared to be sexually submissive, shaving her vulva—but which in fact was a very positive and feminine move. She excited Dean without making him feel that she was being judgmental about his sexual performance, and she took greater control over the way in which they made love without making him feel threatened.

These days—compared with two decades ago, when *How to Drive Your Man Wild in Bed* was first published—the vast majority of women trim or shave their public hair, so it is no longer such a revolutionary piece of advice. But remember that men are very responsive to visual images. They can be turned-on by photographs of a woman's breasts or vagina, even if they can't even see the woman's face. They go to strip clubs and stare at the bodies of women they don't even know, or are ever likely to know.

To see a woman's vulva shaved of all hair and openly displayed is a very powerful erotic stimulus. It communicates all kinds of highly arousing messages, such as "look at me, I'm a woman," and "I'm not hiding myself, I'm proud of what I am," and "I did this for you, so that you could see me."

If you want to improve a routine sexual relationship, then you should be thinking of a "detonator" of your own—something which clearly shows the man in your life that you're still very interested in sex, and that you want more of it. Pubic shaving is one of the more obvious demonstrations of the way you feel. Another is to wear more erotic underwear, or to make sure that he knows you're not wearing any underwear at all.

Here's a checklist of 15 things you can do to a man *today* to show that you're interested in having more exciting sex, without making him feel that you're questioning his virility.

1. Start wearing really sexy underwear, like G-strings and crotchless panties and garter belts and quarter-cup bras, and don't say anything about them. If he asks, say, "I like them, they're much more comfortable and they're fun."
2. Take longer to dress in the morning, and undress sooner in the evening. Do your household chores

in nothing at all, or jeans with no top on, or a short sweater with no bottom on. Flaunt yourself, you're lovely.

3. Shave off all of your pubic hair, and treat it as a perfectly normal cosmetic treatment. You did it because it's neater, cleaner, and because you want to wear those high-cut leotards when you do your aerobics.
4. Make sure you join him in the shower or tub, and give him a generous soaping where he needs it the most.
5. While you're reading or watching TV in bed, reach over and casually start to play with his cock, while at the same time lightly pleasuring yourself with your other hand.
6. Ask if he can rent a porno movie, because you just want to see what they're like.
7. When he's come, show him that he turns you on. Sit on his lap—kiss him, nuzzle him, the way you used to do when you first went out with him. Put your hands in his pants pocket and play with his cock. Men often tend to become very complacent when they're involved in a long-term sexual relationship. They need reminding now and again that you're lovers . . . now and again, and again and again, and again.
8. Tell him that some of your girlfriends use vibrators and other sex toys, and recommend them very highly. You were just wondering, maybe we should try some, too?
9. Give him oral sex whenever you have the time and the opportunity. When he comes home from work, when he's watching baseball on television, when he's in the tub, when he's working on the car, even.
10. When he undresses for bed, rub his neck muscles and tell him that he's really tense. Offer to give him a massage (and make sure that you have some cream or massage oil handy). As any masseuse will tell you, one kind of massage can soon lead to another . . .
11. Tell him about this really sexy dream you had last

night, in which he tied you to the bed with scarves and made love to you for hours. Tell him it gave you the most fantastic orgasm ever, and why doesn't he try it to see if it works just as well in real life.

12. When you're out shopping, tell him that you forgot to put panties on. Say it discreetly, of course—you don't want everyone in Winn-Dixie to know that you're pantie-less!
13. Buy some breast-firming cream (any good body lotion will do, if you can't find any) and ask him to help you to massage it in. Slowly and luxuriantly, please, and pay close attention to the nipples.
14. *Talk* about sex with him. It's amazing how many couples—once their lovemaking is over—return immediately to whatever they were doing before hand (reading a book, watching TV, cooking dinner) as if nothing had happened between them. Sex is the most intense expression of physical love of which two human beings are capable. It should be interwoven into your everyday life, into everything you do and say—yet so many people treat it as if it were separate—almost as if those two people who kiss and caress and have intercourse together aren't really *them,* but another two people altogether. Later, we'll take a look at how you can overcome this common tendency to shut your sex life away from your everyday life, but just for the moment let's say that a good way to start talking about sex with your partner is to tell him about one of your erotic fantasies. It doesn't have to be *too* graphic: one young bride told her husband, right out of the blue, that she had always fantasized about having sexual intercourse with a horse. It was true, but it was too much for her husband, who threatened to go home to his parents. It doesn't necessarily have to be a real fantasy, either . . . just something like "I've always had a fantasy about being a stripper . . . I wonder what's it like to take all your clothes off in front of hundreds of men." Then you can mention the fantasies of

other women you know, and ask him what *his* favorite sexual fantasy is.

15. Wake him up in the middle of the night by caressing his penis, and tell him that you must have more of him. You're aching for him.

Each of these 15 sexy tips suggests a way in which you can "set up" a sexual situation that is intended to arouse your lover and encourage him to go further. But none of them undermines his virility, because each of them requires him to take a positive move in order for full lovemaking to follow. You may give him oral sex, but that doesn't necessarily mean that he has to do anything more than lie back and enjoy it, although it's likely that he will be sufficiently aroused by it to make love to you fully in return.

You may caress his penis in the middle of the night, but it will still be up to him to wake himself up, turn over, and make love to you. Although strictly speaking you will be the one who is initiating sex, you will not be doing it in such a way that he feels you're taking over control.

What you're saying is, in one or more of 15 different ways, is that you want him. It's then up to him to oblige.

Now you can see what I mean by spicing up your sex life without threatening your relationship in any way. I know that there will be plenty of women who retort, "Who cares about his precious virility? What about my right to be satisfied?" But the fact is that your lover's "precious virility" is precious; it's a very important component of his sexual character. The more virle he feels, the more masterful he feels, the more he believes that he has done something positive and decisive and manly in bed, the more excitement and satisfaction he will derive from making love to you, and the more frequently he will want to do it.

I am certainly not talking about "virility" of the violent, macho, uncaring kind. I am talking about the strength of your lover's physical and emotional *maleness*, and how you can nurture and enhance it in order to enjoy better and wilder sex. When a man compliments you on your face, on your figure, on your clothes and your hair, it nurtures and enhances your femininity. It makes you feel better. It arouses you. That's all I'm asking you to do to the man in your life in order to improve your lovemaking.

If your sex life has gone flat, there are three things you must never say, however sorely you're tempted:

1. I don't turn you on any longer, do I?
2. Have you gone off sex?
3. Is there somebody else?

Most sexual relationships go flat because couples grow physically overfamiliar with each other. It's intensely thrilling to kiss a stranger and feel a strange man's erection inside you. But the thrill inevitably wanes, especially when you're not just dating but living together, with all the humdrum everyday pressures of working and cooking and cleaning and bringing up children. Lovemaking becomes routine, unsurprising, and because of that it tends to become much less frequent and much less arousing even when you do manage to get around to it.

In order to rekindle your man's sexual fires, you have to think positive, rather than negative. You may be feeling that you *don't* turn him on any longer, but unless there is clear evidence that he's seriously interested in another woman, the chances are almost 99.999 percent that you still *can* turn him on—if you just start using some of the wilder sex techniques we've mentioned.

Don't ask if he's gone off sex, because the chances are almost 99.999 percent that he hasn't gone off sex, either. In fact he's probably dying for it, if he could just forget about his career worries and all the other problems that have been bothering him lately. It's very easy to get out of the habit of making love frequently, and it's surprising how quickly even a very close couple can become sexually distant from each other—to the point where they can't make love spontaneously anymore. They almost reach the point of feeling that they have to cough politely when they want sex and ask each other's permission.

Men have a tendency to prefer the familiar to the unfamiliar, the comfortable to the challenging. Once they've allowed their lovemaking to lapse, they'd rather spend their leisure time playing golf or watching football or enjoying themselves in the nonthreatening company of other men. Making love requires passion and thought and creativity and commitment, not to mention physical energy. Making love to somebody you have known and slept with for years requires even more physical skill, and even more emotional input. Terrific sex doesn't just *happen.* No wonder so many men find it easier to improve their golf handicap than exciting their women in bed.

Of course, we have to face facts: sometimes a woman's sex life will go flat because there *is* somebody else. In that case, she has to decide whether or not she wants to fight for her lover's sexual affections. If she does, she'll find out how to do it in this book. If she doesn't, then good luck to her. If a man isn't sexually inventive enough to keep a relationship alive and exciting year after year—not just for his lover's pleasure but for his own pleasure, too—then she's probably better off without him. And there *are* ways of finding new lovers, even for more mature women: take a look at my book *Single, Wild, Sexy . . . and Safe,* which tells you all about introduction agencies and voice-mail dating, and how to make the best use of them.

Apart from the way in which they all encourage a man to come up with a strong virile response, the 15 sexual suggestions have something else in common. They are all designed to appeal to a man's sense of what is sexually arousing—not like so many of the "how to turn him on" tips that I've seen in women's magazines, which more often than not are a list of sexual teases which women would like to think that men find arousing.

Some of the major differences between male sexual response and female sexual response are very neatly summed up in *Burning Desires,* a report on American sex by Steve Chapple and David Talbot. They describe the pornographic videos for women produced by Candida Royalle's Femme Productions: "Femme women don't sleep with men until they want to, and if the guys do start things, they usually ask first. And politely. There's a lot of kissing and fondling and foreplay. Afterward, the men rock the women in their arms. Royalle likes cuddling.

"The men dress like models in Calvin Klein ads. The women are hardly the 'Talk dirty to me' fuck-bunnies of older porn but rather normal, if horny, gals with good jobs and 'Dynasty' clothes. The sets seem designed by Laura Ashley, all flowered wallpaper, arranged silverware, antique oaken beds, designer sheets, and yards and yards of expensive lingerie.

"Violence is as forbidden as a male lead with a potbelly. Okay, maybe a little giggly bondage with silk scarves looped around the pipes of that Laura Ashley brass bed. But good God, no 'golden showers' of love—and definitely no nipple piercing.

" 'Women want a situation, a tenderness component,' said Royalle. 'They want a relationship, more than a body and a sex organ.' "

But she's acutely aware of what turns men on. " 'The big fantasy in many adult movies is to have lots of women throw themselves at a man because that kind of thing never happens in real life, whereas for women it's easy to go out and have sex—too easy—so we like buildup and lead-in. Typical porn strives to please men in a society where hot sex is mostly prohibited. Since your wife is supposed to be that lovely, pure woman who wouldn't dream of giving you a blow job, then the male porn movie provides you with that little girl-woman who does offer dirty sex. That's why the visible come shot is so very important in typical porn. It provides men with visible release.' "

The key word here is *visible.* Men are sexually excited by what they *see*—much more quickly and much more intensely than what they feel. By taking advantage of your lover's susceptibility to visual sex, you can liven up your love life literally in seconds.

Helen, 21, a very pretty brunette newspaper reporter from Cleveland, Ohio, told me, "I've always been very romantic. I fell in love with Jerry because he wined me and dined me and treated me like a princess. I guess I assumed right from the very start of our relationship that we were going to get married. My parents loved him! He was so polite and everything, and when we first made love he was so gentle and caring. The trouble was, I didn't know anything about sex at all. I knew about contraception and orgasms and all of that clinical stuff. But I didn't know what really turned men on. One of my best friends at work told me about oral sex, and I wasn't disgusted or anything like that, but I just couldn't imagine myself doing it. I mean, what would Jerry say, if I started sucking his penis?

"We dated for nearly six months, and then we rented an apartment in University Heights. At first I was blissfully happy. It all seemed like a dream come true. We made love almost every night and every morning before we went to work. Jerry is very dark and very hairy. I'd never dated such a hairy man before, and I absolutely adored making love to him. I could run my hands through the hair on his chest, and when he was making love to me I could twine my fingers into the hair on his thighs and tug it until he shouted. And his penis was so hairy! It was like a bald eagle in a thick black nest.

"As I say, we were blissfully happy. But after about three months Jerry was promoted, and his job started to take up more and more time, and of course he was feeling much more tired all the time. We made love less and less, and when we did it was all over so quickly that I scarcely had time to get turned-on. I began to think that Jerry had fallen out of love with me, or that he was seeing another woman."

Helen told me that she and Jerry always made love in the bedroom, almost always in the same position (Jerry on top, Helen underneath) and almost always in the dark or near-dark. What she needed to do first of all was to make their sex life much more varied and much more *visual.* Jerry's fatigue and extra workload had led them to getting out of the habit of having frequent sex, and it's surprising how hard it can be to get back into the habit once you've lost it.

She needed to give Jerry the following Three Turn-Ons:

1. A memorable visual turn-on (so that he would remember how aroused he was and look forward to seeing it again).

2. A memorable physical stimulus (an erotic act that would really stick in his mind, and have him panting for more).
3. A feeling that he had really gratified her (to give him a sense of sexual self-pride and achievement).

Helen's choice for a *visual turn-on* was to buy herself several tiny G-strings. She suggested wearing one of them (and nothing else!) to greet Jerry when he came home from the office, but I advised her against it. If he was really suffering from an overload of work, he would need some time to unwind when he got back home, and he would almost certainly find Helen's appearance to be sexually confrontational—just at a critical moment in his day when he would be looking for relaxation rather than stimulation.

Instead, she left her visual surprise until just before bedtime, when Jerry had eaten, and drunk a couple of glasses of wine, and was feeling "on the edge of mellow." She didn't want to leave him until he was *too* mellow, because then he usually dropped off to sleep on the couch.

"He was sitting on the couch watching television when I came in wearing nothing but a scarlet G-string trimmed with white lace and my white cotton blouse. I unbuttoned my blouse as I came toward him, and underneath it my breasts were bare. I felt quite breathless, to tell you the truth. Scared, even. I don't know why. I think everybody's a little afraid of laying their sexual feelings on the line. You might be rejected or ridiculed or shouted at, and then what?

"I stood in front of Jerry and gave him a kiss on the forehead. I said, 'Like my new panties?' They're transparent, so that he could see my pubic hair through them. I turned around so that he could see the elastic up between the cheeks of my bottom. He said, 'You sure didn't buy them to keep warm, did you?' But I could tell that they turned him on. I kissed him again, and he kissed my stomach, and then my hips, and then he gently pulled down the front of my G-string and kissed my pubic hair.

"I took off my shirt, so that I was completely naked

apart from my G-string. I said, 'I had to take off my clothes to give you a massage. You've been working so hard, your muscles are all knots.' He said he didn't want a massage, he didn't like massages. I said, 'You're going to like this one.' "

I had advised Helen that men respond very quickly to direct sexual stimulus, even when they feel reluctant to make love. The secret of dealing with a tired and unenthusiastic lover like Jerry was first to relax him and make sure that his level of general well-being was very high—what I like to call the "Feel Good Factor." Then to give him some kind of visual stimulus such as Helen's erotic underwear, and a glimpse of bare breasts beneath her unbuttoned blouse.

It is almost impossible to underestimate how effective visual stimulus can be in reviving a sexual relationship. If you have any doubts about it, go to your local newsstand and leaf through some of the men's magazines such as *Playboy* or *Penthouse* or *Hustler*. Go to a strip club and watch the effect that striptease dancers have on their audience. Many women think that men's magazines and stripping are not demeaning to women. But to my mind, they are among the most obvious demonstrations of the way in which men are aroused simply by *looking*. You have a power. You have a beautiful face. You have a beautiful body. The man in your life wants to see your face and your breasts and your vagina. *You are sexy to look at.* You can use that power whenever you like to give your love life so much extra verve.

What is so effective about visual stimuli is that *you* are exercising your control over your sex life by displaying yourself, but *he* will feel that you are displaying yourself to him because he is such a stud. Men rarely realize when they are being sexually manipulated, even if you are manipulating them for no other reason than to rev up your sex life, and to give far greater pleasure and satisfaction to both of you.

It *does* take nerve to expose yourself openly to your lover. As Helen said, she was almost breathless with anxiety. Supposing he didn't like it? Supposing he became angry? Supposing he felt that I was taking over our sex life?

But if you know your man well enough to know what might particularly turn him on (a very short skirt with no underwear? a change of hair color? A pair of tight denim jeans and no top? lipstick? stiletto heels? A rubber skirt? A silky negligee?) then nine times out of ten your visual stimulus will work wonders.

After the visual stimulus comes a direct physical stimulus. I told Helen that she could certainly kiss and nuzzle Jerry, but that she needed to do something that exploited his natural male responses—which are very quick.

If they were first-time lovers, I would have recommended a slow, teasing buildup, with plenty of kissing and caressing and nipple tickling. But Helen and Jerry were already physically familiar with each other, so Helen needed to do something quick and dramatic to keep up his sexual interest.

"I opened his pants and took out his cock. He said, 'Hey . . .' but I said, 'That's all right, I just have to check that you're enjoying this.' His cock wasn't fully hard, but it was very juicy at the end. I knelt down between his legs and swirled my tongue around his cock head, around and around, almost immediately his cock began to grow. I took it into my mouth and licked all around his little hole with the tip of my tongue, and then I slowly (and gently!) sucked his cock, bobbing my head up and down so that my hair brushed the sides of it. I could feel it growing in my mouth. It swelled up until it practically choked me, but I took it deeper and deeper into my mouth until his public hair was brushing against my nose.

"Every now and then I took his cock out of my mouth and licked it like a grape-flavored sucker, real slow and sensual, around and around, so that it was all wet with my saliva. Then I bared my teeth and gently bit it, so that he could see my teeth sinking into it. I reached up and unbuckled his belt, and unbuttoned his pants, and tugged them down a short way, so that I could get my hand into his undershorts. I took hold of his balls and started to pull the hairs out of them, one by one. His cock was deep in my mouth when I started doing that, and it swelled up even bigger. It was so hard it was like a cop's nightstick; and it tasted so good that I could have sucked it all night.

"I looked up at him while I was sucking his cock and I'd never seen that look on his face before. He was staring at me like I was somebody magical, almost. I had kind of kissed his cock once or twice, when we were making love in bed, but I had never knelt down between his legs and sucked it like that, with all of the lights on, so that he could see everything that was happening. I pulled more hairs out of his balls, and they were so tight they were like pebbles. I could swear that he was going to climax at any moment. I could feel the tension in him, all of his sperm building up, ready to shoot out.

"I started to rub his cock with my hand, too, and I could feel how tight he was, bursting with sperm, and for the first time ever I wanted him to climax in my mouth, I wanted a whole mouthful of sperm so that I could swallow it and taste it and suck him dry.

"It took all of my self-discipline to remember what I was supposed to do. I gave his cock one last lick, and then I said, 'Now for your massage.' I have to tell you, he was putty in my hands, and this is without putting him down or anything. I loved him and I wanted him, and I knew that all I was doing was showing him what we could do together if we only knew how.

"He tried to resist me, but I kept on kissing him, and I kept on rubbing his big slippery cock with one hand while I unbuttoned his shirt. While he finished undressing I spread a big bath towel on the couch, and I opened up my jar of massage gel. Then I told him to lie facedown on the couch while I massaged him.

"I filled my hands with this spice-scented gel, and rubbed it all over his shoulders. His shoulders are very hairy so that he looked like a seal by the time I was through. I eased all of the knots out of his shoulders, and massaged his neck and his upper arms, I climbed on top of him, and sat astride his back, squeezing his sides with my thighs and rubbing my G-string against him. I was all greasy and smothered in gel, and I pulled my G-string over to one side so that my cunt was bare, and I massaged him with my cunt, too, squashing my cunt lips up against him. He kept trying to reach around and touch my cunt but I wouldn't let him.

"I was real aroused myself by then . . . it was all I could do to continue massaging him, instead of turning him over and sitting on his cock. But I knew that I had to do this properly, if it was going to work. I slid down him a little ways, and then I smothered the cheeks of his ass in massage gel, and gave him a long, slow squeezing. I reached between his legs and his cock was incredibly stiff. I slid my hand down it, and around his balls, but I knew that I had to leave *that* till later.

"I opened the cheeks of his ass with both hands, and slowly massaged gel into his asshole. It really turned me on, his dark hairy ass with his tight red asshole, and his balls all tight. I rubbed the tip of my finger around his asshole, around and around, and then I slid my finger inside, a little at a time. At first I could feel his muscles clenching, but my finger was so slippery, and he wanted it up there, he really wanted it, and so he relaxed, and I slid my finger up his asshole as far as it would go, and waggled it around.

"All the time I was massaging his back with my other hand, around and around, and he was making these incredible groaning noises. I asked him if I was hurting him, but all he said was, 'If this is hurt, then hurt is heaven.'

"I have to tell you that I had never done anything like this before in the whole of my life. If you hadn't encouraged me, if you hadn't made me feel that sex between people who love each other can never be bad or dirty, I wouldn't have been able to do it. But it was very liberating. It made me free, I mean sexually free, because I learned to love my lover's body and I learned to love my own body—and more than anything else, I lost my fear of doing whatever I felt like doing.

"I slipped a second finger into Jerry's asshole. He wanted it, he wanted it, I could really tell. I massaged deep inside his ass, and he didn't say anything, he didn't say a word, he was deeply gone, right inside his own pleasure. I drew my fingers out again. His asshole looked red and sore, but he reached around and opened it up with his own fingers and said, 'More . . . you're fantastic.'

"I'd read about fisting in one of your books, but I never imagined that I'd ever be doing it. I rubbed more gel on my hand, and then I folded my hand real tight, and I gradually twisted all of my fingers up Jerry's ass, until my whole hand was up his asshole, right up to the wrist. It was amazing. I looked down and there was my own wrist, disappearing deep inside his hairy stretched-open asshole. Inside, he was all soft and slippery and beautiful. I thought: I'm exploring, right inside my lover's body, deep inside. I wriggled my fingers like an octopus, and he started groaning again.

"After a while, I slid my hand slowly out again, and then I turned Jerry over. He was so aroused that he was almost out of his mind . . . and *I'd* done it! His cock was standing up like a big thick flagstaff, and there was white sperm dripping from the end of it, that's how excited he was.

"My G-string was so wet with gel and cunt juice that it didn't get in the way at all. I took hold of Jerry's knob and placed it between the lips of my cunt and sat on it, and when he slid right up inside me I thought that he was going to touch my stomach, he was so hard.

"He held my breasts in both hands, squashing them and flipping my nipples, and all the time this immense cock was pushing up inside of me, it was *huge.* I could feel every ridge, every vein, every inch of it.

"When he came, I felt his cock pump and pump, and I came, too. I thought I was going to die. Everything went black and all I could feel was cock, as if my whole body was nothing but a cunt that was crammed with cock. I lifted my hips up, and his cock slid out of my cunt, and fell sideways against my thigh, all soft and fat and juicy, and then his sperm dripped out of my cunt on top of it, long sticky drips.

"I took his cock in my mouth and I had my wish, a mouthful of sperm. I wouldn't let him get up. I wouldn't let him leave. I lay there with his cock in my mouth, gently massaging his asshole, occasionally dipping the tip of my finger into it, and I almost fell asleep, and so did he.

"I felt like we'd discovered a whole new world, and I guess you could say that we had."

Helen and Jerry eventually married and her latest report was that she was "blissfully happy . . . especially in bed."

She had used very simple and logical techniques in order to transform her sex life overnight. She had been self-disciplined, too. Even when she was giving Jerry oral sex, and felt like making him climax so that she could enjoy swallowing his sperm, she resisted. It was important that she went on to perform a memorable sexual act (in this case, fisting) which would make him especially eager to have sex with her again.

After that act, she went on to straightforward intercourse, to give him the satisfaction of having "possessed" her and brought her to orgasm.

If she hadn't climaxed at that point, there were several ways in which she could have made sure that he *did* satisfy her, all of which would have made him feel equally competent and fulfilled.

Good sex is learning how to make your partner feel better. If your partner feels better, then you'll feel better, too. Wild sex is learning how to make your partner feel so excited that he or she can't *help* but make you feel better. Wilder sex is when you both do everything you've ever fantasized about, and more.

Wilder sex is when you wake up in the morning thinking "Wow!"

THREE

How to Find the Wilder You

Every woman has a wild, exciting personality inside of her. Every woman is capable of being strongly sensual, a tigress in bed.

So why are so many women so sexually inhibited? Even today, in this liberated, sexually-aware age, why are so many women still dissatisfied with their love lives? Especially when they *could* be having wild and passionate sex whenever they feel like it?

We've seen part of the answer already. To realize their full sexual potential, women need men who are skillful, caring, romantic, appreciative, slow, fit, virle, unafraid, masterful, adventurous, slow and romantic, and *slow.* After so many millenia, you would have thought that men would at least have got the message that men are quicker, women are slower. Men quick, women slow. It ought to be printed on a T-shirt. If the man in your life never learns anything else about sex, then at least teach him that.

When businesspeople go to seminars to learn how to be better at management and marketing, one of the first lessons they learn is to know what their problems are, and then to set themselves ambitious but achievable targets in order to solve these problems and put themselves back on the track for success.

You can do the same with your sex life. Take out a pen and paper, and ask yourself the following questions.

1. Am I satisfied with my sex life?
2. If I am satisfied, is there still some way in which it could be even more exciting?
3. If I am not satisfied, why am I not satisfied? (Check as many of these as you need to.) (a) My lover isn't romantic enough. (b) We don't have sex often enough. (c) Our lovemaking is monotonous. (d) He doesn't arouse me enough before intercourse. (e) It's all over too quickly for me. (f) I rarely or never achieve orgasm during sex. (g) I wish he would try some sexual variations. (h) He does sexual things to me that I dislike. (i) I don't know enough about sex to be able to excite him.
4. If my lover isn't romantic enough, would he be upset if I told him, or should I try a more subtle approach? (Remember, I'm not suggesting that it's right to be afraid to talk to your partner about any aspect of your sex life, but sexual shortcomings can be a highly sensitive subject and in real life it is often more productive to use practical techniques to improve your lover's sexual attitudes than it is to confront him with a bald out-and-out statement that "you're not romantic enough." More often than not, a man who isn't romantic doesn't know *how* to be romantic, so trying to *tell* him what's wrong with his sexual approach will not only make him respond to you in a negative way, but will be of no practical use. Better to show than to tell—*that's* the way to get really effective results.)
5. If we don't have sex often enough, why? Is it lack of interest or tiredness on his part? Or lack of interest or tiredness on my part? If I want sex more often, have I done anything about it, or do I always wait for my lover to make the first move? Is it lack of time and/or opportunity? Is it simply because we've gotten out of the habit, and sex

doesn't seem to have a place in our daily schedule anymore?

6. If I don't think we have sex often enough, how often *would* be often enough, and when? (Set yourself a time and a place, and try to make sure that you really do make love when the time comes.)
7. If our lovemaking is monotonous, why is it monotonous? Is it because we always do it in the same place at roughly the same time of day? Is it because my lover always uses the same routine? Is it because he doesn't seem to know how to do anything different? How would he react if I tried something sexually startling?
8. If my lover doesn't arouse me enough before intercourse, what can I do to slow him down? Is there anything special that I would like him to do for me, such as kiss me more, or caress my breasts more, or give me oral sex?
9. If it's all over too quickly for me, is there a reason for this, and can I do anything practical to slow our lovemaking down?
10. If I rarely or ever achieve an orgasm during sex; is there a way in which I can make sure that I do? Is there any way in which I pleasure myself which I could include in our lovemking so that I am more aroused? Can I think of any special fantasies that would heighten my excitement?
11. If I wish he would try some sexual variations, have I suggested them to him? Do I know if he has any special sexual likes or dislikes? Does he know any sexual variations? Is there anything that I can do to encourage him to give me more varied sex, such as changing my position in bed, or giving him oral sex while my own vulva is close to his face (the so-ealled 69 position), or dressing in clothes that will really excite him, such as peephole bras, or garter belts or latex?
12. If he does sexual things to me that I dislike, can I encourage him to change his sexual techniques? Have I thought that what he does might be a very strong turn-on for him, and that I *could* get to like

it if I took greater control of what he was doing? (Women have complained to me more about oral and anal sex than any other sexual technique, but in almost every case there was an element of force involved—their lovers' penises were thrust into their mouths quite arrogantly, or else they were penetrated anally without proper preparation and lubrication.)

13. If I don't think I know enough about sex to excite him, am I prepared to find out what to do? And when I *have* found out, am I prepared to put my newly acquired knowledge into practice?

Let's look first at *romance,* which to my mind is essential for really wild and exciting sex. Even though we have seen that men are much less romantically inclined when it comes to sex, and that they are sexually responsive even to pictures of women whom they don't even know, men actually find sex more satisfying within a relationship that has a strong romantic content. What I found especially interesting was how many men would have found certain sexual variations highly exciting with their own wives or long-term lovers, but did not have the courage to attempt them. Instead, they fantasized about them while they masturbated, or else they visited prostitutes and practiced these variations with them—*even though more than 78 percent of them admitted that "it would have been ten times more erotic with my regular partner."*

And why would it have been so much more erotic with their regular partner? "Because our relationship is a loving relationship, a romantic relationship . . . and the idea of doing something wild with your romantic partner is a terrific turn-on."

So why don't they do it? "Because I don't think she'd like it if I did."

I have talked to many different couples about sexual acts that the man secretly wanted to do but never had the nerve to try. When it seemed appropriate, I asked them to try these sexual acts to see what the woman actually thought of them, but with the stipulation that the man should be as romantic and caring in this approach as he knew how.

Here's David, 29, an insurance salesman from Phoenix, Arizona. David has been married to Bonnie, 27, for three years, although they have been living together for four. "I would say that Bonnie and I are quite a romantic couple, yes. I still bring her flowers. I still take her out for dinner when I can afford it. I guess I'm not the kind of guy who shows his feelings very openly. I tend to take it for granted that I love Bonnie, otherwise I wouldn't be living with her, would I? I hope that Bonnie and I will have a family before too long and stay together for the rest of our lives. I think she finds me too quiet sometimes. She likes to talk a lot. She even likes to talk through sex, which kinds of puts me off. I don't talk during sex.

"Our sex life is pretty good. We make love two, three, sometimes four times a week. I think I would like it if we made love someplace else apart from the bedroom. Sometimes we make out on the living-room rug, but Bonnie is not altogether happy about doing that, especially with all the lights on. I like to see my cock sliding in and out of her. That really turns me on. But what I would really go for is oral sex, to have Bonnie sucking my cock so that I can watch her doing it, and then to come in her mouth.

"I haven't asked her to do that so far; and so far she hasn't offered. So I guess it's one of those things that's always going to stay a fantasy. I have a couple of magazines with pictures of guys shooting their loads into girls' mouths, but I wouldn't go to a prostitute. Guess I'm too scared to, if the truth were known."

Bonnie said, "David's shocked me, I have to admit. I'm not so much shocked by what he wants to do, but by the fact that he hasn't been able to talk to me about it. I don't know very much about sex, but I know what I like, and I'm not at all sure that I want to swallow his come. The whole idea of it makes me feel like he wants to humiliate me . . . or at least make me do something subservient. I thought we were partners, you know, equal partners. I didn't realize he wanted me to be a sex slave."

Bonnie's first response to the idea of swallowing David's semen wasn't at all unusual. But many women whose initial reaction was "yuk!"—just as hers was—later find that they have developed quite a taste for it. Julia, a 23-year-old sculptress from Sausalito, California, wrote to tell me that she regularly asked her boyfriend to masturbate onto her toast in the morning so that she could eat his sperm for breakfast—and, if he ate more honey, would his sperm taste any sweeter? Liza, a 34-year-old homemaker from Denver, Colorado, saved her husband's ejaculate in a screwtop jar in the fridge, so that when he went away on business trips she could drink it while she talked dirty to him on the telephone. "The trouble is," she said, "I liked it so much I used to drink two weeks' worth of sperm in one sitting. It was running down my chin."

Gillian, a 27-year-old designer from Baltimore, Maryland, said that she always turned her lover's condoms inside-out after making love and drank the contents. "I love him, I love the taste of him, why shouldn't I?" And, of course, there was no reason at all why she shouldn't. There was nothing harmful about it—and, as she reported, "It always drove him crazy . . . it made him ready for more lovemaking then and there. He used to watch me licking that condom and his cock used to rise up like you wouldn't believe."

Gillian's sperm drinking took much of the sterility out of lovemaking with a condom. "If I hadn't had his sperm inside me, one way or another, what was the point of it?"

Bonnie was concerned that David might have been using his sex magazines as an aid to masturbation ("and why should he need to masturbate if he can make love to me?"). The answer to that is that many men in long-term sexual relationships find themselves in David's position, unable to voice their sexual fantasies to their wives or lovers, and so they do seek out a substitute in pornographic magazines and videos, and often use them to masturbate. This practice is completely harmless and is rarely a reflection on a man's feelings for his partner. But if he is unable to express such an ordinary and healthy need as a desire for oral sex, then obviously there is a serious lack of communication within the relationship that requires some urgent attention if it isn't going to become any more damaging.

Sex writer Brenda Jones rightly says, "There is one aspect of oral sex that makes it slightly different from other sexual techniques. It does seem that more men than women enjoy practicing it. And although considerable numbers of women do come to adopt it, it is usually at the suggestion of their partners at first. They do not seem to discover it for themselves.

"The man's urge is much more instinctive. There are many women who enjoy a man making love to them this way—it is, in fact, particularly well-suited to a woman's orgasm—but shrink from the idea of returning the favor."

Your lover should be aware that women are much more likely to find oral sex appealing if they are very highly stimulated before they attempt it. Tell him that if he takes the trouble to romance you, kiss you, caress your breasts, and gives you all the foreplay that a woman expects from a skillful lover, his chances of enjoying oral sex will be greatly improved.

And this is not just a game, either. There are real physiological and psychological reasons why—if you are highly sexually excited—you will find not only the *idea* of oral sex more appetizing, you will actually find it easier to do it.

Most people think that when you are sexually excited, your senses are very much keener. In fact, just the opposite occurs. All of your sensation becomes concentrated deep within your nervous system, and your ordinary every day senses such as sight and hearing, smell and taste, all diminish. The pupils of your eyes dilate so that you can only see straight ahead, and you would probably be unable to distinguish between the taste of semen and the taste of vanilla yogurt.

Not only that, a sexually aroused woman will no longer experience the gagging response that most people have when something is placed deep in their mouths. I have talked to many women who strongly disliked the idea of oral sex to begin with, but who were later able to take the whole length of their lover's erect penis into their mouths, with unstinting relish. "Nowadays," said 31-year-old Tina from Houston, Texas, with undisguised pride, "I can swallow Ted's cock so deep that his balls are banging against my chin."

All it took was teasing, cajoling, guiding—and practical sex lessons, women showing their lovers exactly what it was they wanted, and how to achieve it.

For men, fellatio (oral stimulation of the male genitals) has some powerfully-arousing characteristics, which are quite different from those of cunnilingus (oral stimulation of the female genitals.) Fellatio allows a man actually to see his penis being stimulated—and we have already noted how strongly men respond to visual sex. I gathered 50 recent catalogs for pornographic videos from all over the world, containing full-color illustrations of the videos' front covers. Expressed as percentages, 33 percent of the covers show women sucking one erect penis, 12 percent show women giving oral sex to two or more men at once, 3 percent show women with two erect penises in their mouths at once, 23 percent show men ejaculating sperm into women's open mouths, 2 percent show men urinating into women's open mouths, 1 percent show men sucking the penises of other men.

Most of these videos are "classics" of pornography and have been selling thousands of copies for many years. The lesson is absolutely clear: depictions of oral sex sell videos and magazines, and the buyers of pornographic videos and magazines are overwhelmingly male.

Apart from the visual excitement of oral sex, there is no way of avoiding the reality that even the gentlest and most appreciative of men is also aroused by the idea of the woman in his life submissively kissing his penis. Wendy Dennis, the feminist author of *Hot and Bothered* told me when we appeared together on Toronto's *Shirley Show* together that she disapproved of fellatio because it meant that a woman had to get down on her knees to a man. Although I fully understood what she was trying to say, I didn't agree with her, because I have yet to meet a woman who feels degraded by giving oral sex to the man she loves. A woman doesn't "kneel" to a man when she gives him oral sex—not in the sense of paying him homage. She may have to kneel because his penis is halfway down his body, but oral sex is usually performed lying down, and then who's kneeling? Almost always, the so-called submissiveness of oral sex is only a game, and there is no real "domination" involved in fellatio—any more than there is "domination" involved in cunnilingus, a man kissing a woman's genitals.

No matter what sexual fantasy arouses you the most, there will always be some element of domination or submission in it, and most well-balanced lovers are aroused by a little of both. There will be times when you want your partner to woo you, to treat you like a queen—while at other times you feel like nothing more than rough and immediate intercourse, almost verging on rape. Helplessness can be just as erotic as total control; and the accepting of pleasure is just as important a part of an exciting sexual relationship as giving it.

In fact it's surprising how many sexual relationships run into difficulties because one or the other partner finds it almost impossible to accept the erotic stimulation that their partner is trying to give them.

Mary, a 23-year-old teacher from Baltimore, Maryland, said, "I'm quite willing to 'go down' on Paul . . . I enjoy oral sex and I think that I'm good at it, too. It's very intimate and it's a good way of making love when you don't feel like having full intercourse, like when you have a period. The trouble is, Paul immediately stiffens when I start licking and sucking his penis, and I don't mean that he has an erection! He doesn't seem to find oral sex very stimulating, although I can't discover why. I usually manage to suck him into a full erection, but I've never managed to bring him to a climax. My previous lover used to adore it, and I was always sucking him and swallowing his come, but I don't think that's ever going to happen with Paul."

Paul's problem was quite common. He felt that he always had to be in charge when he made love to Mary, and he didn't like losing control of the rhythm or the pace of their lovemaking, or the strength of the stimulation that he was receiving. Despite its appearance, the act of fellatio is in many ways an act of submission for the man, rather than an act of domination. His precious penis is completely in the woman's control (she can bite it if she wants to . . . even to the extent of biting it off altogether), and he has to rely on his woman to judge how fast and how hard he should be aroused.

Many women don't realize that sucking and licking and kissing a man's penis is rarely enough to bring him to a climax, and that he will usually need some strong manual rubbing as well.

But wild sex isn't all about one partner dominating the other: wild sex is all about sharing every second of your sexual arousal—and sharing it with relish.

Wild sex is always swings and roundabouts—not so much domination and submission as giving and taking, initiation and acceptance. Sex is a physical and emotional arena for all of your feelings of tenderness, passion, excitement, and love—and if you are as strongly aroused as you should be, then you will be able to accept and enjoy all kinds of acts that technically break the rules of sexual politics, but which will bring you sensations you never thought possible.

So long as you both fully enjoy what you're doing—so long as one partner isn't physically hurt or emotionally upset for the sake of the other partner's pleasure—then almost anything goes.

David agreed to behave much more romantically toward Bonnie—and she, in turn, agreed to be more sexually adventurous.

David: "It took me some time to accept that I hadn't been very romantic. I always thought I was. But I guess when it was pointed out to me that romance is something a little more than bringing home flowers now and again, and saying, 'That's a sexy dress,' I guess I started to get the message. I'm not a very physical person, in that my family never kissed and cuddled very much. For that reason I find physicality a little hard to deal with. When we're not actually making love, I don't automatically put my arm around Bonnie, or hold or cuddle her or tell her how much I love her. I thought she knew that I loved her just because I did. It didn't occur to me that she needed to hear it out loud, and so often. I feel bad about that, because I've always loved her, and I never wanted to upset her.

"That first night I brought home flowers and a bottle

of Mumm's Cuvée Napa, which is every bit as good as French champagne. She had dressed up specially in a white silk blouse and short black skirt, and brushed her hair loose, which I really like—and this time I told her that I really liked it. I made a point of kissing her when I came in, and holding her close, unlike the quick pecks on the cheek which I usually use to give her. And do you know something, it felt good, kissing her like that? I actually began to feel quite horny."

I had suggested to David that he treat *every* reunion with Bonnie as a prelude to making love, even if he had been away no longer than a twenty-minute trip to the hardware store. It's surprising how many couples forget to smile when they greet each other, and forget to make every reunion pleasurable.

"I felt self-conscious at first, telling her how much I loved her, and making such a fuss of her. But she reciprocated. She kissed me back, she ran her fingers through my hair, she slid her knee up in between my thighs. I suddenly thought: this being romantic, this isn't a drag at all, this is actually very exciting.

"She had cooked us a light supper, chicken and salad with balsamic vinegar, it's one of my favorites. Then afterwards we took the rest of the champagne through to the living room, and I put on some real quiet romantic music. I held her in my arms and I kissed her. I really spent some time kissing her, and I was amazed what a turn-on it was, just kissing. I wouldn't have minded if we hadn't done anything else at all, because I suddenly remembered what it was like just to hold her in my arms and kiss her and feel like I was in love with her, instead of thinking that I had to make love to her instantly, then and there, the quicker the better.

"We drank some champagne and kissed some more. By this time we would usually have undressed, made love, finished, and gotten dressed again. I caressed her breasts outside of her blouse, and I was surprised to feel her nipples sticking up through the silk. At first I thought she wasn't wearing a bra, but then I unbuttoned her blouse and found that she was wearing a lacy white bra with holes for her nipples to stick through. That really turned me on. I can tell you. I stroked and played with her nipples and then I kissed them and sucked them, and all the time I didn't even have to take off her bra.

"I unfastened her skirt and slipped her out of it. Underneath it looked like she was wearing regular white lacy panties to match her bra, but when she opened her legs a little way I suddenly saw that they were open in the middle, and I could see her bare pussy and her blond pubic hair.

"I held open her pussy with my fingers and played with her clitoris, which was stiff like a little bird's beak. Then I slipped one finger up inside her, and she was so juicy that her pussy actually made a squelching noise. I had never seen Bonnie wearing anything like this before. It was white and flowery, very virginal, but at the same time it was really blatant, really whorish.

"I gently stroked her clitoris with my thumb, while I continued finger fucking her. My cock was so hard thought it was going to burst out of my pants. Bonnie opened up my zipper, reached inside my shorts, and took out my cock. She rubbed it up and down a few times, gripping it really hard so that the head bulged even bigger. Then she unbuckled my belt, pulled down my pants and my shorts, and started to massage my balls with one hand while she rubbed my cock up and down with the other. I was getting pretty juicy myself, but Bonnie reached down between her legs and slid her fingers into her pussy next to mine, so that they were all covered in her own juice, and then she rubbed my cock again, so that it was all slippery and shiny.

"She stuck out her tongue, and ran the tip of it all the way up my cock from my balls to the very top. Then she pressed her tongue flat against the underside of my cock, and gave me a long hard lick, all the way up, and then again, and then again, and watching her do that was such a turn-on. Her nipples were sticking out of her bra, pink and stiff, and I played with each of them in turn, gently twisting them and tugging them.

"Bonnie licked all the way around the rim of my cock head, licking every vein and every crevice. Then she kissed my cock, very slow and lascivious, like she was kissing my lips. All the time my finger was working around and around in her pussy. I slipped another finger in beside it, just to make it slippery, and then I started to touch and stroke her asshole.

"At first she resisted, but I kept pushing the tip of my finger into her asshole, and at last she relaxed it a little, and I was able to slide it further inside, and work it around and around. She opened her legs wider, so that her panties opened even wider, too, and I could see my finger disappearing right inside her asshole, right up to the knuckle.

"She went on kissing and licking my cock, and at last she opened her mouth and took the head of it between her lips. She gently sucked it against the roof of her mouth, and very gently bared her teeth and bit it. All the time she was slowly rubbing my cock up and down, up and down, keeping up this rhythm, and I began to feel my balls tightening and that feeling you get when you're almost ready to shoot out your load.

"Bonnie looked at me and gave me a dreamy look with her eyes, and that almost made me climax on the spot. Seeing your wife in a peephole bra and open panties and her mouth crammed full of your cock—that was like a sex fantasy come true.

"She took me so deep into her mouth I could hardly believe it. The feeling was sensational, but it wasn't so much the feeling aroused me, it was seeing it happen. It wouldn't have been the same in the dark. She sucked me and rubbed me harder and harder, and I began to push my fingers even deeper into her pussy and her asshole. We were both sweating and panting and completely wild. And then an incredible thing happened. Bonnie had an orgasm before I did, shaking and jumping and clenching her thighs together. She actually tried to cry out with my cock in her mouth, and I was going to take it out, but she wouldn't let me. She kept on rubbing and licking, faster and faster, until I felt like I was going to explode.

"The first squirt of sperm went straight down her throat. But then she took my cock half out of her mouth, so that the next squirt went all over her lips. She rubbed me again and again, and more sperm squirted onto her cheeks and onto her chin. There was thick white sperm all over her face. She went on licking and sucking my cock even when it was going softer, she didn't want to stop. She gently pushed me so that I was lying on my back on the couch, and she climbed on top of me, so that her pussy was directly in my face, and she took the whole of my soft cock into her mouth, and went on sucking it, very slow and gentle.

"While she was doing that, I kissed and licked at her pussy at the same relaxed pace. We weren't trying to bring each other to another climax, or anything like that. We both felt warm and satisfied and all we wanted to do was to enjoy each other's bodies. I slipped my finger into Bonnie's asshole again, and this time she accepted it readily. In fact she pushed her bottom back a little so that it went in deep, right to the knuckle.

"After a while she climbed off me, but before she did so she took my cock in her mouth and stretched it out as long as it would go, and grinned at me. I never thought I had a wife who could be wild in bed, but I certainly found out different that day . . . and our lovemaking has been so much more exciting ever since."

Bonnie said afterward, "For me, the greatest thrill of what happened that day was discovering that I knew how to turn David on. For the first time, I felt as if I was sexually in control of myself, and sexually in control of David's responses. I always knew that men liked to look. I think all girls know that from their childhood. But I never realized what an important part of lovemaking it is. I never realized that I could show myself off like that, and what effect it would have on him.

"I've seen men's magazines with naked girls in them and I've always thought of them as pretty vulgar and distasteful. I never put two-and-two together and asked myself, why do men buy them, and is there something in them that I can learn to make my sex life better?

"The best part of our lovemaking that day, as far as I'm concerned, was that I was slow and unhurried and romantic and there was a whole lot of kissing and touching. I always knew that David loved me, but it didn't do my ego any harm at all to have him lavish so much attention on me, not to mention champagne.

"I wasn't sure about the sexy underwear at first. I

imagined black stockings and purple garter belts. But this underwear was so white and pretty that I didn't mind wearing it at all . . in fact I still wear it now, out of choice. I found it exciting to wear, particularly the open panties, because I could show off my pussy or not, according to how I opened or closed my legs.

"Another thing that surprised me was how naturally it came to me, giving David oral sex. I was in a comfortable position and in any case he was touching me and fingering me and turning me on, so I wasn't nearly so inhibited about doing it as I thought I was going to be when we were discussing it 'cold.' Once I'd started licking and sucking his cock, I enjoyed myself so much that I didn't want to stop. What I liked more than anything else about it was being able to control how fast or how slow David was being aroused. That meant that I could make our lovemaking go on longer if I wanted to, and since I've always been very slow to become aroused, this was a real bonus.

"These days, when we make love, I often give David oral sex before we have intercourse, which means that I'm almost always very well aroused by the time he actually penetrates me. *He* thinks our sex life is better because he loves me sucking his cock. *I* know it's better for me because I'm always much more satisfied.

"I couldn't believe how easy it was to take his cock deep into my mouth. Normally I'm the kind of person who starts gagging if I so much as push a sundae spoon too far into my mouth. And if I'm really turned-on, I don't mind swallowing David's sperm, either, although I know he likes it when it shoots all over my face or onto my breasts.

"One thing I like so much that I've grown almost addicted to is David sliding one finger up my bottom when we're making love, or even when we're not. About three weeks ago I was resting on the bed after a shower, face-down, almost asleep, because we'd been playing tennis all afternoon. David came and lay beside me and after a while he lifted my towel so that my bottom was bare and started kissing and tickling it. He smeared some hand lotion on his finger, and then he pushed it into my bottom, as far as it would go.

"I just lay there while he squirmed it around and around, my eyes closed, and after about five or ten minutes I suddenly realized that I was well on the way to having an orgasm. I didn't quite make it, but I was amazed how much David could arouse me, just by doing that."

David and Bonnie's sexual relationship was improved because they both recognized that men and women have different sexual needs and that women, as a rule, take longer to become fully aroused than men. Of course there will always be times when you both enjoy quick, rough sex. But for long-term satisfaction and for the ability to vary and intensify your lovemaking so that it becomes really wild for both partners, you need to match your timing so that you both reach a high level of sexual excitement at around the same time.

This doesn't mean trying to have simultaneous climaxes. The simultaneous climax with fireworks bursting in the air and surf washing over the rocks is an invention of romantic fiction, and it is neither necessary nor particularly desirable. What I *am* talking about is making sure that each of you is intensely aroused, so that when you *do* try some of the wilder sexual techniques, both of you are ready and willing—not only physically but mentally, too.

Bonnie, for instance, wouldn't have enjoyed giving David oral sex so much if she hadn't been highly aroused before she started. I have talked again and again to women who are made to feel inadequate because they don't care for oral or anal sex or other variations that their lovers try to force on to them. Almost always, the cause of their unhappiness is their lovers' failure to arouse them sufficiently beforehand. Once they have been properly stimulated, they frequently find that they are able to enjoy all kinds of sexual variations, some of them *very* wild indeed, with enthusiasm, joy, and wholeheartedness.

Here's another interesting couple—Bryan, 34, a technical designer from Pasadena, California, and his wife Renee, 35, a former grade school teacher. Renee was upset because Bryan had managed after five-and-a-half years of marriage to tell her that he wanted her to dress up like a nurse when they made love. She had been aware that men were supposed to have sexual fantasies about women dressed up as nurses or police officers or French maids, but she had always regarded these fantasies as something that existed only in the cartoon pages of *Playboy*. At first, she was unable to take Bryan's request seriously. Then, when she did, she began to have serious doubts about the sexual side of their marriage.

On the one hand, she appreciated his honesty in telling her that he wanted her to dress like a nurse; and she wasn't too shocked to consider doing it. On the other hand, when she *did* do it, she began to wonder if he was making love to her, in a nurse's uniform, or to just a fantasy nurse.

Renee wasn't alone in having doubts about role-playing in a sexual relationship. Many men and women who try to spice up their love lives by acting out fantasy roles have doubts and questions about it. Each individual case is very different, and when one partner is unable to have satisfactory sex without some form of fantasy being played out, this can be a cause for some concern. On the whole, though, fantasy role-playing in a sexual relationship is not only harmless but positively beneficial. In Bryan and Renee's case, it allowed Bryan to introduce some wilder and sexual variations into their lovemaking which Renee eventually admitted that she found "very forbidden, very dirty, very exciting"—because both of them would make the mental excuse that it wasn't Bryan and Renee who were doing these things, it was Patient and Nurse.

There may have been an underlying psychological reason why Bryan wanted Renee to dress up like a nurse when they had sex—a childhood trauma, an experience in hospital—but in my experience psychologists try to look too deep into the past to explain the most obvious examples of human sexual behavior.

Men and women use role-playing fantasies in order to explain to their partners some of their strongest sexual desires—desires they would find extremely difficult to articulate in words, for fear of rejection or embarrassment.

When Bryan told Rence that he would like her to

dress up as a nurse, he wasn't simply saying that he was turned-on by nurses' uniforms, he was telling her that occasionally he wanted her to take charge of their sex life, that occasionally he wanted to feel submissive while she was active. In the Nurse/Patient fantasy there is often a hidden desire for so-called wet sex and anal stimulation, too, which many men find extremely difficult to suggest to their partners outside of the fantasy context.

I was able to reassure Renee that Bryan did not see her as anybody else when she was dressed up in nurse's uniform, that he was still excited by her, Renee. He was simply acting out an erotic role-playing game in which it became possible for him to express his sexual desires more openly.

There's another important point to make, too, in the context of wilder sex. Just because your man wants to try something different, that doesn't mean that he's always secretly wanted to do it, and never told you. It doesn't mean that you haven't been satisfying him sexually up until now. It doesn't mean that he's a closet pervert, and it doesn't mean that if you try it, and he likes it, but you don't, that you'll always have to go on doing it.

But you don't know what any sexual variation is like until you've given it a try—not reluctantly, but with sharing and generosity and a willingness to make it exciting.

As I've repeated many times over the past two decades, you owe it to yourself and to your partner to try anything and everything in bed. Provided you both enjoy it, and provided it's safe, then there is no reason why you shouldn't try it.

If you don't like any particular sexual variation, all you have to say to your partner is, "Please, let's not do that again," and if he's a considerate lover, he won't.

Bryan said, "I've had a nurse fantasy for just about as long as I can remember. I don't think it's anything to do with my childhood. I was never in hospital when I was a child . . . only once, I think, for stitches in my knee. But I just loved the idea of lying in a bed while a beautiful woman in a crisp white uniform takes care of you, and has to do everything for you, because she's a ministering angel and in any case you can't help yourself. I suppose it's the idea of being dominated that turns me on, in a way . . . but it's also the idea that even though a nurse is in charge, and is telling you what to do, she *has* to look after you, it's her job, and she doesn't have any choice in the matter. So I guess it's a fantasy that has its submissive side, as well as its dominant side. I don't know. It's hard to explain why it turns me on so much, but it definitely has a lot to do with being helpless while a strict woman in uniform can do whatever she likes to you.

"I never had a fantasy about any special nurse. When you have a fantasy, you don't think about any particular girl . . . leastways, I don't. You just imagine this fantasy woman. She doesn't have to have a name, even. I like girls with very short blond hair and blue eyes and very big breasts . . . but then that just about sums up the way that Renee looks anyway. That's one of the reasons I fell for her, and that's one of the reasons she turns me on.

"Renee and I have always had a pretty good sex life. She can be very passionate when she's in the mood. The trouble is, she doesn't like to talk about sex too much. If I try to mention the sex we had last night, she always turns irritable and changes the subject. She came from a very conventional family and I guess that may be part of the reason. But it makes it difficult to suggest things to her—even to ask her what *she* wants in bed. For all I know, she may have a fantasy about being fucked by 40 pharaohs, but she's never told me about it, never.

"I guess the nurse thing came up when we were watching a TV movie about a hospital. One of the nurses looked quite a lot like Renee. She had this little starched cap and short blond hair, and one of those white uniforms with buttons all the way down the front. I always imagine they're naked underneath, but I guess they're probably not. She wore white ankle socks and white oxfords, too, and as far as I was concerned that really put the frosting on the cake.

"I said to Renee, 'I'd love you to dress up as a nurse. I mean, talk about sexy,' and that's how I came to make my confession. She teased me about it, and then she got a little angry about it. She said I should have told her years and years ago, if it turned me on *that* much.

"I didn't say anything more about it, and I kind of

assumed that the subject was closed. But then I came home one evening and there she was . . . all dressed up in this white starchy nurse uniform, complete with a cap and everything. She clung on to me and kissed me, even before I'd had the chance to walk in the door. She'd bought the uniform from a regular medical-supplies store, so it was totally authentic. She's very big-breasted, and it was kind of tight across the bust, but I liked that.

"She said I had to undress and get to bed because I was looking sick. She took off all of my clothes for me—necktie, shirt, socks, pants, and shorts. It was still daylight but that added to the feeling of being a patient in a hospital. When I was naked, my cock was totally hard. She stroked it a few times, and then told me that it needed some special attention.

"She told me to lie on the bed, face upward. I did what she said because she was Nurse, and she was supposed to be looking after me. I felt helpless but very strong and excited, too, if you can understand what I mean. I felt that I was doing what I had always wanted to do . . . it was actually coming true. And I was doing it with Renee, too, which made it feel even better. She was actually sharing my fantasy . . . the same fantasy I used to jerk off to, when I was younger. It was coming alive with a real woman.

"I don't think Renee understood it, not to start with, but it was more exciting that I was doing it with her than it would have been if I had been doing it with a woman I didn't know, say a hooker or somebody.

"She said she had to wash me. She brought out a basin of warm water and a washcloth and a bar of soap, and she soaped my chest and my stomach and my thighs. Then she worked up a thick lather between her hands and started to soap my cock, squeezing it up and down. She soaped all around my balls, and she soaped my ass, too. Then she rinsed off all the soap with the washcloth, and used it to grip my cock and give me five or six really hard rubs.

"She said her uniform was getting all wet, so she had to unbutton it. She opened it all the way down, and she was fantastic. Her breasts were bare, and her nipples were all pink and crinkled up. Even though her breasts are so big, they're still very firm. She was wearing a black garter belt and black stockings, but no panties. She always shaves her cunt except the tiniest little fluff of blond hair, just above her clitoris. She opened her cunt with her fingers and I could see that her lips were looking swollen and that she was wet . . . so the nurse fantasy must have turned her on, too.

"She climbed on to the bed on top of me, and took hold of my cock. She rubbed it some more, and then she opened her legs wide, and fitted my cock in between her cunt lips, and slowly sat down on me, so that my cock slid up inside her. I tried to lift up my hips so that I was fucking her, but she wouldn't let me. Every time I tried to do it, she said, 'Keep still! Nurse knows best!' and sat right down on top of me, with my cock still deep inside her cunt. I reared my hips up a bit, so that my cock drove even deeper inside her, but still she wouldn't let me fuck her. She was playing the part, too.

"She said, 'You have to learn how to control yourself,' and she lifted herself up and down on my cock. When she went up, my cock almost slipped out of her cunt, I could see the knob between her cunt lips, purple between pink. She hesitated for a moment, right at the very top of her stroke, when I really felt that my cock was just on the verge of dropping out, and then slowly she sat down on me, as hard as she could, until my cock was so deep inside her that it looked as if my pubic hair was hers.

"She went on doing this, slow and deep, and she almost drove me crazy. I felt like fucking her fast and hard, but she wouldn't let me. After a while, though, she said, 'You can squeeze my breasts if you like . . . just for the physiotherapy. We wouldn't want your fingers to stiffen, from lack of use.' So I reached up and massaged her breasts. They're firm and heavy and I can almost plunge my fingers right into them. I stroked her nipples with my fingertips, and lifted my head up and kissed them, but almost immediately she pushed me back down again.

"Now she was moving up and down on me faster. She was beginning to pant, and her face was flushed pink. Her nurse's cap had come unpinned on one side, and her hair was coming loose. Her eyes were closed and she kept licking her lips. She reached down with both hands between her legs. With one hand she held her cunt lips apart, and with the other she started flicking her clitoris—flicking it so quickly that I could scarcely see her finger.

"So much juice was dripping our of her cunt that I could feel it running over my balls and sliding between my legs. She gripped my sides with those slippery black nylon stockings, and she fucked me and fucked me, deep but still slow, until I felt something like a giant crab nipping me between the legs, and there was nothing I could do to stop myself from climaxing. I just couldn't stop. I started to pump sperm up inside her and she started to shake and shake and she wouldn't stop shaking.

"I thought it was all over. But she climbed off me almost at once, and buttoned up her uniform again, and said, 'That's very bad of you . . . now I'll have to wash you again.'

"I said, 'Can't we take a break now? I could use a drink, and I have to go to the bathroom.'

"She said, 'I'll bring you a drink, and I'll take you to the bathroom.'

"She led me to the bathroom, and stood me in front of the john, and held my cock for me. I started to kiss her but she said, 'First things first.' You have no idea how difficult it is to piss when a woman is holding your cock for you. I started with two or three spurts, but at last I managed to get going, and when I did, Renee kept massaging my cock while I was doing it, and playing her fingers in the stream of piss, and massaging my balls with piss. By the time I was finished I was hard again. We went back to the bedroom without even hesitating and fucked all over again, except this time I was on top, and Renee had her legs around me.

"It was the greatest sex we'd had for a long time, we both knew it was. Renee had really gotten into the spirit of the fantasy. But a couple of days afterward, when I suggested we do it again, she said she didn't want to. She said I wanted the Nurse, not her, as if the Nurse was a separate person altogether.

"I asked her if she liked playing the Nurse, and she said sure she did, but she felt as if she didn't turn me on anymore ... not the Renee that I'd first been attracted to, not the same Renee that I'd married. She said, 'Is this the only way we're ever going to get great sex, by playing hospital?'

"Renee as Renee still turns me on just as much as she ever did. For myself, I don't see any difficulty with playing out your fantasies. Anything that makes life more exciting. But there's no question. Renee sees it different. She likes the game, she enjoys playing it. She's very creative when she's playing it, she takes the initiative. I bought an enema syringe so that she can give me an enema, and she says that she will, which is a pretty wild thing for a girl like Renee to do. But there's no doubt that we have a problem there, and I don't want to upset her. Most of all, I don't want our marriage to fall apart, just because of some stupid misunderstanding. Renee's too valuable to me. I love her too much."

So what did Renee think about all this? I told her that I was surprised that she had entered into the spirit of David's nurse fantasy so enthusiastically—given that she now had doubts about it.

Renee said, "I was very sexually excited by what I was doing—more sexually excited than at any time since David and I very first made love. I was so turned on that I was trembling! That was the big plus about it. The other big plus was that I could do whatever I wanted ... by that I mean it was always my decision whether I rubbed him by hand or whether we had intercourse or whether we had oral sex ... and it was also my decision *when* we did things.

"I think David's a very considerate lover but there are plenty of times when it all seems to be over far too quickly. When we are playing out this nurse fantasy I could stretch it out for as long as I wanted, and if I liked doing something I could go on doing it, or I could go back to it and do it again. I do happen to like very long, slow intercourse, dragged out as long as possible, stopping when you feel you're just about to have an orgasm and then starting again after the feeling's subsided. I really enjoyed that—that was beautiful, and I was able to go on doing it for as long as I felt like it.

"I was in charge of whatever we did because I was the nurse and David was the patient and if he wanted the game to continue he had to obey me.

"In spite of all that, though, I didn't feel like I was having to play the part of the dominant partner. I don't feel that everything that happened was down to me. After all, I was playing *David's* game. I was dressed up like a nurse because he wanted me to dress up as a nurse, and I was doing the kind of things to him that a very sexy nurse would do.

"Up until now, I think I've been quite reserved and shy about sex. I was brought up that way. I didn't know anything about sex until I was 16 or 17, and it was a long time after that before I found out about oral sex and anal sex and gays and all that kind of thing. Certainly a plus point about a role-playing fantasy is that you feel you can do some very far-out things without feeling embarrassed. After all, it isn't *you* that's doing all these kinky things . . . it's the person you're pretending to be."

Sometimes the give-and-take required in a sexual relationship can strain it to the limits, but if you both work very hard at giving, and work just as hard at taking, too, the results can be *very* wild indeed.

FOUR

How to Discover (and Satisfy) His Secret Desires

Everybody has their own secret sexual fantasies. But having a fantasy doesn't necessarily mean that you want it to come true. A very common fantasy that women tell me about is the fantasy of being raped by one or more men—the fantasy of being taken by force. Not one of these women, however, has ever said that she would *really* like to be raped. In fact they consider the threat of rape to be one of the greatest sexual fears.

Some men and women, however, suffer long-lasting frustration and guilt because they have a secret sexual fantasy that they long to share with their partner—yet which they're too embarrassed to talk about.

Here's Ray, a 33-year-old auto mechanic from Seattle, Washington. You couldn't hope to find a brawnier, more masculine-looking husband. Yet until he wrote a letter to me, Ray hadn't told his 31-year-old wife Sylvia that he longed to make love to her while dressed in women's underwear.

"How do you explain to your adoring wife of five years' standing that you have the strongest urge to put on stockings and garter belt and G-string and bra? I know I'm not a homosexual. I'm not a transvestite in the sense that I want to put on a wig and a dress and paint my face—although I can understand the feelings of men who do, and I feel a whole lot of sympathy for them. They're just like me, in the sense that they get aroused by something which everybody else seems to regard as disgusting or ludicrous or both.

"I've had this feeling all my life, ever since I was an adolescent. I was staying with my cousins once, in Spokane, and I snuck into my 16-year-old cousin's bedroom. Her name was Jenny and she had blond hair in a kind of Prince Valiant cut and she was beautiful. When she was out I borrowed her garter belt and her stockings and her panties. I can remember everything now . . . they were tan-colored 15-denier stockings, a lacy garter belt, and little pink panties made of see-through nylon with a white lacy frill around them. I had a huge hard-on, and I could hardly fit my cock inside.

"I dressed myself up, and paraded in front of the mirror. I don't know what it was that turned me on so much . . . seeing my own body in lace and frills . . . or maybe imagining that I was a girl, showing myself off to a whole lot of imaginary men. It's very complicated, psychologically. I don't understand it myself.

"What made it worse was that I could never talk to anybody about it. Can you imagine me sitting around with my pals in the shop and saying, 'Hey, guys, guess what *I* did this weekend? Strutted around in bra and panties.'

"While I was wearing my cousin's underwear, I knelt down in front of the mirror and masturbated, squeezing my cock inside of her panties. I pushed my other hand inside the back of her panties, and stroked my balls and my asshole. I imagined that I was being raped, and I forced one finger up my asshole, and then another, and then a third, until it really hurt. I was beating my cock like crazy, and I climaxed right inside her panties, filling them up with sperm. I wiped sperm around my thighs and inside her stocking tops . . . it was a very exciting experience, but it made me feel ashamed, too, like I was some kind of pervert.

"Her panties were soaking wet and of course they reeked of sperm so I kept them. I put back her stockings and her garter belt and nobody ever said anything about them, so I guess that she never found out. I kept those panties for months afterward, and wore them regularly. Sometimes I wore then to school—except on days when I knew we were going to have gym.

"When I left home, I started to buy women's underwear pretty regularly . . . mostly stockings and garter belts and panties. I used to like see-through nylon panties because I could see my cock through them, or else open-crotch panties.

"I'm not gay. Men don't turn me on at all. Yet I do enjoy anal stimulation. I have two vibrators, one very thin one like a finger, and another very long, thick one, and when I'm dressed up in my panties and stockings I enjoy greasing them up with KY jelly and sliding them up my ass. I can't describe what goes through my mind. I feel as if I'm two personalities almost, both rolled into one . . . a man who's fucking a woman and the woman who's being fucked, both of them, both at the same time."

I asked Ray whether he had ever felt the urge to "come out" (at least with his wife Sylvia) and tell her about his liking for women's underwear. He said he thought about it "pretty much every day," but he was afraid that she would consider him to be perverted. Eventually, however, he decided to do it—provided that I could give Sylvia a full and objective explanation of what his sexual fetish was all about.

As it turned out, Sylvia had felt for a long time that, sexually, Ray was hiding something from her. At one time, she had even begun to suspect that he might have another woman. But the truth was that Ray's guilt about his interest in women's underwear had led him to misrepresent to Sylvia the true nature of his sexual personality. Quite understandably, this had caused him enormous frustration, and even more guilt.

Women like Sylvia often write to me and say, "I'm beginning to wonder if my husband has homosexual tendencies. I've found women's underwear hidden in his closet." Or else, "I discovered some terrible pornographic magazines in my boyfriend's apartment. They showed all kinds of disgusting acts. We're engaged to be married but now I'm seriously beginning to think that I ought to call it off." Or, "I found a vibrator under our bed. I've never seen it before and my husband has never used it on me. Do you think he's seeing another woman? Or is he a closet gay?"

I explained to Sylvia that the simple fact is that millions of men are sexually aroused by fantasies and fetishes that appear to women to be perverted or strange. Not many men will openly admit to their interests, because they are afraid that their partner's reaction will be one of bewilderment or disgust. Rather than risk the stability of their relationship, they keep quiet.

Their interests may be extremely mild. In Ray's case, he wanted to do nothing more bizarre than dress in women's underwear now and then, so that he could fantasize about sexual arousal from both the man and the woman's point of view. His fetish was so common that it barely registers on the sexual Richter Scale as a deviation. There are umpteen men who wear women's underwear under their normal clothes, and umpteen more who would like to try it. It doesn't mean that they're homosexual. It doesn't mean that they're transvestite. It doesn't mean anything at all, except that they become sexually excited when they do it.

It certainly doesn't mean that they don't love the women in their lives (you). Usually, it means quite the opposite. But it can be a cause of discontent and anxiety and imbalance in a sexual relationship, and if it continues without being openly satisfied, it can have damaging consequences for your partnership that go far beyond something as innocent as wearing women's panties.

I explained to Sylvia that most male sexual fantasies and fetishes are not illnesses and they certainly don't need curing. They may seem weird or threatening if you have been given a very conventional sexual education, but in fact they are perfectly within the parameters of "normal" sex.

What's more, wives and lovers can use their partner's special sexual interests to improve their sexual relationship quite dramatically.

Sylvia was very dubious about Ray's underwear fetish when I first discussed it with her. But when she understood why it excited him to wear women's underwear and how she could use his sexual predilection to make her love life even sexier, she became more than enthusiastic about it.

I told her that there was absolutely nothing wrong with him, either physiologically or emotionally. There was nothing wrong with their sex life, either. But just as some people are excited by one sport and not by another—just as some people adore one kind of food and dislike others—some people are turned on by one kind of sexual activity, when others might leave them cold. Ray was aroused by the silky texture and the thin fabric and the overall flimsiness of women's underwear, as well as the incongruity of seeing his own stiff penis in tiny see-through panties. He also enjoyed the femininity of garter-belt elastic, and the feeling of enclosing his legs in slippery stockings. In his head, as he masturbated, he could be both man and woman, dominant and submissive. Sometimes he imagined that he was actually a woman. At other times he imagined that he was a man forced to dress like a woman. Sometimes he was a man, forcibly imposing his sexual will on a woman. Then again, he was a man humiliating another man.

Sometimes he was both man and woman at once.

What I asked Sylvia to remember was that Ray's fantasy was only a fantasy. It was only a way of achieving sexual arousal. It didn't involve any harmful or injurious acts. It didn't involve anybody else, neither was there any question of infidelity. It didn't put their marriage at risk in any way.

In fact—once Sylvia had understood that Ray's underwear fetish was not a sexual problem at all, she could see that it was a golden opportunity for her to inject some real wildness into her love life.

"The evening after you'd explained Ray's liking for women's underwear to me, I talked it over with Ray, and told him that it was something I'd like to share with him—something I'd like to include in our sex life. After our shower, we went into the bedroom and I opened my pantie drawer and asked him to choose something to wear. He chose a little pair of white nylon panties with lace edging. We were both naked, and even while he was choosing them his cock started to rise. I knelt down in front of him and helped him step into them, and at the same time I gave his cock two or three kisses and it rose up even stiffer. It was so big I could hardly cram it into my panties. It had to lie sideways, with the head of it rearing over the top of the elastic.

"I dressed him in a white lace garter belt to match, and a pair of sheer white stockings. We stood side by side in front of the bedroom mirror . . . I was naked, he was wearing my panties and my stockings. I guess it was kind of bizarre. I kept thinking to myself, this is so wild. This is so *kinky,* and it's me doing it! I began to get really turned-on . . . and what turned me on even more was that Ray was so turned-on. His cock was *huge,* and I could see that he'd already wet my panties with his love juice.

"I took out a little black G-string, and Ray helped me put that on. It's so small that my pubic hair bushes out at the sides, and the string disappears right up between the cheeks of my bottom. I put on black stockings and a black garter belt. I didn't put a bra on . . . I liked having my breasts bare. We stood in front of the mirror and kissed and caressed each other, and then we climbed onto the bed.

"Ray lay on his back and I sat astride his chest. I leaned forward and kissed him, and he was so excited that he almost ate me alive! He reached up with both hands and squeezed and caressed my breasts, gently pulling my nipples between his fingers. Then I shuffled up and sat astride his face. He kissed and licked my G-string, sucking the elastic that went between my legs. He wriggled his tongue underneath the little nylon triangle and licked my cunt lips and sucked my pubic hair. I loved it when he does that, it gives me a gorgeous tugging feeling between my legs. He licked my clitoris, too, very light and quick, and by that time I was really turned-on. I pulled my G-string over to one side, and squashed my cunt around and around against his face, until his whole face was covered in love juice.

"I climbed off him, took off my G-string, and lay beside him on the bed wearing nothing but stockings. We rubbed our legs together and it was incredible because we were both wearing stockings. Our legs felt all slippery together and made a kind of zizzing noise. I reached into Ray's panties and took hold of his cock. It was hard and hot and the knob was dark red and very wet. I squeezed his balls and they were hard and tight, too, as if he was almost ready to climax.

"By this time I'd completely lost any of my inhibitions about Ray dressing up in my underwear, I was enjoying myself too much. It was sexy and wild and absolutely fantastic.

"Ray took his cock over the top elastic of his panties, leaving his balls inside. He climbed on top of me and I wanted him so much that I held my cunt lips open for him. I lifted my head up so that I could watch his cock sinking into my cunt. My cunt lips were juicy and all swelled up, and I don't think I ever saw anything so sexy as Ray's cock head sliding in between them, and with him wearing my panties and a garter belt and all.

"He fucked me very slow but hard. Every time he went in deep I felt as if he was touching my stomach. I slid my hands into his stocking tops and stroked and scratched his thighs. Then I took hold of his panties at the back, and pulled them up tight between the cheeks of his ass, so tight that they pulled on his balls, too.

"I massaged his cock and my cunt lips so that my fingers were all juicy, and then I slid my hand inside the back of his panties and tickled and massaged his asshole. I slid one finger inside, but his reaction was to clench up tight, and I had to say 'Relax, come on, relax,' and when he *did* relax I was able to slide another finger into his asshole and pull it and stretch it and push my fingers in real deep, and churn them around inside his ass. When his asshole was really relaxed and open, I took out my fingers and reached for my G-string. It was damp and chilly from when he'd been licking me, but I wound the elastic around my fingers (just to make sure that I didn't lose it!) and I pushed it slowly up his ass. Over his shoulder I could see that, too—the black nylon disappearing inch by inch into his bright red asshole, until the whole G-string was up inside his ass.

"He said, 'Oh god,' and he climaxed. His cock jerked out of me and great warm blobs of sperm were flying everywhere, all over my stomach, all over my stockings. At the same time I pulled my G-string out of his ass, not too fast, and he quivered and his cock reared and shot out even more sperm.

"He bent over me and licked all of his own sperm off my stomach, until it was dripping from his lips, and then he kissed me, and I stuck my tongue right inside his mouth and we shared the taste of his come. We'd never done that before and I don't know why we did it then, but it's the best thing ever, sharing a mouthful of your lover's sperm.

"Afterward, we lay side by side for almost a half-hour, just touching and stroking and kissing each other. I didn't feel at all weird about the way that Ray was dressed. If it turned him on as much as that, and if it turned *me* on as much as that, I was all for it.

"Now I buy him women's underwear and stockings of his own, and he models them for me. Sometimes he wears them when we go out, and that turns me on . . . thinking that I'm the only person who knows that this hunky-looking man is wearing a flimsy little pair of girl's panties underneath his jeans, barely large enough to keep his cock in."

Sylvia's open-minded willingness to indulge Ray in his harmless sexual fetish not only saved their sexual relationship from increasing frustration and gradual deterioration, it gave them both a refreshing erotic lift, and a huge amount of satisfaction. As Ray said afterward, "We felt like young lovers all over . . . horny and frisky and ready to make love anytime day or night."

Sometimes a sexual fetish can become an obsession. That is, it can become more important than any other sexual activity in an individual's life, and the individual (almost always male) is actually incapable of achieving sexual fulfillment without it. Although underwear is one of the more common objects of sexual obsession, fetishists have been known to be sexually aroused by an extraordinary variety of artifacts, from leather britches to rubber miniskirts to boots and shoes and even certain smells.

A man who is incapable of achieving sexual satisfaction without the presence of some kind of fetish is in need of psychiatric counseling. But there is nothing at all wrong in having a taste for some particular erotic clothing or behavior, and as we have already seen from Ray and Sylvia's experience, it can add a great deal of zest to a humdrum sex life.

It is interesting to note that Sylvia had an instinctive understanding of what men find sexually arousing. Many women share that understanding, but are too shy to put their understanding into action. Men can be intensely stimulated by anal penetration and manipulation—a fact that even sex researcher Shere Hite found "astonishing" when she discovered it. I don't know why it should astonish her when homosexuals have been practicing anal intercourse since the dawn of time. But anal stimulation of a man by a woman during the normal course of lovemaking can not only greatly intensify the man's pleasure, it gives the woman the opportunity actually to penetrate her lover's body, to get inside him, which is one of the joys of physical sharing.

Sylvia's instinct led her not only to stimulate her lover's rectum with her fingers, but to use her G-string to make an improvised version of that age-old sexual plaything known as Greek love beads—a long string of beads that are inserted into the anus during lovemaking, and then slowly pulled out at the moment of orgasm.

Her sense of sharing also included the mutual swallowing of her lover's sperm. This kind of wholehearted relish of everything that happens during lovemaking is always exciting and rewarding, once you've acquired the taste for it. Men can be highly sexually excited by kissing their partners just after they have given them oral sex, then their mouths and faces are liberally covered in vaginal lubricant. Yet many women regard the idea of "tasting my own cunt" as repellent. I suggested several years ago that both men and women should develop a taste (or at least a tolerance) of their own sexual fluids by masturbating now and again and licking their lubricants and their semen. Since then I have received considerable numbers of letters in which women have talked about the excitement of tasting their own excitement.

Female vaginal juices are harmless, almost tasteless, and as 27-year-old Mary from Minneapolis, Minnesota, put it, "Tasting myself made me feel proud of myself. I used to shudder at the idea, and whenever my boyfriend tried to kiss me after going down on me, I used to turn my face away. But when you explained that it was clean and harmless and natural . . . and if my boyfriend liked it so much, how could it possibly be repulsive? I gradually grew to like it, and then to find the taste of it really arousing."

It is not within the scope of this book to discuss cross-dressing—men who go the whole way and dress up fully in women's clothing and makeup and even take on a female name and persona. But it is worth mentioning that a very high proportion of women who have discovered that their lovers or husbands are cross-dressers and have reacted with understanding and tolerance have found that a little understanding and tolerance can reap tremendous rewards.

It's the same with sexual preferences. Don't ask yourself whether your partner is "weird" or "kinky" or "abnormal." Ask yourself whether his sexual tastes are physically harmful or emotionally distressing. If they are neither, and if you feel on reflection that you could include them in your sex life without too much discomfort or embarrassment, then you could at least give them a try.

Pippa, a 24-year-old dental nurse from St. Louis, Missouri, had an unusual problem with her live-in boyfriend Dean, a 27-year-old media accountant.

"I thought our sex life was perfectly normal until one evening I was standing naked in the bathroom brushing my teeth when I heard a noise right outside the bathroom door. It sounded like a cough or something. I opened the bathroom door and there was Dean kneeling on the floor with his pajama pants open and his cock in his hand. He had been spying on me through the bathroom keyhole and masturbating.

"I couldn't believe it. I said, 'Why the hell are you peeping through the keyhole to look at me when you could have opened the door and come right in?' I was really mad. I thought I was living with some kind of pervert or something.

"Dean was very embarrassed. It took us a long time to make up, especially since I kept asking him why he was spying on me like that and he wouldn't tell me. He said that he didn't want to discuss it, and that was that. But after that I used to get really jumpy whenever I was in the bathroom or getting dressed because I always felt that he was watching me. Why should he need to watch somebody he's already living with?"

I explained to Pippa that Dean was sexually aroused by voyeurism—that is, by spying on a woman doing something personal without her being aware she is being observed. What he found exciting was not so much her nudity or what she was doing as the fact that she didn't know that he was watching her.

Pippa understood what I was talking about especially since she and some of her high-school friends had once climbed onto the roof of the boys' locker rooms so that they could spy on the football team taking showers. Not only did she understand, she was prepared to play a sexual game with Dean so that his voyeurism could become part of their foreplay

Obviously—once she was aware that Dean was going to be watching her—some of the secretive excitement was going to be lost. But she could make up for that by letting him watch her do things that normally she would have done completely in private.

Dean's initial reaction was one of embarrassment and anger, but to her credit Pippa managed to cajole him into trying it. She assured him that *she* would find it sexy, too, and as it turned out, she did.

"That evening, I went into the bathroom and I *locked the door,* like you said to."

Locking the door was very important because it meant that the only way Dean could see Pippa was through the keyhole: he couldn't just open the door when he felt like it and walk in. Because he could spy on her but not reach her, a high sexual tension was created which more than compensated for the fact that she now knew that she was being watched.

"I tried to act as if I didn't know that he was there. I took off my skirt and my pantyhose first, like I always do. I was wearing only a short sleeveless T-shirt on top, so I walked around the bathroom for a while, half-naked from the waist down. I did make a special point of teasing him . . . giving him a quick glimpse of my pussy and then moving out of sight.

"I took off my T-shirt and my bra so that I was completely naked. I sat on the toilet for a pee, and the only thing I did different from usual was that I opened my legs wide apart, so that he could see me. In fact I held my pussy open with both hands so that he would be able to see it jetting out. I have to admit that I felt strange, doing that, because I'd never been to the toilet in front of Dean before—especially not like *that!*—but at the same time it made me feel kind of powerful, as if I had a hold over him, and that was a thrill.

"After I flushed the toilet, I got into the shower. I left the curtain half-open so that he could see me. I washed my hair and then I massaged soap all over myself, especially my breasts and between my legs. Then I stepped out and dried myself, and walked around the bathroom for a while wearing nothing but a towel around my waist.

"When I came to bed afterward, Dean was already there. He didn't say a word, but his cock was as hard as a rock, and he couldn't wait to make love to me. There was nothing strange about the way we made love, except that it was very passionate, and very strong. I kept thinking about him watching me, and I guess he was thinking about him watching me, too, because we had the best sex we'd had for months and months.

"We were so pleased with the way that everything had worked out that we tried it again a couple of days later. I went into the bathroom and locked the door, and then I undressed completely, except for my white satin slippers with the little heels. I stood facing the keyhole. I didn't know whether Dean was watching me yet or not. That's the exciting part about it, from my point of view.

"Anyway, I snipped my pubic hair with nail scissors until it was cut really close. Then I took Dean's shaving foam, and I squirted it all over my pussy. I massaged the foam around and around my pussy with my fingers. Then I took Dean's razor and carefully shaved off all of the rest of my pubic hair. When I reached the hair right down between my legs, I spread a towel on the floor and sat on it with my legs wide apart, pulling my pussy lips to one side so that I could shave off every last scrap of hair. After that I went down on my hands and knees and squirted more shaving foam between the cheeks of my bottom, and reached between my legs with the razor so that I could shave off the fluff around my anus. Just for fun I poked the razor handle into my anus and pushed it in and out a few times.

"I leaned up against the washbasin and splashed warm water on my pussy and between my legs to rinse off the foam. Then I sat down on the toilet like I had before, because I knew that had really turned Dean on a whole lot. I opened up my bare pussy lips with one hand, as wide as I could, and with my other hand I played with my clitoris and slid two or three fingers up inside my vagina.

"At first I was so excited that I couldn't pee, but then I managed it, and I spurted out all over my hand, and rubbed myself at the same time. I could guess how much Dean was turned-on, and I nearly had an orgasm there and then, sitting on the toilet. Once I'd started, I just seemed to go on peeing and peeing, and it was gushing all warm through my fingers. I half-stood up, so that Dean would be able to see me more clearly, and it was dripping from my pussy lips and running down my legs. I held my pussy lips wide open so that he could see exactly what I was doing . . . I was gently pinching my clitoris between my finger and thumb and tugging it downward and outward, which is the way I've always masturbated, and which always turns me on the most.

"That evening was even better than the first evening. Dean adored my bald pussy, he couldn't stop touching it and stroking it—yes, and licking it, too! We went to bed as soon as I came out of the bathroom . . . he didn't even give me time to dry my hair. He opened my legs wide and held open my pussy and pushed himself right inside me, and he fucked me so hard I was bouncing up and down on the bed, and my breasts were bouncing around, too.

"We don't play 'Peeping Tom' very often, but occasionally I feel like it, and Dean always knows because I lock the bathroom door. I always put on a really sexy show for him . . . last time I masturbated in front of the keyhole with this really huge carrot that I'd bought in the market. It was enormous, more than a foot long and about three inches thick. I greased it up with shower gel and slowly fucked myself with it, only a few inches away from the keyhole. I managed to get most of it up inside me, so that only the bright orange stub was showing, then I sl-o-owly drew it out again, then pushed it back in. The feeling was fantastic . . . it was so huge I could hardly get it in. I tried to push it up my anus as well, but I couldn't get it in, it was far too big. I hope Dean wasn't jealous!

"What I like about 'Peeping Tom' is that I can act totally uninhibited in front of Dean, and do things that I never normally would have dared to do. It's changed our sex lives completely. I never thought that I could be so daring."

One of the most inhibiting factors in sexual relationships—even in long-term sexual relationships, in which a couple have been intimate for years and years—is lack of confidence in your physical looks. Although women's magazines exhort women to "striptease for your lover," it isn't always as easy as it sounds, being openly provocative, and I know from two decades of experience that even the most passionate of women can be painfully shy when it comes to showing off their bodies.

Very few women are completely content with their figures. Discuss a woman's looks and she will tell you that her breasts are either too big or too small, her hips are either too heavy or too bony, her thighs, are either too flabby or too skinny. She doesn't like her hair, she doesn't like her chin. She *hates* her nose.

Of course, much of this self-deprecation stems from a need to hear a man say "Don't be so ridiculous, your breasts are perfect," or "How can you say that, you have the most beautiful legs I've ever seen in my life." But it still takes a great deal of confidence for many women to stand naked in front of the man she loves and give him the visual thrill which (as we have already seen) is a very important part of driving a man wild.

However, almost all men are aroused by a sexual performance of the kind that Pippa gave Dean. His personal predilection was to watch her through a keyhole, to give him the feeling that he was spying on something forbidden. But the "keyhole" arrangement also suited her, because it gave her the confidence to display herself sexually without feeling—as she put it—that "Dean was staring at every mole and every wrinkle and every bulge that wasn't supposed to be there."

If you *do* have the confidence to put on a sexual act for your partner, then you should try it. Men are turned on by looking at their partners intimately, even men who have been living with the same partner all their lives.

Do one of these 10 things tonight, and see what effect it has on your lover.

1. When he comes home, greet him at the door wearing nothing but a sweater or T-shirt and high-heeled shoes.
2. Serve him dinner topless. Tell him you just felt like it.
3. While you're watching TV, lift your skirt and slide your hand into your panties and start to pleasure yourself. If he expresses surprise, invite him to slide his hand in, too, and join in.
4. Put on some slow, sexy music and dance with him—but while you're dancing, slowly strip yourself, until you're dancing naked.
5. When it's time for bed, give him a long, slow, tantalizing striptease.
6. Ask him to soap you in the shower. Tell him to make sure that he pays extra attention to the exciting bits.
7. Shave off your pubic hair so that he can watch you doing it.
8. When he's finished taking his shower, make sure that you are lying naked on the bed waiting for him, legs open, playing with yourself. Let him watch you while you do it.
9. Sit naked astride his face so that he can give you oral sex (and have a close-up look at your vulva, too).
10. Give him oral sex, so that he can watch you sucking and licking his penis.

What do all these suggestions have in common? They all have a high *visual* content. They will turn your partner on because they will appeal to his eyes. Whatever you think of the way you look naked, the man in your life likes the way you look naked or else he wouldn't stay with you. Therefore you can prance around nude or semi-nude as much as you like, and your sex life will only get better.

Pippa gave Dean some highly-arousing visual images that stayed in his mind long after each episode of playing "Peeping Tom." Even if you don't arrange to do it through a keyhole, you can still do the same for the man in your life by giving him some unexpected visual delights.

This is Margie, 21, a supermarket checkout cashier from St. Cloud, Florida. "I know that I'm overweight. I've been dieting for nine months now and I've managed to lose almost 17 pounds, but I'm naturally plump and it is a struggle. I had boyfriends when I was thinner . . . that was when I was 16 and 17. But I broke up with this one guy Chet that I really liked a lot, and after that I didn't seem to do anything but eat all the time. I guess it was a way of drowning my sorrows. The trouble was, the more I ate the more I wanted to eat, it was like a vicious spiral. I could eat a whole package of donuts in one sitting. In the end I got so big I had to ask my doctor for a special diet.

"I couldn't believe it when Jude asked me out. I thought he was just funning. But he took me to the Cracker House for a country-and-western evening and we had a real good time. He told me that he'd always liked big girls . . . liked them in a big way, that's what he said. He kind of surprised me, Jude, because he's tall and good-looking in a dumb-ass way, like Clint Eastwood's retarded brother if you know what I mean, and that's not being rude to him because I love him. I love his slowness and the way he always answers a question with another question, like I'll say, 'Take your clothes off, Jude, and he'll say what for?' I mean, what the hell does he *think* what for?

"But Jude is good to me and kind and loyal . . . even though I never wanted to make love to him with the lights on, not to begin with. I was nearly 180 pounds and I was wearing bras that were 46DD and I was still too small for them. The worst thing I was ashamed of was my hips. I thought they looked so goddamned enormous, like I was carrying somebody's couch inside of my jeans.

"Jude always treated me like a lady, right from the start. But one day he said, 'I'm real tired of this. We never make love with the light on. I never get to see you taking a bath or a shower. I never get to see you naked, ever. I'm beginning to think that you don't love me.

"Of course this wasn't true at all because I adored him. The only trouble was I didn't want him to see my big fat body. I guess in the end I managed to explain what the problem was. But he said, 'I *know* you're fat. I'm not stupid. I like you fat. I like you the way you are. I want to see you. I want to see what you look like. In fact he said he was starting to get real frustrated because I always made sure that I jumped into bed before he did, and I always wore a robe, and I always switched off the light before we had sex."

Pride and self-confidence are essential to an active and satisfying sex life. The very first thing I said to Margie was that she should take off all of her clothes, take a good look at herself in the mirror, and say to herself, 'This is me . . . this is the way I am today. I'm a loving, attractive woman. Jude wants me and I want Jude, and I'm proud of myself."

I told her to take stock of her grooming . . . to pay attention to some of those little details that sometimes we tend to forget, particularly as if we haven't been feeling too good about ourselves (and this goes for men as well as women). I told her to have her hair fixed, manicure her fingernails, and go look for some fresh makeup. One way of helping yourself to feel better is to go to the cosmetics counter at a big store and arrange for a face makeover. Usually, these store cosmeticians put on far too much makeup, but they do look at your face with a new eye, and they can often give you some excellent pointers for making your appearance just a little more glamorous. In Margie's case, a cosmetician was able to show her how to use a slightly darker blusher to trim down her cheeks, and how to pluck her eyebrows a little higher so that her eyes looked wider and she lost that heavy-browed look that actress Kathy Bates deliberately cultivated for the movie *Misery.*

I also recommended that she rethink her wardrobe. Larger women have an understandable tendency to choose clothes that are comfortable rather than fashionable, such as T-shirts and jogging pants, but these tend to emphasize a woman's size rather than diminish it, and that little bit of extra fashion-consciousness, such as a loose, pretty blouse or a pleated skirt can make a remarkable difference. Sexually, most men pay far less attention to a woman's weight than you would think. Some of the most popular nude models that I have met during my career with *Penthouse* and other men's magazines were positively chubby—but they were proud of their bodies and proud of themselves and it was their pride that gave them so much of their sexual glow.

Of course, it is healthier to watch your weight. The diet that Margie's doctor had given her was straightforward and very sensible—a varied low-calorie diet that didn't leave her feeling bored, deprived, or miserable. I have often been asked for diets to improve sexual drive, but the plain fact is that sexual drive is increased only by general well-being and fitness, which can be achieved with any diet that gives you balanced proportions of protein, carbohydrate, and fiber.

I recently discussed the idea of a "sex diet" with my diet specialist in London's Harley Street, and his view was eminently simple: If you eat more calories than your body requires for its daily routine, then you'll put on weight. If you eat fewer calories than your body requires for its daily routine, then you'll lose weight. It doesn't actually matter *what* you eat, provided you don't eat more than you need.

I'll add just one coda to that. Any diet that is intended to improve your sex life should be very sparing on alcohol. Not only is it very fattening and of no nutritional value, it always dulls your sexual responses (even if it makes you feel less inhibited).

Margie said that she had read in several of my books the suggestion that, now and again, a woman could try shaving off her pubic hair. She had been anxious to try it for a long time but hadn't had the nerve. She was worried what Jude would think about it. I reassured her on that score, saying that he almost certainly *would* approve. Shaving her vulva would clearly demonstrate to him that she was proud of herself sexually and that she wanted to show herself off to him. In any case, even if he *didn't* like it, it wouldn't take long to grow back again. I suggested that she might want to leave a small plume or tuft of hair, like many women do when they depilate to wear bikinis. but Margie wanted her vulva completely bare.

Finally, I talked to Margie about her sexual techniques. Many larger women are inhibited about sexual variations because of their weight and because they feel ungainly. But most men who are involved in sexual relationship with larger women are perfectly happy about their partners' bodies—in fact many of them would be quite distressed if they suddenly became thin.

Give him the opportunity to enjoy your body to the utmost, in the same way that you should enjoy it to the utmost. When you're making love, make the best of what you've got. Big breasts? Use them to massage his face and his penis. Big bottom? Let him bury his face in it. Be active and adventurous, and never hesitate to try anything you feel like. You're not a thin person, so stop trying to pretend that you are—otherwise you'll resist and inhibit your every move.

Jude said, "When I saw Margie that evening I thought she was a different woman, completely different. Her hair was all curly and her face was so pretty. She was wearing a new blue dress with loose sleeves and she looked just fine. We had a drink and some BBQ ribs and some salad on the way home, and she told me everything she'd been doing, painting her nails and all, and she said she truly felt better about herself already. I said I was surprised she'd ever felt bad about herself. So far as I was concerned, she was always the girl that I liked the most. She's not skinny, and that's for sure, but she has the prettiest face and the sweetest nature, and she's always considerate and loving. Doesn't mean she doesn't have a temper. She knows what she likes and she knows what she doesn't like. But I never met a girl like her before and I don't think I ever will again.

"We went home and put on some music and kissed and cuddled some, and then Margie said, 'I have a surprise for you.' She stood right up in the middle of the living room and she let her dress fall around her ankles. Underneath she was wearing a black bra, about the smallest and most transparent bra you could find in her size, which is a 44 plus. She wasn't wearing a petticoat or panties or anything else at all. What was more, she'd shaved off all of her pussy hair.

"She did a twirl for me and then she came over and kissed me. She said, 'You can undo my bra if you like, it fastens at the front.' Well, I didn't need a second telling. I unhooked it, and those big beautiful breasts of hers swung out. She held her left breast in both hands, and fed me her nipple. She has the sexiest nipples . . . very wide and pink, and they get really stiff when you suck them. I sucked the whole of her nipple right into my mouth and rolled it up against the roof of my mouth with my tongue. She gave a little moaning sound and I knew she was enjoying it, she loves having her nipples sucked, but before then I didn't get to see it as well as do it because she always wanted to have sex with the lights off.

"I went on sucking and pulling on that nipple and then I changed to the other one, although I kept on massaging the first one, which was all wet from my sucking it. I felt like I wanted to stuff her whole breast in my mouth—almost like I wanted to suffocate on big, pillowy breast. My cock was already hard as a bone.

"Margie sat down on the couch next to me. It's black leather, so it's pretty slippery, but it's soft, too. She opened her thighs wide, so that I could see her pussy, and she said, 'What do you think, do you like it shaved?' Like it? It was blowing my mind. I'd never really *looked* at her pussy before, not *looked* at it, close-up, with all the lights blazing—let alone without any hair on it at all. She has a beautiful plump pussy, like a ripe peach, and she opened herself up with her fingers so that I could see her clitoris, which doesn't stick out too much, it's just this gorgeous little pink button, and her inside lips, which were neat and pretty. I could even see her pee hole, and then her actual vagina, which she held wide open with the fingers of both hands so that I could see inside where it was brimming with juice.

"We'd made love dozens of times, but when you can actually look at your woman's pussy and marvel at how beautiful it is, that's something else. I wish I had a full-size color photograph of it to hang on the wall at work, I could look at it all day. I couldn't resist opening her pussy lips and stroking her clitoris, and then slipping my middle finger up inside her vagina. She was warm and juicy inside, and my fingers came out all wet and slippery.

"She unbuttoned my shirt and unbuckled my belt. Between us, we managed to get my clothes off in world-record time. I knelt between her thighs and kissed her and started to fondle her breasts. But she reached down between her legs, so that her hand was covered in her own pussy juice, and she smeared it between her breasts. Then she said, 'Here . . .' and she lifted her breasts up in both hands and squeezed them together, and said, 'you can fuck me here.'

"I sat astride her, and slid my cock into her cleavage. It was so tight and soft between her breasts, and so slippery with pussy juice, that it was almost like pushing my cock into her vagina. I took hold of her breasts myself, they're absolutely enormous, and pressed them harder and harder together, twisting and pulling her nipples at the same time. My balls were banging against her chest, and she was panting. But she didn't flag, no way. While I was fucking her breasts she reached around and gripped my ass, scratching my cheeks with her fingernails and poking my asshole. She took hold of my balls, one in each hand, and gently clawed at them, and stretched the skin of my ball-bags. She stretched it so far I almost had tears in my eyes . . . then she dug her fingernails into my skin and played with my balls. She turned me on so much I was almost ready to come. I'd never had sex anything like it before. She's a big girl, for sure, but how can you fuck a girl's breasts if she doesn't have any breasts?

"She said, 'Come on, fuck me prop[illegible] she

pushed me back so that I was sitting on the sofa. She straddled me, and opened up her pussy with her fingers, and guided my cock up into her pussy. I saw it with my own eyes, sliding inside that plump bald pussy, right up to the hilt; and then she lifted herself up again and out it came; and then in again; and out again. Her breasts were jiggling right in my face, her nipples stiff, and she was squashing me and hugging me and kissing me. She was totally sensational . . . and there is no feeling in the world like burying your bone-hard cock into the juicy pussy of a really fleshy woman—nothing.

"I thought I was going to come, but she said, 'No, no . . . I want everything.' She climbed off me and she knelt doggy-fashion on the leather couch, her face against the cushions, and she said, 'This way, too. Please. I want everything.' She reached behind her with both hands and pulled her ass cheeks wide apart, and smeared pussy juice all around her asshole.

"We'd never done this before, and I was afraid of hurting her. But she kept on begging me and begging me, she was so excited. I knelt up behind her, and positioned the head of my cock up against her asshole. She was too tight at first, she kept squeezing it tight so that I couldn't get it in. But at last she relaxed and I managed to push the head of my cock into her asshole. It was stretched pretty wide, and she was whimpering, but I pushed again, and this time it went into her asshole another inch. 'More,' she said, 'more!' and this time she really opened herself, and I pushed the whole length of my cock into her asshole, right up to the balls, and she let out such a sexy moan.

"I fucked her asshole very slow, so that I wouldn't hurt her. She closed her eyes and murmured sweet nothings, and I went in and out of her ass just like fucking a girl for the first time. I couldn't believe we were really doing it. I could feel her ass muscles gripping my cock, gripping and squeezing. I pushed in again and again, and she reached around behind her with both hands and pulled her big fat ass cheeks wide apart, so that I could fuck her even deeper. It was just like burying myself in total flesh . . . fantastic.

"I [illegible] my climax coming so I went deeper and

deeper, and I reached around her and took great handfuls of her stomach and her breasts. I kept on squeezing her left breast with my left hand . . . I plunged my right hand deep between her thighs, and took hold of that beautiful plump bald pussy. She was so juicy that I couldn't believe it. I flicked her clitoris, not too hard, quicker and quicker, and then she suddenly reached an orgasm. And that was some orgasm, believe me. She shook and she shook, and her ass gripped my cock so tight that I felt I was never going to get it out of here. Her ass kept squeezing and squeezing and then I was climaxing, too, I was pumping sperm right up inside her ass, it was like she was squeezing every last drop right out of me.

"Afterward, we lay side by side on the couch, holding each other, sweaty and hot, but satisfied. Margie was kind of embarrassed that I'd fucked her up the ass, but when I told her how much it had turned me on, she said she'd do it again, anytime, it had hurt her some but she loved it. I can tell you, I held her in my arms and she was just as plump as she always was, but she was something else, she was everything that any man could ever want."

How did Margie feel afterward? "I felt like a huge weight had been lifted off of my life. I didn't feel guilty or secretive about my body any longer. So I was fat? What do those PC people call it—'differently-sized?' I was fat, but I was proud of myself, and I was so excited that I could turn Jude on so much. I felt a little sore afterward . . . I had never had a man's cock up my bottom before. When Jude was asleep that night I touched my bottom because it was feeling tender, and it was then that I realized that it was wet. Jude's sperm was dripping out of my bottom, and that was proof of just how good it had been."

Margie found her sexual confidence almost overnight. She did it because she decided that it was no good putting off her sexual happiness until tomorrow. She wanted to be sexy and exciting with the body she already had *now*.

How many times have you said to yourself, "I'll go buy some new clothes when I've lost another 10 pounds." Or, "I'll have some of my friends over for dinner when I've lost some more weight and I feel more confident." If you do that, believe me, you will *never* buy those new clothes. You will never have those friends over for dinner. And your life will be the poorer for it.

It's the same with sex. No matter how overweight you happen to be, there is a man who will want to make love to you—that's if you don't happen to have a man already. If you're proud of yourself, sexy, uninhibited, and glamorous, you will always be able to turn men on. What's more, that spirit of confidence and pride will help you to overcome those eating problems that are associated with low-self-image and a lack of self-esteem.

Remember, there is no specific diet that can radically improve your sex drive. But if you indulge your sex drive, you can find a new interest in life—an interest that helps you to stay trimmer and to feel much better about yourself. Originally, I devised this routine simply to help women become wilder lovers, but it does have the beneficial side effect of making you feel much more relaxed with the body you've been born with—of giving every woman of every size and every age and every imaginable appearance a feeling I call The Sex Glow.

FIVE

The Sex Glow—What It Is and How to Have It

You would be amazed how many women feel that they are somehow "missing out" on sex. Every time they write or talk to me, they express their anxiety that everybody else is having a varied and passionate sex life, everybody else is having more fun and more satisfaction, and somehow they weren't invited to the party.

Much of this anxiety is caused by the enormous emphasis that magazines and newspapers place on sex. How many times have you picked up a copy of a woman's magazine and seen articles such as "How to Have Multiple Orgasms Every Time," "How to Satisfy Three Lovers at Once," "Sex in the Office . . . How to Have a Great Career and Great Sex, Too."

Leafing through a selection of new magazines for women *and* men, you would be forgiven for thinking that everybody else was having an orgy but they forgot to invite you.

The truth, however, is quite different. Articles and stories are simply aimed at selling magazines, and they are very far from the reality of most women's everyday sexual experience. Most women have only a handful of sexual lovers in their lifetimes, and most couples make love no more frequently than two to three times a week. What's more, most of the couples to whom I have spoken over the past 20 years have admitted that most of those acts of love are "straightforward, no-nonsense intercourse."

However "left out" you feel, your experience of sex isn't much different from that of most other people of your own age and social background. Of course there *are* people to whom sex is virtually their principal pastime, and who indulge themselves in swinging and swapping and watching porno videos, but people with sexual appetites like these are an exception, rather than a rule.

It doesn't particularly help the sexual self-confidence of the average woman when babe feminists like Katie Roiphe and Naomi Wolf so fervently advocate their particular brand of dominant sluttishness. Unlike radical feminists like Andrea Dworkin and Catherine McKinnon, who regard all men as potential rapists, babe feminists say that it's okay to wear lipstick (even though the lipstick industry is an instrument of oppression) and that it's okay to push up your breasts with a tight-fitting bustier so that men stare at you at parties (provided that men don't stare at you when you don't feel like having them stare at you). It's okay for a woman to tell a man that she is carrying a condom with her. "We need sluts for a revolution," says Naomi Wolf.

There's a lot in what babe feminists say. The battles for equal pay and equal opportunities can mainly be taken as read, and it's time for women to take charge of their sex lives—to enjoy gratuitous, pleasurable sex, not feeling guilty and taking full responsibility for their own actions. They talk about using men instead of being used by them. As one female writer put it, the maximum of babe feminism is "I'm too sexy for you, but I'll have you on Thursday at 8 P.M."

Babe feminists haven't yet worked out how to prevent men from staring at them when they don't want to be stared at (what do you do? poke their eyes out?). Neither have they overcome the biological response that causes most women to become aroused by male sexual strength—just as men are aroused by women's femininity. When I say sexual strength, I mean *strength,* not aggression. Showing men that they can be gentle and considerate as well as strong is one highly commendable part of babe feminism.

On the whole, though, I am totally in favor of women acting in a sexually positive and upfront way—of exploiting their sexual attractiveness to the hilt, and of taking whatever sexual pleasures they want, without feeling ashamed or guilty about it. The only problem is that it's a hell of a lot easier to say "go out and strut your stuff" than it is to do it, particularly if you're lacking in sexual self-confidence, or you're easily embarrassed. It's also a hell of a lot easier to talk about female potency and the right of sexual self-determination if you know exactly how potent you can be, and what particular sexual acts you want to be self-determined about. Twenty years ago, when I wrote *How to Drive Your Man Wild in Bed,* I received anguished letters from middle-aged women who had never known that they could have orgasms. These days, I receive similar letters from women who have never had oral sex from their lovers or husbands and never had any anal stimulation, and feel desperately cheated.

So the first step toward being a sexually potent woman is to get that Sex Glow. It's the glow of *pride,* the glow of *knowledge,* and the glow of *skill.*

Getting the Sex Glow for yourself starts with some very simple but positive acts. First of all, some serious thinking about your appearance. Are you happy with your hair? Your face? Your makeup? Your breasts? Your stomach? Your thighs? Write a quick list of anything you're not contented with, and decide that you're going to do something about it. Something positive. Make up your mind that you're not going to put up with anything you dislike about yourself a moment longer.

Think about *what* and *who* you've always wanted to be. By that, I'm not suggesting that you try to mold yourself into the likeness of another woman, such as Julia Roberts or Madonna or Donna Tartt or whoever you happen to admire. Think about your own distinctive characteristics, the things that make *you* special. Your interests, your sense of humor, your accomplishments, your personality. Make a quick list of the way you would like a man to describe you to another man. "She's a good listener, and she's always laughing. She makes me feel confident." That kind of thing.

Think about some positive aspect of your personality that you've allowed to lie dormant for too long. It could be simply your flirtatiousness. When did you last flirt with the man in your life? With any man? It could be your sense of fun and adventure. When did you last suggest going someplace exciting or doing something wacky? It may be your sense of culture. When did you last visit an art gallery or go to a concert?

You have a sparkle within you. You must have, because people with no sparkle don't dare to read books like this. This is a book for women who want excitement and thrills and an intense degree of erotic pleasure—and it takes sparkle just to feel the need for such things. Do yourself the greatest favor of your life, and allow that sparkle to show. Smile more. Laugh more. Show the man in your life your zest for living and your zest for sex.

Now think about what you want out of your sex life. More romance? More kissing? More frequent lovemaking? Longer-lasting lovemaking? More unusual lovemaking? Make a list of all of those, too.

Finally, write down the very wildest sexual act that you would be prepared to do. Stretch your imagination to the limit. Now stretch your imagination a little farther, and write down a sexual act so wild that you *wouldn't* do it—not yet, anyway.

Let's see how Sandra, a 25-year-old travel agent from Madison, Wisconsin, developed her own Sex Glow. Sandra is petite (5 feet, 2 inches) with blond, shoulder-length hair. She was married at the age of 19 but divorced when she was 22. She has been living with Burt, a 28-year-old professional musician, for two-and-a-half years. She thought that their relationship was "happy . . . but maybe kind of routine." She was beginning to worry that she didn't excite Burt as much as she used to, and that he was making love to her less and less frequently. "I don't think he's having an affair with anybody else, not yet. But I'm worried that if he met the right girl at the right moment, he might be tempted to."

Sandra went through the sexual self-assessment that I outlined previously. First of all, she decided that she *liked* her hair, although she had always wanted it cut very short but never had the nerve to do it. She liked her eyes (blue) and she didn't mind her nose, although it had a little bump on the bridge. She thought her lips were too thin and her chin too square. She admitted that she had never been very good at makeup and tended to use the same eyeshadow and blusher most of the time. On weekends she wore only eyeliner and sometimes no makeup at all.

She thought her neck was too short and her breasts too big ("they grew enormous when I was 14 and I've been thinking about a reduction ever since"). She went to aerobics classes three times a week before work and she had kept her stomach flat, and she was proud of her legs. She admitted that she "wasn't as conscientious as I ought to be" about keeping her nails manicured and pedicured.

She dealt with everything she disliked about herself, and she had to admit after only 24 hours that she was feeling "radically better" about herself already. She went to the best hairstylist she could afford and had her hair cut the way she had always wanted it but never dared—very short, with a full head of blond highlights to bring out her natural color. At the same time she had her finger- and toenails manicured.

She went to an expert cosmetician who showed her how to relieve the squareness of her jaw with subtle use of foundation. She was also taught how to use different colors to very her appearance from day to day and to reflect her changing moods. Not only did her cosmetic makeover give *her* more confidence, it made Burt sit up and look at her afresh, which was just the sexual effect she was looking for.

Sandra decided that she wanted to keep the little bump on her nose even though it could have been "ironed out" with a relatively inexpensive and simple operation, but she did opt for collagen injections in her lips, which she was able to have within a week. Fuller lips not only helped additionally to reduce the apparent heaviness of her jaw, but gave her a "wonderful, pillowy, kissable look." For the first time, she started to wear a bright scarlet lipstick.

Her concern about the length of her neck was very easily dealt with by wearing more open-collared blouses and lower-cut sweaters. She had always liked polo-neck sweaters, particularly in Wisconsin's bitterly-cold winters, but she achieved the same warmth and the same look with sweaters that had larger, more open collars.

The question of her breast size was very interesting. I persuaded her to visit a corsetiere, a woman who makes personalized underwear for those who can afford such luxuries. This corsetiere had previously shown me statistics produced by some of the country's biggest chain stores, which show that most women wear the wrong size bra. Not a few women—*most* women, up to 76 percent of the bra-wearing population. Particularly these days, when the average breast size is increasing, a well-fitting bra is essential not only for looks but for comfort. More than half the women interviewed for this trade survey accepted discomfort as an everyday part of wearing a bra, whereas the corsetiere assured me that even the biggest-breasted women, in the correct-size bra, should feel no discomfort at all—and she fits women up to size 52H.

When she was properly measured and fitted, Sandra was amazed at how comfortable she felt, and how much better supported her breasts were. "I can walk around without them jiggling all the time, I can run without them bouncing up and down." She decided against a breast reduction on the spot (much to Burt's relief, because he adored her breasts). Ask yourself: Are you absolutely sure of your correct bra size? It really is incredible what a difference a professional remeasurement can make.

While most of the adjustments that Sandra made to her appearance may seem obvious, we all know how easy it is to get into a rut with our clothing and our grooming, especially if we are shy or defensive or don't particularly like to stand out in a crowd. But dressing "safely" doesn't mean you have to forfeit sexiness, especially if you enhance your best features and make up your mind that you're going to do something positive about the features you like the least.

Sandra had always wanted to appear smart but not "power-smart." "I never wanted to look like those domineering women with padded shoulders and short skirts." Instead, when she chose some new clothes for herself, she opted for a casual, pretty, look, with unstructured tweeds and linens, plenty of layers, and lots of natural fabrics. Combined with her new short haircut and her new makeup, she looked absolutely stunning—and, what's more, she *knew* she looked stunning.

What she actually did was to change and enhance her appearance so that she looked sexy to *herself*. "I didn't buy anything because I thought 'this is going to turn Burt on.' I bought it because it made *me* feel sexy." This was a critical part of building her sexual self-confidence, of making herself feel sassy and sexually attractive but far from cheap and available. So much of igniting your own Sex Glow depends on your own pride in the way you look—in developing the sure and certain knowledge that you're exciting to men.

Sandra wrought dramatic changes underneath, too. Apart from buying herself four new well-fitting bras, she went through her lingerie drawer and threw out most of her old underwear in a wholesale act of eth-knick cleansing. "I threw away *all* of my panties. I bought six new G-strings for wearing under jeans or slacks, or whenever I wasn't wearing pantyhose, but I've never seen the point of wearing panties as well as pantyhose, and I thought that it was time that I was confident enough to go without them."

In fact, when she was wearing anything but miniskirts, Sandra dispensed with panties altogether. "Nobody ever saw anything. Nobody knew, except Burt, but then I made a special point of telling him. It never failed. It turned him on so much that he couldn't leave me alone all evening!"

Her body hair was very fine and blond, but she removed all of that, too. "I read in one of your books years ago about shaving off your pubic hair, and I'd always wanted to try it, but I never knew what Jim (her first husband) would think about it, so I never quite dared. But if I'm going to do what *I* want to do, then I want to shave it off. I love having a clean-shaven cunt. It's exactly that, clean—and the first time that Burt saw me, his eyes came out on stalks, and he wanted to make love to me then and there. It's also a terrific feeling, walking around the bedroom naked and no pubic hair at all and just *knowing* that the man in your life can't keep his eyes off your cunt. It's a way of sexual showing off, isn't it? A man can walk around with his cock hard, but a woman can show that she's interested in sex and ready for sex if she shaves off her pubic hair and shows her man her bare cunt."

With a new hairstyle, new makeup, and a head-to-toe makeover, Sandra could now turn her attention to her sexual self-knowledge, which was the next essential step in kindling her Sexual Glow. She had to spend some time learning about her own body and her own sexual responses, and what she could do to drive her lover even wilder in bed. I have recommended "sexual self-discovery sessions" in a variety of forms for many years, and they have proved to be extraordinarily instructive, therapeutic—yes, and erotic, too. They are designed to be completely self-indulgent, and to give you some sexual "quality time" in which you can find out what sexual varieties of stimulation excite and satisfy you the most—and what new sexual ideas you could bring to the bedroom when your lover comes home. You don't have to have a lover or a husband to practice these Sexual Glow self-discovery techniques, so do try them. You'll be more than ready to give your new man a really wild time in bed when he does walk into your life.

You need privacy and you need time. A whole day would be ideal, but try to give yourself a minimum of three to four hours, so that you don't feel rushed or pressured. If you think that a whole day is too long, think of what you're actually trying to do—change your sex life into the most exciting and enduring relationship that ever was, with fireworks every time. Is that worth 12 hours of your time or isn't it?

Privacy is essential. Find a location where you won't be interrupted, either by personal callers or by telephone, and where you feel completely secure. If you have children, find somebody to take care of them while you indulge yourself. You should assemble the following aids for your sexual self-discovery session, too: a lotion or massage oil in your favorite fragrance, or (if possible) a new fragrance that you adore, but which you usually can't afford—remember, this is a time when *your* pleasure is all that matters! Make sure you have a variety of music available, some dance music and some mood music. Maybe a little wine to relax you, if you like wine. Maybe a glass of champagne, or sparkling wine.

If you have access to a sexy video, it would be a good idea to have that ready, too. Preferably a *new* sexy video, one that you haven't seen before. If you have a vibrating penis-shaped dildo, that would help. If you have *two* dildos, or a double-dildo, even better. If you can't easily acquire a dildo, however, you can improvise with a large candle or a giant-sized cucumber, peeled and carved to give you a knoblike end, and sheathed in a condom for comfort and safety.

Last but not least, you should try to obtain a camcorder—so that you can actually *see* for yourself how you sexually respond.

In the past few years, the camcorder has become a useful and exciting aid to sexual self-understanding. I have recommended its use to many couples who have been unsure about the physical geography of their own bodies, and the finer details of sex. A camcorder can be used to enhance your sex life in dozens of different ways. You can use it together with your partner to record your lovemaking. You can make videos independently of each other, and play them while you're making love, as part of your foreplay. You can use them to act out your erotic fantasies. Or else you can use it—as you will be using it during your Sexual Glowtime—to find out more about your own body and your own sexual responses.

If you don't own a camcorder, do beg or borrow one for your own hours of sexual self-discovery. It will be an invaluable aid in learning about your sexual self. As Sandra said afterward, "I never even knew myself before. I never knew what I really looked like. I never knew what was really happening, when I was making love. And I never, ever knew that I could take anything so big inside of myself, and so far up!"

Your Sexual Glowtime takes you through nine separate stages. One, relaxation. Two, self-revelation. Three, nudity. Four, self-examination. Five, self-pleasuring. Six, sexual drama. Seven, controlled orgasm. Eight, repeated orgasm. Nine, relaxation.

Rather than give you a list of cut-and-dried instructions, let's follow Sandra, and how she went through her Sexual Glowtime, and what she felt about it when she'd completed it.

Sandra and Burt live in a quiet first-floor apartment in an older building, with polished-wood floors in the living and dining area, but a warm, well-carpeted bedroom in back. Burt was away for two days, playing for a wedding in Milwaukee, so Sandra was able to take all the time she needed without any fear of interruption.

"It was three o'clock in the afternoon. I came back to the apartment after marketing, and spent the first half-hour relaxing on the couch, drinking a glass of sparkling wine and eating a couple of praline chocolates. Then I went to the mirror in the hallway, and stood in front of it, and admired myself, the way you said I should. I was well-dressed in a coral-colored short-sleeved sweater and a fawn-colored skirt. I lifted up my skirt, hitched it right up so that it was up around my hips. Underneath I was wearing one of my G-strings, a little white one with flowers embroidered on it. I turned around a few times, and admired my figure—admired my bottom and admired my thighs, and admired the look of that pretty little G-string. It scarcely covered my cunt, and I thought that it looked truly sexy.

"I unfastened my skirt, and stepped out of it. I suppose I must have been nervous still, because I folded it up so carefully! I don't know why I was nervous of myself. There was nobody else in the apartment. But maybe we're all a little afraid of our own sexual feelings; and I know that I was a little afraid of mine.

"I set up the camcorder so that it was facing toward the mirror, not to me. I strutted up and down in front of the mirror, wearing nothing but my sweater and my G-string. Then I turned my back in the mirror, and bent right down, and looked at myself between my legs. I thought my legs were in pretty good shape. Those aerobic workouts really help. The string of my G-string went deep between the cheeks of my bottom and didn't quite manage to cover my asshole, but then that's not the point of them, is it?

"I turned around again, and lifted up my sweater, and took it off. I squeezed my breasts through my bra, and pressed myself up close to the mirror, so that I could admire myself up close. You told me to look in the mirror and love myself, so I did. I even tried kissing my reflection, and I left a big crushed-strawberry lipstick mark on the glass. It was quite sexy, in a way. I could look at it and think, 'Did I kiss the girl in the mirror, or did the girl in the mirror kiss me?'

"I took off my bra, and held my bare breasts in both hands. I lifted them and pressed my nipples against the mirror and they both went hard as bullets. I squashed my breasts against the glass, and massaged them around and around against the glass . . . you don't have any idea how sexy that can be, especially when there's a reflected girl squashing her breasts right up against yours.

"I squeezed out a small drop of KY jelly on each nipple, and then massaged them up against the mirror again. That was tremendous: that was 10 times better. Most of the time, when Burt massaged my breasts and my nipples, his fingers were dry, and I didn't find that particularly exciting. But I loved squashing and squeezing my breasts when they were all slippery. It was such a turn-on. I smeared them around and around against the mirror, making circle marks with Ky on the glass. The camcorder recorded it all.

"Now I took off my G-string and sat down in front of the mirror with my legs apart. I moved the camcorder so that it was pointing at *me*, now, instead of my reflection. I focused it so that it would take a really sharp close-up of my cunt, the way you suggested, and I lay one of Burt's desk lamps on its side on the floor so that it would shine right up between my legs for extra illumination. Oh, it worked, too. The videotape was incredible. You can see my cunt in pin-sharp detail. You can see my clitoris and my lips and pee hole . . . you can even see right inside my vagina, right up inside there, all pink and shiny.

"I think every woman has some idea of what her cunt looks like, but when you see it on video, the way your lover sees it, that's totally different. I spent five or ten minutes just spreading my cunt lips apart with my finger, and running the tip of my finger around and around the entrance to my vagina . . . just seeing what I looked like and where my touching tickled me the most.

"You asked me to pleasure myself in the way that I normally pleasure myself. To tell you the truth, I haven't masturbated at all since I first met Burt. I've felt like it, sometimes. But it seems kind of disloyal, if you understand what I mean. Like, if he doesn't satisfy me, then why am I living with him? I should tell him the truth, or leave . . . not secretly masturbate behind his back. What relationship ever benefited from secrecy?

"I opened my legs wide and drew back my inner cunt lips with my fingertips. I hadn't realized that they were so connected to my clitoris. If you take hold of your inner cunt lips and tug them downward, rhythmically, you get that same kind of feeling around your clitoris as you do when your lover's fucking you . . . at least I do. I hadn't realized how connected they are, and that you can actually bring yourself off by pulling down on your cunt lips . . . at least, I can! and I know at least one of my friends who can.

"I pleasured myself in the way that always makes me come the quickest, and I was really surprised to watch the video of it afterward, how complicated it looks. I use the middle and third fingers of my left hand to pull my left cunt lip to one side, while I quickly flick my clitoris with the tip of my index finger. And when I say quickly, I mean quickly. When you look at the video, my fingertips flying faster than a hummingbird's wing, and scarcely touching my clitoris, even though my clitoris is sticking out really pink and hard and incredibly long, I never realized it came out that much. I rest the tip of my left pinkie directly up against my pee hole, although I wasn't aware that I was doing it before, it just felt nice when I circled it around and around my pee hole, very very lightly, it made me feel like I wanted to pee even though I didn't.

"With the index and middle fingers of my right hand, I hold my *right* cunt lips open, while my third finger is up inside my vagina, and my pinkie is very quickly stroking my asshole. As I get more and more excited, I pull my cunt lips wider and wider, and my right-hand pinkie starts to dip into my asshole, only a little way, but very fast. You can see the juice running out of my vagina, and now and then I slip my *left* pinkie down to lubricate it with juice, and circle it around my pee hole.

"I was amazed when I watched it. I just used to think that I rubbed myself. I never realized there was all of this touching and flicking and dipping and stretching going on. The only time it stops is when I come. I open my thighs really wide, pulling my vagina open, and then I take all of my fingers away except for the finger which is stroking my clitoris. I close my thighs tightly together and that's when I have an orgasm. I'm always very wet when I climax. On the first video I took, you can see me lying on my side with my knees drawn up and my legs clenched, and juice is pouring out of my cunt and down my thighs. I always knew that women didn't come like men . . . they don't actually shoot out sperm. But I couldn't believe how much juice came out of me."

Although women don't and can't ejaculate in the same way that men do when they reach orgasm, they can, if highly stimulated, produce copious amounts of fluid—so much so that some of them are worried that they have "wet the bed." There are all kinds of medical arguments about where this fluid comes from. Some doctors say Bartholin's glands; others say Skene's glands. They still haven't made up their minds. But it doesn't really matter, because they're all *your* glands, and there is nothing more exciting for you or your lover than a copious gush of fluid when you climax.

Some women (like Sandra) achieve it naturally, whenever they're highly excited. Others achieve it now and again, on special occasions—when their lover touches them just the way they like best. But almost every woman *can* achieve it—especially if she's feeling very sexy, and especially if she or her lover can find that particular place (popularly but not accurately known as the G-Spot) which stimulates the clitoris from *inside* her vagina, as well as from outside.

The pleasure of expressing a climax by releasing a copious amount of fluid had led to an increased interest in so-called wet sex, or urination for sexual enjoyment. Since I first openly discussed the subject several years ago, an extraordinary number of women of all ages have written to me, describing the freedom and enjoyment of openly urinating when they reach orgasm, or simply urinating in front of their lovers as part of their foreplay. As Jane, a 31-year-old dental nurse from Austin, Texas, wrote me: "I often used to wet the bed just a little when I reached my climax. One afternoon, I went to bed with Rod, a man I really liked, and he excited me so much that when I climaxed I pissed everywhere, all over his cock, all over his balls, all down his legs, all over the bed. Instead of being angry, he thought it was the most exciting thing that had ever happened to him, and he always loved it when I did it. In fact, he used to be disappointed when I didn't."

We'll discuss "wet sex" in more detail a little later, but there is no doubt that for many women it has strong connotations of sexual freedom and self-expression. As Jane said, "Once I'd learned that I didn't always have to crouch down to relieve myself . . . once I'd understood that I could do it anyway I liked, and that I could use it to express my sexuality . . . I gained much more confidence in myself. I experienced the same feeling that I had when I first walked into a bar on my own, ordered a drink, drank it and enjoyed it, and said 'No, thank you,' to every man who came up and asked me if I wanted company. I experienced the same feeling that I had when I first went out without a bra. Of course you can't do it all the time, but now and again every woman should take a piss standing up, wet her panties, who cares, just do it for the hell of it."

In her first exercise in self-pleasuring, Sandra had seen for the first time what complicated stimulation she needed to excite her to orgasm. This helped her to understand what kind of touching and caressing she needed during her mounting progression toward an orgasm.

When her lover Burt saw the video she had made, he too realized that he needed to know when and how to touch Sandra in order to give her the very best erotic excitement—in other words, manipulation that was gentle, accurate, and never left her (even for a second or two) feeling sexually impatient.

The special benefit of the camcorder is that it enables you to see for yourself how you sexually respond. You can learn more from recording your sexual self-pleasuring in one afternoon than you can in a lifetime of sex lessons. Many powerful physical changes take place within your body as you become sexually excited. Watch your own responses on your video recording, and see if you can match them to the responses that have been recorded by sexual researchers who have observed women becoming sexually excited under laboratory conditions.

Excitement phase: When you first become sexually excited, your heart rate steadily quickens. Place your hand against your heart to feel it. Your nipples stiffen, and there is a slight increase in the size of your breasts. Some women feel no perceptible swelling, but others say "my breasts feel really bigger, and tighter, and my nipples stick out and feel really sensitive." It's interesting to note that the women who experience the greatest proportionate enlargement of their breasts during the early part of sexual excitement are those women who normally think of themselves as having quite small breasts. Zoe, a 21-year-old fashion student, told me, "My breasts are very, very small. I'm more like a boy. I never have to wear a bra. I don't even own a bra. But when I make love to my boyfriend Paul, I'm really conscious of having breasts. I feel like a woman. I want him to touch my nipples and squeeze my breasts and I swear they really do get bigger." Charlene, a 25-year-old dancer and photographic model, has had her breasts enlarged to 46DD by silicone implants, but she also reports that her breasts grow bigger during sexual excitement. "I was always big . . . I have very big nipples . . . when I'm turned on, they stick right out and they don't get soft again, not until I've climaxed. My breasts always swell out, too, sometimes they feel like they're going to burst, almost, they seem like they're huge. My breasts have always been sensitive. I think that most women feel the same way. But the funny part about it is that men are always looking at women's breasts, but when it comes to having sex, they always seem to ignore them. I could spend a whole afternoon having my breasts tickled and stroked and sucked and massaged, and that would be more than enough for me."

During the excitement phase, some women like to have their nipples very lightly brushed and flicked, while others want their nipples to be pulled and pinched and even twisted. Marcia, a 33-year-old research chemist, admitted that she was excited by having her nipples hurt during intercourse. "I do like biting . . . my boyfriend bites my nipples and that sharp pain really excites me. Sometimes he used crocodile clips, too, and clamps one on each of my nipples, or six or seven of them all around my areolas. I suppose I just like a little pain. Not too much . . . you couldn't say that I was a masochist, but it sharpens the experience, you know, just like Tabasco sauce on your hamburger . . . sometimes I like him to fasten four or five crocodile clips around my anus when we're making love . . . he pulls on them when I'm close to coming, and it always makes my orgasm so much more intense."

While the idea of having your nipples pulled or pinched or crocodile-clipped may not appeal to you, your Sex Glow video will show you and your lover quite explicitly how you *do* like to have your breasts stimulated. Do you like your breasts squeezed and massaged? Do you like your nipples tickled or flicked or gently pulled?

Whether your breasts swell noticeably or not, you will often find that your sexual excitement will be betrayed by a rosy flush across your chest. You may have other rashes on your back or your thighs. These are caused by vasocongestion—congestion of the veins. The sex researchers Masters and Johnson described them as "the sex flush."

This flush will appear not only across your breasts. As you become more excited, your clitoris and your inner vaginal lips will begin to swell, and may become redder in color. Your outer vaginal lips will draw back, making your vagina more accessible to your lover's thrusting penis. The inside of your vagina will become increasingly lubricated with "love juice."

While we're discussing your vaginal lubrication, it's worth mentioning that I have had many queries over the years from women who have experienced vaginal dryness—either because of illness or stress or simply because of increasing age. These days, any reputable drugstore can sell you a vaginal lubricant, some of which feel extremely natural and enjoyable.

While you are pleasuring yourself, see how long it takes you to reach this stage of excitement, because only now are you completely ready to take your partner's erect penis inside you. As Sandra said, "One of the problems that I've been having with sex is that Burt is often so eager to push himself into me. Quite often he's entered me before I'm juicy enough, and that can be uncomfortable and off-putting. It doesn't turn me on, for sure. And the trouble is that when he's as eager as that, he reaches his climax even before I feel like making love, and so it's all over before I know what's hit me. That's really frustrating, but I don't like to criticize him . . . he'd take it all the wrong way, and he'd probably end up arguing and sulking about it for weeks."

The beauty of your Sex Glow video, of course, is that you can show your lover how you like to be stimulated without having to make any slighting remarks about his sexual performance. In my experience, it doesn't matter how mature and understanding a man may be, he will *never* take kindly to criticism of his lovemaking. He has to be guided, rather than censured. One way in which you can make sure that his technique improves is to say "Do you remember that time when you kissed me and stroked me and touched me for ages and ages before you put yourself inside me? That really turned me on so much . . . you must have such fantastic control to be able to make love like that." Any lover who doesn't take the hint after *that* must have futon filling for brains.

While you're pleasuring yourself, you can try giving a running commentary of everything you're doing—and, more importantly, of everything you're feeling.

Here's an excerpt from Sandra's commentary. She's

lying back on her black leather couch, completely naked now, and she's succeeded in manipulating herself beyond the excitement phase into what sexologists called the *plateau phase.* This is the phase during which your arousal steadily increases until you reach orgasm. Your breasts swell even more. In some cases, an increased breast measurement of more than 25 percent has been noticed, although the swelling tends to be less pronounced in women who have suckled babies.

Your areolae, the pinkish rings around your nipples, also swell up so that the erection of your nipples become less obvious. Your clitoris, which at first was very prominent, draws back and almost disappears, which can cause problems if your lover is pleasuring you with his fingers, and is a little uncertain about the exact location of your clitoris (another reason why it's so important to *show* him how you like to be aroused).

During your plateau phase, the muscles of your vagina relax, making it large enough to accommodate your lover's penis, and your womb rises so that the head of the penis can plunge more deeply into your upper reaches.

At this point, Sandra picked up the dildo she had bought for her Sex Glow session, and smothered it with KY jelly. It was a "Rambo" vibrator, described as "ten inches of pulsating erection that never gets tired . . . well-veined for ultra-realism." She says, "when I saw this in the store, I thought twice about buying it. Not because of the price . . . it was only $29.95, but because of the sheer size of it. It's much bigger than Burt's cock and I simply didn't think that I'd be able to get it inside me . . . but anyway, I'm feeling very sexy now, I feel that I really want it inside me, even if it *is* too big.

"I've made it totally slippery, so it shouldn't be *too* difficult . . . after all, if they make them this size, *some* women must be able to get them up their cunts. Look, I'm holding my cunt lips open, and I'm sliding the head of the dildo up and down in my cunt slit, so that I'm really slippery, too. Now I'm lying back on the couch with my legs as wide apart as they can possibly stretch, and my cunt wide open, and you can see right into my vagina, right inside, it's all pink and wet and open, like it's just begging to be fucked, like it's just begging to have a huge big cock right up inside it. I'm stroking my clitoris with the tip of my finger, very gently, kind of a slow, gentle downward movement, and my clitoris is still very stiff and sticking out. Now I'm positioning the head of the dildo right up against my cunt hole. It feels huge, it feels enormous. I'm sure it won't go in. It's much bigger than Burt's cock, and Burt isn't exactly under-endowed. But I'm going to try to push it in now . . . I'm pushing it in. My cunt's stretching wider and wider, you can see my lips stretching, look. Oh God, it's too big, I can't take it. It's far too big. I'm taking it out again, but I really want it in. I really want it up me. Look, I'm pushing it in again, and it's going in. The whole head's disappeared now, and look how wide my cunt lips are stretched open, it's unbelievable. I'm going to push it in further and further, not too fast; it hurts a little because it's so big, but it's a good hurt, believe me. I'm pushing it further and further in, it's halfway in now, and I can really feel those veins. It's not like a real cock because it's so hard, and it doesn't quite feel like real skin . . . but it's filling me up. I never felt filled up like this before, ever.

"I'm pushing it in now, as far as it will go. All you can see now is the red handle sticking out of my shaved, stretched-open cunt. It looks amazing, doesn't it? Look at my cunt lips, how swollen they are, and completely bare, and shining with KY—and this enormous vibrator filling up my cunt hole so that I can hardly breathe, it's so big. That's 10 whole inches I've got up inside me, 10 whole inches long and 3 inches wide.

"I'm drawing it out now, all the way out, sliding it out of my cunt hole—and look, my cunt hole's actually gaping open in a perfect circle, where it went right up me. Now I'm pushing it in again, and it's easier this time. I'm pushing it all the way in, and switching on the vibrator. Oh . . . you don't have any idea what that feels like . . . you don't have any idea. Oh God, I don't think I can stand it. The whole of my cunt is tingling, it's *tingling*! I don't have to play with my clitoris anymore, my whole cunt is electric.

"I'm pushing the vibrator even further up, so that it's right up next to the neck of my womb, and now it's making my whole *womb* tingle. I can't believe it. I can't believe it. My cunt's started to squeeze the vibrator, tighter and tighter, these squeezes. It's almost like it's trying to squeeze it out. Oh God, something's happening to me . . . I don't know what I—"

In Sandra's video, you can clearly see her pressing her thighs together, bending forward, and beginning to shake in an orgasm that she later described as "the best orgasm ever . . . I never had one like it . . . it was like being lifted up on a tidal wave made of warm molasses."

This was her *Orgasm.* Some sexologists think that a woman's orgasm is more pleasurable and more profound than a man's; and it's true that some women actually lose consciousness for a few moments when they climax. However, there is no empirical way of telling whether the female climax is really more enjoyable than the male, and it really doesn't matter if it is. Both experiences are highly pleasurable and deeply satisfying, and when a man and a woman are climaxing together, the sharing of their ecstasy greatly enhances the pleasure for both of them.

Kay, a 24-year-old teacher from New Orleans, Louisiana, put it very succinctly when she said, "Whenever I rub Norman's cock, and his sperm comes shooting out all over my fingers, I experience almost as much pleasure from *his* pleasure as if I were having a climax myself."

And John, a 31-year-old lecturer from White Plains, New York, said, "Sometimes I bring Helen to orgasm with my finger. She loves it, but I love it, too. More than once, I've come close to coming when she comes, without even touching my cock at all, and about a month ago I ejaculated all over her leg, even though neither of us laid so much as a finger on my cock, from beginning to end. I just had this stunningly erotic tingling sensation in the end of my cock, and I start pumping out sperm, more sperm than I can ever remember."

After her orgasm, Sandra entered the *resolution phase*—that is, the period of recovery. The length of the resolution phase is another of the fundamental sexual differences between men and women—even more dramatic, in some ways, than the difference in time it takes for a man and a woman to become sexually excited.

After *his* climax, a man loses his sexual urge almost completely. This is why so many men, after the most passionate intercourse, can abruptly "switch off"—turn over and go to sleep. A woman on the other hand is capable of another orgasm almost immediately—sometimes without any interruption at all—and can technically go on having orgasm after orgasm until she is totally exhausted.

This is why I so strongly recommend that loving couples have at least one vibrator or artificial penis in their nightstand drawer. A man is simply incapable of having climax after climax after climax. Once he had ejaculated his semen, Nature decides that he has done his job for now, and makes sure that he gets plenty of rest in preparation for the next impregnation. But because Nature has short-changed men when it comes to multiple climaxes, there is no reason at all why *you* shouldn't have them, and this is where "10 inches of pulsating erection that never gets tired" comes into the picture.

If you can persuade the man in your life to learn the skills of stimulating you not only with his penis, his fingers, and his tongue, but with a vibrator—if you can both learn to enjoy the vibrator as an adjunct to your love life that's fun, willing, and extremely practical—then you, too, can discover the shattering (if exhausting) pleasure of multiple orgasms.

It's interesting to note that if a man *does* have a way of continuing to stimulate you after his climax, his next erection will almost certainly come sooner, especially if you use the vibrator on him, too. Once you've climaxed for the second or third time, stroking the shaft of his penis with the side of the vibrator, try nudging it around his balls, and then see how far you can push it into his bottom. If he can't achieve another erection after *that,* then he really does need to get some sleep. Never mind, you can always try again in the morning.

Sandra had never experienced a multiple orgasm before she made her Sex Glow video. When she did, she couldn't stop, and she discovered heights of sexual ecstasy that she hadn't believed possible. "For over an hour, I was coming and coming and coming. I wanted it to stop but then I didn't want it to stop, ever. I wanted to go on having orgasms until I passed out, or died. The more excited I became, the more excited I became. I was full of myself. I felt that I could do anything, fuck anyone. I felt almost like I was reborn, or in one of those dreams where you know you can do whatever you like. And I felt so much of a *woman.* I felt so feminine. That was the most arousing thing of all. I was a woman with breasts and nipples and a cunt and a clitoris, and I could give myself the kind of pleasure that most people never even dream about."

After her first orgasm, Sandra relaxed for a moment, but then she gently started running the vibrator up and down her vaginal lips. "Just playing at first . . . it wasn't even switched on. But then I switched it on and very, very gently let it buzz between my legs, with no more presure than its own weight. After only a short time, my clitoris started to stiffen again . . . my cunt lips were sore because I'd been pulling them wide open with my fingers, but they weren't *that* sore, and I really did feel like having that vibrator up inside me for a second time. It was so long, so fat. I loved the way it filled me up.

"Look—here I am, sliding it back into my cunt again. Look at my face! Talk about the cat that got the cream! That's a Sexual Glow if ever I saw one. This time I'm doing it much more slowly, but pushing it very deeply in, and holding there, and then sliding it right out again, and pausing for a moment before pushing it back in again. But my legs are much closer together . . . I don't have my cunt spread wide."

While Sandra was doing this, she deliberately clenched her vaginal muscles as tightly as she could around the shaft of the vibrator. This is the secret of achieving second, third, fourth, and even more orgasms one after the other—keeping your vagina fully filled with a large object (a real penis, if your lover still had a hard one), while at the same time keeping your thighs as close together as possible. If you're actually having sexual intercourse, your lover can help by inserting his penis into your vagina and then placing his knees on each side of you, so that you won't be tempted to open your legs wide.

The reason for keeping your legs together is that this

position enables you to exert much more of a muscular squeeze on the object inside your vagina, whether it's a penis or a vibrator or a condom-covered cucumber. Start the squeeze at your perineum (the area between your vagina and your anus), and then see if you can rhythmically "ripple" it all the way up to your womb. If you do it in time to the slow in-and-out penetration of a penis or vibrator, you will find that you will rapidly become very strongly aroused, and that you are well on the way to experiencing a second orgasm.

What you're doing, in fact, is continuing to produce the same muscular spasms that you enjoyed during your first orgasm—except in a rhythmical and controlled way.

Some women find that they need a little extra stimulation, such as clitoral tickling. Sandra used a small, soft makeup brush, which she flicked very quickly and lightly from side to side across her clitoris. "When I'm going for my second or third orgasm, I don't like to be rubbed too hard. It makes me jump in the same way as the first orgasm, but by then my cunt's feeling too sensitive for anything rough. I jump, but I don't enjoy it very much."

What Sandra did specifically (and very usefully) learn from watching her Sex Glow session on video was that she can reach an orgasm much more quickly if her lover's penis (or, in this case, her Rambo vibrator) is angled slightly upward as it thrusts into her vagina, so that the glans presses more forcefully on the front wall than it does on the back. This of course has the effect of stimulating her clitoris from inside her vagina. The visible part of the clitoris (the glans) is only the tip of a deeply buried organ that in some women can be an inch long, or even longer: there is considerable variation in clitoral size from one woman to another.

"Normally, when Burt and I were making love, I didn't really notice any difference in how long it took me to reach an orgasm," said Sandra. "But when I was able to do it at my own pace, and try out so many different angles and speeds, I found out what really aroused me and kept me aroused. Sometimes Burt would change position during sex, and the new position wasn't as exciting as the first, and so of course it would take me even longer to reach an orgasm, and there was always the chance that Burt was going to come first.

"I especially like it when I lie flat on my stomach on the bed or the couch, with my legs apart, and pushes his cock into my cunt from behind. Because he's kneeling, his cock pushes into my cunt at just the right angle, and I can feel his balls bouncing against my cunt lips, too, which is really a turn-on."

I asked Sandra to tell me about any sexual fantasy which she might have had about Burt, but which she had so far been too shy to suggest to him. Without any hesitation, she said, "Being tied up, that's my fantasy. Being tied to the bed with silk scarves or handcuffs or something like that, and having Burt do whatever he wanted to me, fucking me any way he wanted to, fingering me, spanking my bottom, anything, and not being able to get free. That's a big, big fantasy for me."

And how about a fantasy that turns her on, but which she's not at all sure that she'd actually like to try?

Again, she didn't hesitate. "Going to bed with two guys."

At the end of her first Sex Glow session, Sandra had already emerged with a new groomed look, a more relaxed attitude toward her sexual feelings, a positive pride in her ability to achieve one orgasm after the other, and a very detailed and intimate understanding of how she could be most quickly stimulated. She also ended up with an extremely erotic video, which she showed to Burt the same evening.

Burt's comment? "It was such a turn-on, I've asked Sandra to film some more. But apart from that, I learned a lot. I genuinely did. I never realized how much a woman's sex organs change during intercourse, and I never realized what a big difference a very small change of position could make, or how hard you kiss, or how roughly you touch.

"It was like somebody giving you an advanced driving lesson. You always thought you were really skillful at driving, and then suddenly somebody shows you that you were just a beginner."

That, of course, is the tremendous advantage of using video. One partner can show and explain his or her feelings at a time when they are not actually making love. On many occasions, watching your Sex Glow video *will* lead to lovemaking, and rather quickly, too! But you can both look at it again and again and begin to understand your own needs and your own favorite ways of getting excited.

By the way—a brief word about multiple orgasms. Sex researchers Masters and Johnson showed in their laboratory experiments that women of all ages are capable of experiencing multiple orgasms—in fact, unlike men, whose ability to have repeated ejaculations falls away sharply with increasing age, older women frequently experience multiple orgasms (as many as 50 in one case.)

However, if you *don't* or *can't* have multiple orgasms, don't worry about it. Every act of lovemaking is exciting and satisfying in its own way, and I don't agree with those people who want to put sex in the same level as a pie-eating contest. One good pie is enough for anybody.

This doesn't mean that you can't experiment, and *try* to have multiple orgasms. Who knows, you may surprise yourself, and your body, too.

Let's continue with building your Sex Glow by looking now at those wild and sexy things that you've always fantasized about, but probably never had the nerve to try.

SIX

No More Ms. Inhibited!

The essence of developing a sexy glow is learning to have pride in yourself. Pride in your appearance; pride in your attractiveness; pride in your sexual personality.

The many ordinary women who have generously helped me with my books over the years are not nymphomaniacs or sex-mad freaks. If you could meet them face-to-face as I do, you would see that they look and talk just like you or me. Behind the sexual anecdotes in these pages, you would find women who are startlingly pretty and women who could only be described as not pretty at all—not in the conventional sense. You would find skinny women and plump women. You would find blondes, brunettes, and redheads. You would find women of all races, ages, and backgrounds.

What they all share is a strong desire to have a fun and fulfilling sex life. They're tired of being shy and inhibited about their lovemaking. They're tired of routine. They want to feel that incredible erotic rush of doing something really daring.

Once they've found their pride, once they've found their Sex Glow, they're capable of taking their love lives into their own hands and experiencing whatever it is they want to experience. And you ought to hear some of their testimonials: "Not in a million years did I ever think I could do *that!*" "I always thought that was absolutely disgusting, truly disgusting. But you opened my eyes and showed me that whatever two people enjoy doing together, so long as they're both willing and so long as it doesn't hurt them, can *never* be disgusting. I look back on my old self now and think what a prude I must have been."

It's genuinely exciting to see the look in the eyes of a woman who has come to recognize at last that she's very sexy, and that she can drive any man wild in bed—or even wilder, if she wants to. Yes, even those women who have always been deeply inhibited about lovemaking because of their physical appearance.

Weight is by far the most common inhibiting factor. "I don't like to take off my clothes in front of him." "I think I look like an elephant." "I hate my body . . . I've dieted and dieted and I never seem to lose any weight. How can I be wild in bed if I'm 175 pounds?"

Well, remember Margie, earlier in the book? She had the best time in bed, in spite of her weight.

I've always been a fervent believer in balanced eating and sensible exercise. But I am very much opposed to the kind of commercial diet routines which promise that "you'll see the weight drop off in just seven days, or your money back!" Keep your money and recognize that most women have a weight problem because of other problems altogether—boredom, unhappiness, stress, and a low sense of self-esteem. The routine is, they tend to eat to relieve all of these problems, but all they do is make the problems worse.

It's not at all easy for a woman to feel like being wild in bed when she has low self-esteem. But the cycle has to be put into reverse somehow. You can't go on for the rest of your life feeling bad and then eating to feel better but then feeling worse.

You don't solve the problem by dieting. Most commercial diets are hard, depressing, and nine times out of ten you put back everything you've lost and then some. You're encouraged to diet by a multimillion-dollar industry that markets diet plans and diet books and so-called diet foods. The plain truth is, they don't want you to lose weight. They have no interest in *you* whatsoever, except to keep you as a customer who constantly chases after that elusive dream figure.

Start looking at your life from another angle altogether. Forget about your weight and your statistics and how you can never get into the clothes you want to wear. A healthy and uninhibited attitude toward sex is a tremendous help in overcoming other problems in your life. And the way to start feeling sexy is by *acting* sexy.

Acting sexy starts with *talking* sexy. Some people express surprise that the men and women who have talked and written about their love lives can use words like "fuck" and "cunt" and "cock" and "asshole" and "pussy" without being embarrassed. The truth is that most of them *are* embarrassed, to begin with. But using plain, straightforward words that everybody understands is the first step to demystifying sex and giving yourself the verbal equipment to drive your man wild in bed. Once you get used to the words, it's surprising how much easier it is to get used to the deeds.

Make yourself a Sex Glow video. Take some time with yourself, cherish yourself. And promise yourself that as often as you can—every day if possible—you'll do something sexy. Make it a time to look forward to, a time when you can indulge yourself. Do it alone or do it with a partner, it doesn't matter which. But try doing some of the things you were always inhibited about doing before.

Here's Greta, a 33-year-old bank clerk from Orlando, Florida: "I was quite skinny when I was a young girl, but when I was at high school I put on a whole lot of puppy fat just when all my friends were looking slim and beautiful. I had only one boyfriend, Clint—no, not Clint Eastwood! .and he was about the same size as me. We kissed sometimes but we never had sex. In fact I didn't have sex with anybody until I was 24. Can you imagine being a virgin until you're 24? Some of my friends were sleeping with boys when they were 11.

"Anyway I read one of your books and it said a whole lot about self-image and self-esteem and being proud of who you are. That stuck in my mind. I did that thing where you tell people to take off all of their clothes and look at themselves in the mirror. I always used to imagine that was for skinny people, but you were right. I looked at my plus points. I may have been fat, but I had a pretty face and lots of curly brown hair. My breasts were enormous, but they were firm, and nicely rounded. I had a tummy, for sure, and a big bottom, but big compared to what? You were right: they looked okay on me. In fact I decided then and there that I looked pretty good all over.

"I went through the whole self-examination, routine, right in front of the mirror, with the book on the floor beside me. I opened my legs wide, and I parted my cunt lips with my fingers, and I touched myself openly for the first time in my life. I used to masturbate before, maybe two or three times a month, but I always did it by squeezing my thighs together, and I didn't always have an orgasm. But now here was a book which was telling me how to touch my own clitoris and how to put my fingers up my cunt and even up my own bottom. I couldn't believe it. I thought it was all so *rude*!"

That night, for the first time in her life, Greta masturbated with her fingers and reached an orgasm. "I'd had orgasms before, but they were nothing at all like this. Boy, you don't know how sexy I felt! You don't know how *great* I felt! Of course I went back to the bank the next morning and I was still tubby old me in my brown stretch-nylon polo shirt and my skirt the size of P. T. Barnum's spare tent. I knew I hadn't changed in physical appearance, but something about me *was* different—and that was the fact that I had made up my mind to learn more about sex, and about that incredible orgasm I'd had.

"I'll tell you what it was: when I was coming, I *felt* beautiful. And afterward I thought to myself, well, if I feel this beautiful, I must be beautiful. And do you know what was the first thing that happened to me when I walked into the bank that morning? The security guard said, 'You're shining today.' "

Greta didn't have a man in her life at the time, but I suggested that she stop worrying about that and concentrate on whatever sexual pleasures she could give to herself. Up until then, Greta had always believed that self-pleasuring was at best disgusting and at worst a mortal sin. She had also regarded self-pleasuring as an admission of defeat—an admission that she wasn't attractive enough to find a man of her own.

All of this, of course, is complete nonsense. Self-pleasuring is amusing, exciting, and completely harmless. It helps you to concentrate your sexual thoughts on yourself and your desires, and it gives you an accurate measure of your own physical needs. Greta began to enjoy self-pleasuring so much that she did it every night, and sometimes mornings, too. Through a mail-order sex-toys company, she bought herself first one vibrator and then a second, so that she could pleasure herself with one vibrator in her vagina and the other in her anus.

"I still longed to have a man make love to me: nothing could take that feeling away. But I tried pleasuring myself in all kinds of different places and different situations. I bought myself some sexy black underwear, too—garters and stockings and G-strings. I bought a G-string that had a hole in the middle of it so that I could slide a vibrator into the hole and up inside me without even taking it off.

"You suggested that I pleasure myself every time I felt like eating a candy bar. Well, I didn't succeed totally. I think I would have rubbed my cunt away if I'd stuck to that! But it's a great idea, it's fun to do, and I genuinely began to lose a little weight. It wasn't a landslide, but my face began to look less chubby, and I lost a few inches off my hips. The weird thing was, I hadn't consciously dieted in any other way. I just started feeling less stressed, and less hopeless about myself.

"I met Alan totally out of the blue. It was totally unexpected. He came into the bank to withdraw some money on his credit card and it took some time because the computers were down. We got to talking and he told me he was working for one of the big hotels on the OBT (Orange Blossom Trail). He was new in Orlando and asked me if I knew anyplace good to eat. The next thing I knew, he was asking me to have dinner with him.

"We had a dream of an evening. He was friendly, he was smart; but he wasn't too pushy. Every time I'd dated a man before, I had always had the feeling that he was tolerating me because I was fat. But Alan paid me a whole lot of compliments and none of them had anything to do with my size. Before, I used to feel like a thin person trapped in a fat body. Now I just felt like me.

"He took me home and he asked me out again the following evening. In the car, he kissed me, and he said, 'You're one of the most attractive women I've met in years. You *glow.*'"

Greta met Alan the following night and he asked her to come back to his hotel room. "For a split-second, I panicked. I thought: maybe I can pleasure myself okay, but can I do it with a real man?

"I needn't have worried about it. He had pink champagne ready in an ice bucket, can you imagine it? He took me in his arms and he kissed me, and when we started kissing it was a long, long time before we came up for air. Alan kissed me and caressed me and ran his fingers through my hair, and let me tell you I thought I was in heaven. I was wearing this simple red button-down dress, and Alan unfastened the buttons one by one, and then he slipped it off my shoulders. I don't think he could believe what he saw. I was wearing a red lacy bra, matching red garter belt and stockings, and no panties.

"I held him close and unbottoned his shirt. I could feel his cock inside his pants, it was sticking right up like an Apollo rocket. I stripped off his shirt, and there was this beautiful muscular suntanned chest. He was big, like me, but he swam and worked out some, and his body was in terrific condition. He reached around and unfastened my bra, and drew it off, and he took hold of my bare breasts in both hands and touched my nipples and I thought, I hope I don't come here and now! My nipples were unbelievably stiff, but they went even stiffer because Alan dipped his fingertips in his pink champagne and touched each of my nipples, one after the other, and then he lifted up each of my breasts and licked the champagne off them, and then sucked them, too.

"I took off his pants. His cock was sticking out of the opening in his shorts. I was breathless at the sight of it. It was big, really big, and the head was dark red, almost purple. I could see that it was wet, too, a little drop of juice was dripping from the opening. At that moment I was so frightened I didn't know whether to touch it or not. But then I remembered some of the things you'd said in your book. I remembered that you'd said about doing the things you wanted to do, and not being ashamed to do them. I knelt down on the carpet in front of Alan, and tugged down his pants and his shorts so that he could step out of them. Then I took hold of that big thick cock in my hand, and I kissed it, and licked it.

"It was strange-tasting, salty-sweet like some kind of tropical fruit, but it was delicious. It was one of those tastes that you can't describe but which you know you're going to get addicted to. I squashed my red-lipsticky lips right up to the head of his cock, and then I opened my mouth and took it right inside, and sucked it. He ran his fingers into my hair, and made this groaning sound. I took his cock out of my mouth and asked him if he was all right, I hadn't hurt him, had I?

He said, 'Don't stop. Stop. You're going to have to stop, otherwise you're going to make me come before we've even started.'

"We went to bed. I didn't take off my stockings or my garter belt or even my high-heeled shoes, I knew Alan liked them. I lay back on the bed and he kissed my lips and my neck and my shoulders and my breasts. He adored my breasts. He loved sucking my nipples and lifting his head up while my nipple was still caught between his lips, so that my breast was lifted, too, and my nipples stretched.

"He caressed me down the side of my thighs, and then his fingers strayed up between my legs. I could feel my heart banging so loudly that I was sure Alan must be able to hear it, too. I opened my legs wide, and I held my cunt open for him. I could hear how juicy it was. Alan lowered his head and licked my cunt all the way from my asshole to my clitoris in one long smooth wet lick, and that was the very first time that a man ever licked my cunt.

"I was so excited I was almost passing out. I wanted him to lick me again and yet I desperately wanted him to put his cock inside me, too. He climbed on top of me, and I reached down between his legs and held that great stiff gorgeous cock, and I helped him to put it into me. He leaned his weight forward and his cock went right up inside, right up inside me, until our pubic hair was all tangled together, and that was the first time a man ever went up inside me, and I thought it was wonderful.

"He rode me so forcefully—you know, so rhythmically. Every time he pulled himself a little way out I found myself begging for him to push it back in again, and then he did, and then that was almost too much, but then he was pulling it out again, and I wanted it back, I *needed* it back.

"He fucked me so rhythmically that my breasts swayed up and down, up and down, and he loved that, he really loved it. He buried his fingers in my breasts and squeezed my nipples.

"I turned over onto my hands and knees, doggy-fashion, and stuck my bottom up in the air, and he fucked me from behind. He thrust his cock in again and I couldn't believe how deep it went in, even deeper than before. He started to fuck me faster and faster—too fast for me, but I didn't like to tell him, not then. This was only my first-ever time. He fucked me harder and quicker. My breasts were swaying and jiggling around. I could feel an orgasm begin to rise up between my legs, but Alan couldn't hold himself back any longer. He clenched my bottom tight, and then I felt him shooting his come into me. I actually felt it—I never thought I would!

"Alan didn't know that I was virgin until I told him, much later. Even then he found it hard to believe me, because I knew so much about sex. When I told him I'd got it all from a book he just laughed.

"That was a good relationship, with Alan. It lasted almost three years. then Alan was sent to another hotel in Tampa and things just kind of fizzled out. We parted friends, though, and I'll never forget that very first night. I'm living with Marcus now, he's an electronics engineer, he works at Cocoa Beach. Marcus says I'm the sexiest thing that ever happened to him. What he loves best of all is when I sit on top of him and suck his cock, I can take it right into my mouth, right down to the balls, and then when he's coming I lower my bottom over his face and almost suffocate him! He says it would be a good way to die, with his mouth full of hot wet cunt.

"I never thought that I would ever be like this. Look at me now, I'm just over 162, and I'm so pleased with my life that I can't even begin to tell you. I eat what I like, but I do try to be sensible, and I walk whenever I can instead of driving, and I do go swimming whenever I have the time to spare. I still think my greatest triumph is that I've managed to stop grazing. Whenever I feel the urge to eat anything between meals, I do what I did when I first read your book—I hide myself away someplace, I take down my panties (if I'm wearing any), and I masturbate. It always leaves me feeling better—and not only that, it has no calories whatsoever!"

Greta managed to summon up the nerve to believe in her sexuality—to have pride in what she was, rather than what some dieting article said she thought to be. She admits that she was "totally terrified" when she first dated Alan. In fact she was so frightened that she doesn't even remember where he took her to dinner. But she remembers (with an ever-increasing glow) the night that she won her self-esteem, and the night that she lost her virginity to a man who genuinely found her attractive (which she is).

Let's take a look now at a sample of women who all had strong sexual feelings, yet felt to inhibited to bring those sexual feelings into their relationships with men. In some cases they were simply too shy to express their desires. In other cases, they were concerned (and often rightly) that their partners might take offense, or think that they were nymphomaniac or perverted in their sexual tastes. In all cases, however, they lacked sexual self-confidence . . . that inner glow that we have been learning to develop . . . that strength that comes from understanding your own body and your own sexual urges and being proud of them instead of anxious about them.

However wild you think your secret sexual urges may be, there is simply no such thing as a sexual act that is "wrong" or "perverted," so long as that sexual act is carried out with the enthusiastic agreement of everybody involved, and causes no injury or harm.

In fact, far greater harm is caused to sexual relationships because one or the other partner has sexual urges that he or she is too inhibited to reveal—when all the time those sexual urges could give the relationship so much extra excitement.

If you use the Sex Glow session or a similar program of sexual self-examination in order to come to terms with your physical desires and then summon up the courage to satisfy them, you could experience erotic pleasure such as no erotic pleasure you've ever experienced before. If there is some sexual variation that *you've* always wanted to try, something that you've been too inhibited to admit to your lover, remember as you read these firsthand reports that all of these women felt just the same way as you, but used their new Sex Glow to overcome their inhibitions. They all said to themselves—I'm me, I have my own sexual desires, no matter how wild they may seem to other people, and I want to satisfy them.

Your desire may not be particularly extreme. It may only be as exotic as that of Maria, a 22 year-old hairdresser from Tucson, Arizona. "I have been living with my boyfriend Wayne for two years now. He's a great guy, a good-looking guy, and all the rest of the girls really envy me. The only trouble is, he likes me to go down on him. He could lie back while I suck his cock for hours. But he has never gone down on me. And I mean, *ever*. I would really like him to do that. I'd love him to lick my cunt. But how can I ask him, without making him feel like a fool, and spoiling everything? Maybe he knows how to do it but doesn't like doing it. I don't know. I always feel like our sex life isn't complete, not till he kisses my cunt."

I am reliably told that a few men actively dislike cunnilingus (oral stimulation of the female genitals), but I have to admit that I have never met one. The taste and aroma of the female vulva are powerful aphrodisiacs, and almost all men have a very strong natural instinct to bury their face in a woman's vulva.

Some women don't like it. Sex authoress Jenny Fabian once told me that she couldn't stand the idea of a face staring at her between her legs (and this from a woman who gave oral sex to so many men that she had the taste of sperm permanently on her tongue!).

I suggested three courses of action to Maria. The first was simply to climb astride Wayne while he was lying on the couch, lift her skirt, and present him (at very close quarters) with her exposed vulva. If he didn't get the message immediately, she could then ask him to give her a kiss. If he still showed signs of reluctance to give her oral sex, she should try to find out *why* he was so reluctant. Was she always scrupulously clean? Many men are strongly sexually aroused by the smell of a woman's vulva, whereas others wrinkle their noses. Maybe Wayne was a nose-wrinkler. Would she consider shaving off all or some of her public hair? Maria was a dark-skinned girl, with quite luxuriant black hair, and I assumed that her pubic hair was much the same.

Maria tried the first approach. "Wayne was lying with his feet up on the couch watching television and having a drink. I was wearing nothing but a small white sleeveless top and a very small green miniskirt. I climbed onto the couch and knelt right over his face, so that he could see right up my skirt. I was nervous, for sure. I wasn't nervous of what he might do. Wayne's never violent and he hardly ever loses his temper. I was nervous about being embarrassed. Supposing he said something that made me feel about a half-inch high?

"But I remember what you said about self-esteem . . . and I also remember that Wayne and I had both watched my Sex Glow video together and it really turned him on.

"I lifted my skirt and looked down at him and said, 'How about a kiss, sweetheart?' The tip of his nose was only an inch away from my open pussy, so I don't think he could have missed the point. But he shook his head and kind of twisted out from underneath me. He kissed me on the lips and grinned and said, 'Maybe later.'

"My first reaction was to feel embarrassed and angry and put-down. I'd offered him my pussy on a plate and he didn't want it. If I hadn't been full of sexual self-confidence, I would have started to nag him and argue with him and ask him if he didn't find me sexy anymore. But I knew there were other options, and I was sure that I was attractive and sexy. I was completely confident about myself, physically. Whatever the reason for Wayne's reluctance to give me oral sex, I was pretty sure that it wasn't because *I* was lacking in any way.

"That evening, in the bathroom, I shaved off all of my pubic hair. I was going to leave a small tuft but in the end I decided why bother. I brushed up my hair and tied it in ribbons, and there I was, ready for bed, completely naked except for my bangles, with a plump hairless pussy that looked just like a ripe peach. Surely he couldn't resist that!

"I slipped into bed, making sure that Wayne just glimpsed me. He was watching television at the time. But after a moment's pause he switched off the remote, and he turned toward me and ran his hand over my bare body, all around my breasts, across my stomach, and then down between my legs.

"He looked me right in the eye. He didn't say a word, but he kissed me, and all the time his hand kept cupping and stroking my bald pussy. After a moment or two, he slid down the bed, his lips fluttering kisses over me all the way down to my stomach. He gently parted my thighs with his hands. I could feel his warm breath on my bare pussy lips. The suspense was incredible. Then I felt the first wiggling probing of his tongue. He was opening up my inner lips so that he could lick my clitoris and circle his tongue around my pussy hole. He licked me for almost twenty minutes, and it was so-o-o beautiful. His tongue just kept on washing and flapping and probing and teasing. He even lifted my bottom cheeks with his cupped hands and licked all around my anus. He rolled his tongue up and stiffened it and actually pushed it up my ass. In the end he concentrated on my clitoris, and used his fingers to stimulate my pussy and my ass. I could feel his breath getting faster and faster. He kept my pussy lips wide apart with his fingers so that he could keep on licking my clitoris really well, right till the very end, when suddenly everything rushed together and everything went black—and then, there he was, licking and drinking the juice that was running out of me.

"As we were cuddling afterward, I said, 'Why didn't you ever do that to me before?' He said he would have done, but he had suffered a bad experience with the very first woman he had slept with, who had been four years older than him. He had gone down on her just like he had gone down on me, but when he had looked up at her she had screamed with laughter. 'Little man with the big bushy mustache!' He had lost his erection in embarrassment, and after that he could only think of oral sex with an unshaven woman with a feeling of terrible embarrassment. So that was the answer. I promised him that I would always stay shaved. And I have. I prefer it now. I wouldn't have a hairy pussy for anything."

As amusing as this anecdote may be, the fact is that many serious sexual inhibitions are the result of just such minor humiliations. However well-meaning and affectionate your amusement may be, do be careful if your lover does anything sexual that makes you feel like laughing. Men who are normally easygoing and unself-conscious can be surprisingly quick to feel rejected when their sexual prowess is involved. An important part of driving your man even wilder in bed is making him feel virile and sexually skillful—never forgetting to compliment him on the size and the hardness of his erection, or his skill in arousing you in bed.

When was the last time you said, "Oh, darling, your cock feels so huge inside me . . ." or "You make me want to come, and come, and go on coming forever"? Or words to that effect? Phrases like that are always worth saying, because just as *you* feel more confident when your lover compliments you on your hair or your dress or on anything you do, *he* feels more confident when you tell him how well he makes love to you. Nine times out of ten, the result will be that he makes love to you better.

In reality, your man may be far from perfect when it comes to making love. He may be short on ideas and short on skill. But you can give him those qualities—you can ignite his imagination and you can dramatically improve his technique—just by forgetting his shortcomings and concentrating on what he likes best and what he can do best. You can teach him to give you what you want, too. When you've succeeded in doing that, and he rally starts to excite you in bed, your excitement will quickly communicate itself back to him, and excite him, too, so that he feels more confident about making love to you, and much more easily aroused. When they're making love to you, men need to feel that their touching/kissing/licking/rubbing are having an immediate effect. In other words, if they're sending you into seventh heaven, they need to *know* that they are. The erotic feelings that are exploding inside your head may not be so obvious to the man who's playing with your breasts, kissing your lips, licking your nipples, or rubbing your clitoris.

Always remember that good sex is about *response,* about showing your partner just how much he excites you. You can show your response in the way that you greet him when you see him, the way you kiss him and touch him. You can show your response by dressing in a sexy way. Not necessarily blatantly, but by wearing erotic underwear, or by wearing no underwear at all.

Jemima, 29, an insurance executive from Denver, Colorado, said, "I'm really turned on by the idea of wearing rubber. I don't know why. I mean, who can ever explain why they think that one thing's sexy and another isn't? I know when it started, though. Or at least, when I first became aware of it. When I was 18 I went to a college fancy-dress party. My date was going to dress like Batman so I wanted to dress like Catwoman, right? A friend of mine used to sing with a college rock group and she said she had a black rubber dress she used to wear on stage, and I was welcome to borrow it, which I did.

"If you've never worn anything made out of rubber, you ought to try it. That dress was amazing. It was tight and stretchy and it clung onto me like a second skin. It makes you sweat, makes your skin slick, and it has this amazing smell. It's like perfume, only it's much more exciting.

"The rubber dress was so tight that I could hardly get into it. I couldn't wear any underwear because they would have shown through the latex. I made a cat mask out of black vinyl, and I borrowed a pair of black leather thigh boots, and I made a terrific Catwoman. None of the guys would leave me alone. In fact my boyfriend was furious because I got all the attention and he was supposed to be Batman.

"But, for me, there was something more to that rubber dress than just a fancy-dress costume. It turned me on. I loved the feel of it on my naked skin because it was so tight and I felt like a prisoner inside it. Like a slut, if you like, like a slave. What kind of a woman wears a black rubber dress? A woman who's interested in sex, I guess. A woman who wants to show men that she wants them to own her, and take her; but at the same time a woman who's sexually dominant, too. It's hard to explain. When I was wearing that Catwoman costume I realized that men were fascinated and frightened at the same time. There were some pretty obvious hard-ons walking around.

"I had to return the dress, but I never forgot what it was like to wear it. Whenever I smelled rubber it excited me, I don't know why. I used to buy condoms and use them to masturbate by stretching them out real thin and long and sliding them backward and forward between my legs, so that they would slide against my clitoris and right between the cheeks of my bottom. It wasn't just the feeling of rubber, it was the smell, too. Kind of surgical and—I don't know—forbidden. It's hard to explain.

"By accident, I came across an advertisement for a rubber-wear catalogue in one of my boyfriend's magazines. I sent for a rubber miniskirt and a pair of tight-fitting rubber panties. When they arrived I could hardly wait to get my boyfriend out of the house so that I could try them on!

"When I was feeling in a sexy mood, I wore the rubber panties to work, under my skirt, but I only wore the rubber miniskirt at home. I used to put it on when I was doing the housework on Saturday mornings, this little black rubber miniskirt and nothing else at all, my breasts were bare. Whenever I bent over, my cunt was bare. I used to fantasize that I was a slave who was forced to clean this apartment wearing nothing but a short rubber skirt. By the time I got to the bathroom and the bedroom I was incredibly turned on. I was vacuum cleaning with one hand, and masturbating with my other hand, with this tight rubber skirt right up around my waist.

"In the bathroom, I used to sit on the edge of the tub and slide my electric toothbrush up my cunt, handle first, but buzzing all the time; and sometimes when I was really feeling horny I used to lubricate the toilet-brush handle with liquid soap and slid that up my bottom, too. It was chrome, and it was very cold, and I could feel the coldness right up inside my ass. I used to have orgasms just sitting on the edge of the bath like that. I thought that what I was doing was filthy, sitting there dressed in rubber with a toothbrush in my vagina and a toilet brush sticking out of my bottom; but it was the filthiness that made it so exciting.

"I never dared to tell any of my boyfriends what I was doing. It was a very private fantasy and in any case I was ashamed of it. After I'd climaxed, I would take out the toothbrush and the toilet brush and pull off the skirt and take a long shower to get rid of the smell of rubber. I always used to promise myself that I would never do it again. But of course I always do, it turns me on so much.

"Even when I met Peter and he started to live with me, I never told him about it, even though I loved him madly and we were both talking about marriage. I still did it, when he was out of the house. I still wore my rubber panties and my rubber skirt. I bought some rubber stockings, too—black rubber stockings that came right up to thigh level. But I still didn't want to tell him about it, because—well, because I was embarrassed, I guess. Because he would think that I was some kind of sex freak, some kind of nymphomaniac, and he wouldn't want to marry a woman like that.

"I used to fantasize that I could tell him how much rubber turned me on, and that I could dress up in rubber when we made love, and once I even got as far as showing him a catalog of rubber wear and asking him what he thought of it. He didn't seem to be especially interested in it, so I didn't pursue it. But that night, when Peter was away at a sports club meeting, I put on my skirt and my stockings and I masturbated in front of the mirror with five wooden spoons in my bottom (handle first, of course) and a wooden rolling pin covered with a condom in my cunt. By the time I finished I was lying on my back gasping and screaming, furiously rubbing my clitoris with my right hand, and stirring the spoon handles with my left. I was stretching my legs apart as wide as I could, and part of the thrill was the way I had to stretch so hard because my rubber skirt was so tight."

To meet her, you would think that Jemima was a normal, well-adjusted woman with no far-out sexual tastes. In fact she *is* normal and well-adjusted, although her sexual tastes are quite unusual for a woman. Many people are sexually excited to a greater or lesser extent by the smell and feel of rubber clothing, although the majority of them are men.

Jemima's interest in rubber wear is closely intertwined with a slightly masochistic urge to be treated like a slave, and to have "filthy" things done to her, such as toilet-brush handles pushed into her anus and rolling pins pushed into her vagina. Both men and women quite commonly use artificial objects for sexual stimulation. A catalog of all the items that women have inserted into their vaginas and their anuses would probably run to 500 closely printed pages. Women have told me of inserting shampoo bottles, flashlights, sausages, rolled-up magazines, hairbrush handles, exercise-bike handles, and even lighted cigarettes (filter first), which they allow to burn down until they feel the first twinge of heat.

There is absolutely nothing wrong in using an artificial object to give yourself erotic pleasure, provided that you're sensible about it. Don't insert anything into your anus that could be irretrievably "swallowed." You can buy special vibrating "butt plugs" and anal vibrators that flare out into a very wide base to prevent them from being lost inside your rectum. If you lose anything inside your anus, its removal may necessitate surgery, which is not only acutely embarrassing but extremely painful. Never insert anything that could inflict internal abrasion or pierce the intestinal wall—an injury that could prove fatal. Inserting lighted cigarettes is a very bad idea indeed, especially since it involves the added risk of exposing your sensitive rectal tissues to tobacco tars.

Don't insert anything breakable (even candles can be broken by strong anal muscles), and don't attempt to insert anything (such as a broom handle) that could accidentally penetrate far deeper than you intended.

Never insert any object into your anus and then immediately into your vagina without washing it first—and that includes your lover's penis, too. While your rectum may contain no obvious fecal matter, it is still teeming with virulent bacteria that could give you a nasty vaginal infection.

Jemima went through a Sex Glow session and analyzed her own feelings and her own fantasies. She acknowledged that she was highly aroused by masochistic acts, and especially the wearing of fetishist clothing such as rubber panties and stockings. However, she was not a real fetishist, who is incapable of achieving sexual satisfaction without the object of his or her fetish. Neither was she a real masochist. She and Peter had a healthy, athletic sex life, and Jemima believed that she could happily continue their relationship even if Peter never knew about her private sexual activities.

In spite of this, she *did* want Peter to share in her sexual specialty. "It's my fantasy," she said. "It would be so much sexier if Peter could make love to me while I'm wearing rubber, and Peter could do all of those things to me. But I'm very, very afraid of losing him if I try to explain it to him."

The problem with Peter was that—although he enjoyed sex with Jemima, and was both enthusiastic and vigorous in bed—his lovemaking tended to lack variety and any of that quality that excited Jemima so much: the idea that she was doing something forbidden and "filthy." He had been born when his parents were comparatively old, and his upbringing had tended to be formal and straitlaced.

One of the most important parts of developing your own Sex Glow is that you *show* rather than tell. Most people find it very difficult to put their sexual feelings into words, even with their closest partner—especially with their closest partner. What moment do you choose to say, "By the way, I love wearing tight latex miniskirts and pushing spoons up my ass"? And how do you say it? Usually, it's far easier to demonstrate your desire, without using words.

To that end, I suggested to Jemima that she introduce Peter into her private world of sexual fantasy not so much by showing him that *she* enjoyed it, but by encouraging *him* to enjoy it, so that in the end he would feel that she was dressing in rubber and performing "filthy" acts for *his* pleasure and at *his* imagination. In other words, we're back to the problem we talked about right at the very beginning of this book: how do you take the initiative in a sexual relationship without making your partner feel that you're acting in a domineering way and diminishing his virility? And, of course, as we've seen, it's relatively easy.

Jemima did it by introducing Peter into her world of rubber step by step, a little at a time. She bought a pair of small black rubber panties. These panties, however, were different from the pairs she had bought before in that they were open-crotched, with two separate openings for her vulva and her anus.

"I wore them on the evening we were going out to dinner with four other couples from Peter's company. I put them on and they were fabulous! They were cut in a low V-shape at the front, almost down to my pubic hair, and they were so tight that you could actually see the detail of every hair right through the rubber. The rubber was very new and black and shiny, but right between my legs my pubic hair tufted out, and there were my cunt lips bulging out, too, bright pink and just as shiny! They were absolutely the sexiest thing I had ever worn. I turned around in front of the mirror and you should have seen the way the rubber clung to the cheeks of my bottom. If I bent over in front of the mirror you could just see the little hole in the rubber at the back.

"I wore a short black cocktail dress. It was low-cut but I guess you could say that it was quite demure. I didn't need to wear pantyhose because my legs were so suntanned. And that was all I had on! Black rubber open-crotch panties and a little black dress. I felt very sexy, very confident. In fact I had that Glow you talked about because I no longer felt that I was some kind of nymphomaniac, but just a woman who wanted more exciting sex.

"Like you suggested, I waited until the evening was

in full swing before I said anything. The champagne had been flowing, everybody was laughing and joking and flirting . . . and, yes, I remembered what you said about flirting a little with Peter's friend Murray, so that Peter would be just that little bit more possessive and attentive. Murray's one of these life-and-soul of the party types, and he always makes Peter feel a little edgy.

"Anyway, I was talking to Murray when Peter came up and put his arm around me and murmured in my ear, 'Are you going to spend the whole darn evening with Murray?' But I whispered back to him, 'You don't have to worry. I'm not wearing my ordinary panties tonight.'

"His eyes opened wide, and he looked at me for a while with this funny interested look and then he said, 'What do you mean you're not wearing your ordinary panties? What kind of panties *are* you wearing?' I said 'Rubber panties.'

"This really had him going. *Rubber* panties?' he said.

"I said, 'For sure: but not ordinary rubber panties. These are rubber panties which are'—and I really whispered this into his ear—open between the legs.'

" 'Open?' he said. He couldn't keep his hands off me. 'What do you mean by open?'

"No crotch, I whispered. 'If you put your hand up my dress now, you could feel my rubber panties, but you could also feel a hole in the middle of them, and touch my bare cunt. I'm a good little girl and I'm wearing panties; but my cunt's completely exposed. And more than that, it's very wet, and it wants you."

"At that moment Murray came over and put his arm around me and I think Peter could have punched him right then. My wife's wearing nothing but crotchless rubber panties and you dare to put your arm around her? He was so possessive that it almost made me laugh. But I didn't, because I liked it, and I knew that I had really turned him on. I mean, I had turned him on so much that all he wanted to do was leave that party and take me back home and fuck me.

"We left as early as we decently could. All the way to the car Peter was kissing me and squeezing me. He was crazy for me, and I loved it. It was just like the time when we first met, when we couldn't keep our hands off each other. In the car, we buckled up but Peter didn't start the engine directly. He said, 'Show me, honey. Let me take a look.'

"I pulled up my dress so that he could see my shiny black rubber panties. Because I was sitting down, my cunt was bulging out of the hole in my panties even more than it was before, and my lips were open wide. Peter leaned over and kissed me—a long, deep, passionate kiss, tongue-in-the-mouth. Then he reached between my legs and caressed my rubber panties. He said, 'These are *right,* aren't they?' And I said, 'Yes, they're supposed to be . . . the tighter the better.' He ran his fingers over the latex, feeling how smooth and shiny it was, and then he touched my cunt lips. I couldn't help shuddering. My cunt was very juicy and slippery by now, and the parking lot wasn't all that warm. Peter kissed me again, and ran his fingers into my hair, as if he wanted to *eat* me, almost. He opened my cunt lips with his fingertips, and slid one finger inside my cunt, and then another. He stroked my clitoris and I could feel it stiffen up. My cunt was so juicy that I was embarrassed . . . it had never literally *dripped* with juice before. I put my own hand between my legs, too, and slipped a finger into my cunt, right beside Peter's finger, and the two of us slowly masturbated me, which is something we never would have done or even *thought* of doing up until then. I pulled my cunt open one way and Peter pulled it the other, until I was sitting in the car with my cunt stretched open wide. Anybody could have walked past and seen us, but fortunately they didn't!

"We drove home *very* fast. We went through to the bedroom and Peter kissed me again and started to unfasten my dress. I hadn't seen him so eager to make love, not ever. He was like a hurricane—Hurricane Peter. He lifted my dress over my head and then he just stood there for a moment, looking at me in my rubber panties. He said, 'Where did you get those? They're incredible.' I said, 'I saw them in a magazine . . . I thought you might like them, that's all.' '*Like* them?' he said. 'You must be kidding me!"

"I started to peel them off, but he said, 'No—keep

them on. They're amazing.' He stripped off his clothes and laid me back on the bed. When I was lying with my legs together it looked like I was wearing ordinary decent black panties. But then Peter opened my legs wide, and my cunt was completely exposed. Peter climbed on top of me and his cock was rearing up. The head of it was all slippery, and I took it in my hand and massaged it around and around. Then he slid his cock into me, all the way in. I can't tell you what it felt like, it was sensational. He'd never felt so big and hard before.

"He fucked me deep but very slow. I knew why—because he wanted it to last as long as possible! My rubber panties squeaked every time he pushed into me, and he kept squeezing the cheeks of my bottom through the rubber. He found the little round hole in the back by accident, and he actually gasped! He slipped his finger into it, and right up inside my bottom. I love that feeling: it makes me go all squirmy.

"I began to get very seriously turned-on. I was so turned-on that I was almost panicking. I began to push my hips up against him so that his cock would go deeper and quicker. After a while we were fucking really wildly and I was crying out because I felt like I wanted to be totally filled with hard cock, nothing else but hard cock. I thought I could feel every vein on his cock rubbing against the inside of my cunt. I thought I could feel the big fat head of it pushing up against my womb. I was shouting out 'fuck me, fuck me, fuck me!' over and over again, and then suddenly I climaxed. It went all the way through me like a huge black wave.

"As soon as my cunt started rippling, Peter climaxed too. His first spurt of sperm went right up inside me. I was sure I could feel it, but then his cock slipped out and I saw the second spurt shooting all over my cunt and all over my rubber panties. Then he spurted again, it's fantastic to watch it actually spurting out of the hole in his cock. I reached down between my legs and I rubbed sperm all over my cunt and all over my rubber panties, and I kissed Peter again and again and again, because that was the best lovemaking that we had ever had."

Jemima didn't rush Peter into her private world of

erotic pleasure. But once he had enjoyed one act of love that had involved rubber, he was very much more open to the idea of doing it again. The first article of rubber clothing that Jemima bought at Peter's suggestion was a new black miniskirt, which she wore in combination with her black open-crotch panties.

"Gradually, Peter began to find rubber exciting, too. He began to understand what it was that turned me on—the smell, the slippery texture, the tightness. It didn't take long before he started suggesting that we try to act out some fantasies—like he was running this high-class brothel and he wanted a slave. I just adore fantasies like that, they really excite me. I want to thank you for showing me that I'm not weird and I'm not perverted and how to get Peter involved in all of the things that really turn me on."

Although Jemima's fantasies were more extreme than those of most women who come to me for advice, I wanted to include her story to show you that you never need to be ashamed of any of your fantasies. Sexual fantasies are a normal and useful function of human sexual arousal, no matter how "dirty" they may seem when you think about them at times when you are not so aroused.

Here's Emma, 36, a writer from Florence, Alabama: "Ever since I was 19 or 20, I've had a fantasy about making love to six or seven men at once. Not just two, not just three, but six or seven, so they're all trying to fuck me at the same time. A friend of mine told me that there were porno stars who could take two cocks into their pussies at one time, and two cocks up their ass, and two in their mouth. I don't think I'd like it if it really happened to me, but I *do* have this fantasy of being filled up with cocks, and all these men around me who desperately want me."

Here's Fay, 26, a store assistant from Jasper, Indiana: "When I'm really excited, I have a fantasy that I'm in charge of a coal mine where all these naked sweaty men are digging for coal. Every few hours I take a tour of this mine to make sure that they're working hard enough, and I can feel their muscles to make sure that they're strong enough. I can feel their sweaty stomachs, all streaked with grit, and their rock-hard asses. I can feel them as much as I like, and they can't complain, because I'm the boss. They all have huge penises, and when I'm feeling their muscles I can feel between their legs and weigh their great big balls in my hand, and rub their penises until they're almost hard. Their cocks are all black with coal dust, but when I pull back their foreskin, the heads of their cocks are still bright pink. I walked from one to the other, holding the cocks that I like the looks of, and ignoring the ones that I don't."

Here's Rita, 41, a teacher from Rockville, Maryland: "I used to have a recurrent fantasy about putting on a sex show for a very grand audience. Maybe it came from my research into Greek and Roman entertainments! I used to have this fantasy in my head even when I was making love to my husband, Ken. I would come dancing onto a stage in front of hundreds of men, and I would be wearing nothing but a loose robe of white silk and sandals. All the men would cheer and clap and shout out all kinds of suggestive things. I would tease them for a while, but then I would twirl around and let the robe fall wide open, and underneath I would be completely nude. I would have blusher on my nipples and all of my pubic hair shaved off (which it is anyway, since I first read one of your books!) and I would dance right up to the front of the stage and open my legs wide so that every man in the audience could see my cunt. I would squeeze my breasts and pull out my nipples as far as they would go. The audience would go crazy! Then I would slide my hands down my stomach and around my hips, and pull open the lips of my cunt so that all these hundreds of men could see right inside. I would strut slowly from one side of the stage to the other, with my cunt held open, and all of these men would be cheering and waving their fists, and some of them would be openly taking out their cocks and masturbating because I turned them on so much. Finally, I would kneel down at the front of the stage, with my cunt still held open, and sit on this enormous polished-marble phallus that was placed in the middle of the stage . . . and all the men would go silent as I sat right down on it, this huge marble cock, and then lifted myself up again. I used to like that fantasy. I used to *love* that fantasy. I still have it now, sometimes, in different forms. It's a kind of 'power-over-men' fantasy. Maybe more women should have a fantasy like that, because it's true. Men find women exciting, and what's the harm in that?"

Here's Joanna, a 28-year-old graphic artist from New York: "My mother was very involved with the women's movement and so she brought me up to believe that men were all pigs and rapists. I had a very confused idea about men when I was a teenager. I knew I liked them, but I always suspected their motives. Because of that, I had very few relationships with boys when I was younger, and when I was older, my relationships were always fraught with doubt and accusations and misunderstanding. I could never really believe that men wanted me, just for myself, just as a woman; and that physically I could give a man pleasure. I used to think, why should I give them pleasure? It didn't really occur to me that if I gave them pleasure, they would give me just as much pleasure in return. But I started to have a fantasy about walking home late at night, and these black men following me. Very big men, with shaved heads and muscular bodies and tight pants. Handsome, you know, but brutal. I try to run but they catch me. They take me into an alley, a really filthy alley. One of them grips me from behind, and he's so strong that I can't even move, he's got me locked. The other one pulls up my skirt and drags off my pantyhose. I'm completely helpless, completely exposed. I can feel their muscles, feel their breath. The one who pulled off my pantyhose pulls open his jeans and brings out his cock. It's black like polished wood and it's *sweating* almost, and it's so big that I know that I can never take anything so big inside me. But he pushes himself up to me, and stares me directly in the eyes, and says, 'I'm going to fuck you harder than you were ever fucked before,' and he forces this *huge* cock right up into my vagina, I can feel it opening, I can feel my vagina being stretched apart, I can feel the head of his cock ramming right up against the neck of my womb, and pushing further, and further, even though it *can't* go any further. But this isn't all. His friend—the one who's holding me—he takes out his cock too, and suddenly I'm terrified because he's pushing his immense cock head up against my anus. I don't want it. I can't take it, I'm already filled with one big cock. But he spits on his cock head to make it slippery, and he pushes it into me, and pushes it into me, and I can hear him grunting, but most of all I'm thinking, no, no, no, I can't take all this, my body can't take all this. But then his cock forces its way right into my anus, right up to the balls, and I can scarcely move because my vagina and my anus are so cramful of cock.

"They start to fuck me, these two black men, even though we're standing up. They start to push themselves in and then pull themselves out. It's like their cocks are having a fight with each other, with only the thin skin between my vagina and my anus to keep them apart. Their cocks start to fly right in and out of me, battling with each other, one cock head banging against the other cock head, and my vagina and my anus stretched as far as they can go. The trouble is, I start to like it, I start to *more* than like it. I'm holding onto this black man in front of me, I start to cling to him, and I say to him, *'you can beat him, you can beat him.'* He's sweating and grunting and he's ramming his cock into me harder and harder, while his friend is ramming his cock harder and harder into my anus, the two of them gripping me tight. Then suddenly we're all screaming, all three of us, because we're all coming, all at once, they're pumping gallons of hot sperm into my vagina and right up my ass, and I'm climaxing too.

"Now what do you think of that? That's my fantasy. I never told anybody that fantasy before. I never told my husband that fantasy before. Do you think it's disgusting? Do you think it's crazy? I'm supposed to be a women's liberationist and I'm having fantasies about two men raping and sodomizing me in some back alley someplace?"

Of course there's nothing disgusting or unusual about Joanna's fantasy. Neither is there anything disgusting or unusual about the fantasies that Rita, Ray, and Emma use to arouse themselves. Everybody has sexual fantasies, and the sharing of these fantasies can be one of the greatest sexual pleasures that a couple can experience.

That's why I've always said: no more inhibitions, no more secrets, no more holding back. A fantasy is nothing more than a stimulating idea. It does no harm to anybody; and at the same time it can inspire you to improve your sex life almost overnight.

Just because you've *thought* about something sexual inside of your head, just because it's turned you on, that doesn't mean that you actually have to act it out to fulfill yourself (although, like Jemima, you may like to try out parts of it). It certainly doesn't mean that there's anything sexually wrong with you, or that you're sexually deviant. It's time for us to stop being afraid of our own sexuality. It isn't sex that causes problems in relationships, it's personalities and circumstances, and good sex can help to improve both of those.

If you have a strong desire that you have always been too inhibited to tell your partner about, why not try showing him you feel—and why not try showing him tonight? If you've wanted him to make love to you as soon as he walks in the door, why not try greeting him wearing a basque and sheer black stockings and nothing more? If you've wanted him to touch your breasts more often, why not walk around topless? If you've wanted him to make love to you more often, why not rub his cock through his pants while he's watching TV, or even take it out and suck it?

Women naturally expect the men in their lives to take the sexual initiative, but the plain reality of the matter is that they rarely do. They're tired, after a long day at work. They've gotten out of the habit. They're worried about money. There always seems to be some excuse why a man can't be wild in bed.

The answer is: no more Ms. Inhibited. You feel like good sex. You're entitled to good sex. Show your lover what you want, tell him how you feel.

And don't put it off until tomorrow. You want his cock inside you, don't you, and you want it tonight, and you want it good? So show him tonight!

SEVEN

How to Have It *Your* Way

In the 20 years that I have been talking to men and women about their sex lives, the single most common complaint from men is that their partners "don't seem interested in sex"; and the single most common complaint from women is that their lovers don't make love to them often enough.

Something is wrong here, right? How can so many men complain that their women don't want it, while their women are complaining that they never get it enough?

The answer is very simple. The sexual responsiveness of men and women, as we have seen, is very different. Men can respond almost instantly to erotic images and sexual suggestions, whereas women generally need much more time and much more emotional involvement to become fully aroused. Obviously there will always be exceptions to the rule. I have met many men who need to feel genuinely loved before they are prepared to enter into a sexual relationship, and I have met many women who would be quite gleefully prepared to pull down their panties at the first sight of a handsome guy.

Women *do* have fantasies of instant sex with a total stranger. There is a famous scene in Anais Nin's *Delta of Venus* in which a girl named Bijou, recently abandoned by her lover, is leaning over a wall to watch the barges on the river, when she is approached by "a tall, handsome, well-dressed man."

He says to her, "You don't know how beautiful you look, with your breasts crushed against the wall, your dress so short behind you. What beautiful legs you have."

She feels his hand, gently passing over her leg and under her dress. "He pressed a little against her and, seeing her pliant, began to move behind her so as to cover her with his body. Bijou was suddenly afraid and sought to escape from his embrace. But the man was powerful. He forced her head and shoulders down on the wall and raised her skirt.

"Bijou was again without underclothes. The man began to murmur words of desire that soothed her, but at the same time he held her down, entirely at his mercy. She felt the strength of his two legs, and she heard his voice enveloping her, but that was all. Then she felt something soft and warm against her, something that did not penetrate her. In a moment she was covered in warm sperm. The man abandoned her and ran away."

There are dozens of scenes in women's erotic fiction in which women surrender themselves to men's perverse and casual sexual desires. The same Bijou is taken to a public park by her lover and two other men, and forced to lie on the grass, while a big dog licks between her legs. "His tongue was rough, much rougher than a man's, and long and strong." Her lover also shaves off her pubic hair in front of his friends, and when she refuses to open her legs so that they can look at her naked vulva, he stimulates her clitoris with his shaving brush. "The Basque meticulously brushed her vulva and the tip of her clitoris. Then the men saw that she could no longer contract her buttocks and sex, that as the brush moved her buttocks rolled a little forward, the lips of the vulva parted. The men could see the moisture oozing from her."

For most women, however, the notion of instant sex with a stranger is an exciting fantasy rather than a reality—a fantasy which, if it actually happened, they would not particularly enjoy. Susan, a 27-year-old pharmacist from White Plains, New York, summed up the feelings of many women about instant sex when she said, "I'd love to be fucked by a stranger so long as he was really my boyfriend." The same goes for women who have fantasies about group sex. "I'd adore to be fucked by three men, so long as they were all my husband Jim."

So here we have this distinct difference between male and female sexual responses, and it doesn't just affect how long it takes either partner to reach a climax once they're making love—it affects the number of times they make love.

Women are not only shy about initiating sex; they feel that their lover should do it, and it makes them feel less feminine and less sexually attractive if he won't.

As we discussed at the beginning of this book, women *do* feel sexually excited by male virility and by male sexual dominance. It's completely natural, and it doesn't mean for a moment that women are socially or sexually inferior. The trouble is, many men today feel very reticent about "coming on strong" because of the feminist backlash against date rape and rape within marriage; and even more men become lazy and complacent about making love when they are comfortably settled in a long-term relationship.

Although we have all become more outspoken about sex, and although our expectations of an exciting and fulfilling sex life have become much greater, the truth is that more than three-quarters of the women to whom I spoke during the course of preparing this book felt dissatisfied with their sex lives and wished that their partners would be more positive, more romantic, more aggressive, more daring, more caring.

I was taken aback by Helen, a 36-year-old teacher from Jefferson City, Missouri, when she wrote me: "I enjoy your books . . . they always help me and turn me on . . . but I want to know more about more perversions. I may not want to try them, but I want to know about them, just in case I do. I'm not frightened of sex anymore. I'm eager to try anything and everything. What else can I do to drive my husband wild in bed?"

The greatest change in sexual attitudes over the past

20 years is that ordinary women are prepared to be much more daring in bed—much more daring than men. They have discovered that they are physically and emotionally capable of really explosive lovemaking. But the problem is that they can't be explosive on their own. They need a man who knows how to woo them, how to arouse them, how to stimulate all of their senses. They need a man who is sexually knowledgeable, strong, sensitive—and has a good hard erection, too.

The trouble is, they have to be daring without domineering. They have to involve their men in their newly uninhibited sex lives without diminishing their partner's sense of virility and "taking charge"—which is a very important part of lovemaking for both of them.

Let's take a look at what *ought* to be happening in your sex life.

In bed (or wherever two people make love) all of their affection and all of their meaning as a couple can come together. During the act of love, there will always be a certain degree of sexual dominance on the man's side and sexual submission on the woman's side. These are demonstrations of your passion for each other—your man's manliness and your womanliness. They are not all the same as dominance and submission in politics or in the workplace or in the apportioning of domestic chores. Because a man has a penis instead of a vagina he is not automatically exempt from cleaning the kitchen floor. But—as a lover—he has a role to play. He must be physically strong, emotionally stimulating, and technically skillful. He must be attentive and inventive. He must be *persuasive.*

Jeanette, a 25-year-old corporate lawyer from Cleveland, Ohio, told me, "I never liked the idea of anal sex . . . a man pushing his penis into my bottom. But one night Garth and I were making love and he tried to do it to me, he positioned the head of his penis up against my asshole, and tried to force it inside me. I said, 'No, don't,' and he didn't. But I wanted him to persuade me. I wanted him to say 'Yes, let's do it, I want to feel what it's like inside of your ass. But he didn't. He wouldn't. And there were other times, too, when I wanted him to make love to me—just slide his hands inside my blouse and squeeze my breasts. I've unbuttoned my blouse and walked around with no bra. Sometimes I've even walked around the apartment topless. He looks, and obviously he likes it, but what do I have to do to stir him into some action?"

Jeanette's problem is not uncommon. Many men are very cautious about initiating sex—even with their wives or long-term lovers—because they feel that they may be rebuffed. One reason for this is that, quite often, they *are* rebuffed, not because the woman in their lives doesn't want to have sex but because she wants to be seduced. She wants to be wooed, courted, flattered, and aroused before she makes love.

The same applies to sexual variations, such as oral or anal sex. Many women are extremely anxious to try some wild sexual variations, but they want to feel that they are being *persuaded* to try them. They don't want to feel that they are taking the initiative—that they are doing all the leading and their lovers are simply doing what they're told.

Jeanette said, "If only Garth had persisted . . . if only he had cajoled me into anal sex, I would have loved it, I know. But it's not one of those things that you want to try all the time, only when you're very aroused, and somehow that never seems to happen to us very often these days."

Hedda, a 32-year-old fitness instructor from Akron, Ohio, said, "I've always been turned on by spanking. I don't mean a hard beating, I just mean a few smacks on my bare fanny. I guess it started when I was married to my first husband. I was only 17 and he was 11 years older than me. He was a great-looking guy, and he had a good sense of humor, but I was much too young for him, and I used to irritate the hell out of him sometimes because I want to play rock music all night or fool around or just behave like a 17-year-old. One day I teased him so much that he put me over his lap, lifted up my skirt, pulled down my panties, and gave me six or seven hard smacks on the bare bottom. Of course I'd been paddled by my parents when I was a kid but this was something altogether different. Each time he spanked me I felt this warm, stinging feeling, and a sexy feeling between my legs that I can't describe. I wanted him to go on and on—and of course he didn't understand that at all because he thought he was punishing me. I sat up and climbed astride him and took hold of his hand and said, 'feel me.' I guided his hand in between my legs and I was wet because I was so excited. I pulled open his pants and took his cock out of his shorts. It was rising up right in front of my eyes. I gave it two or three quick rubs to harden it up, and then I pushed him backward on the bed and sat on his cock, so that it went right up me. My bottom was hot and stinging and I absolutely adored it. I turned my head around while I was fucking him, and I could see my bottom reflected in the closet mirror. It was flaming red with handprints on it, and there was my husband's cock ramming in and out of my cunt, and his balls between my red-hot bottom cheeks.

"I wouldn't like to be spanked every night; but the idea of it still turns me on. I don't know how to describe it. It makes me feel—I don't know, kind of helpless and girlish and excited. But Dave, my present partner, doesn't get the message at all. I keep teasing him and annoying him and telling him how naughty I've been and doesn't he think that I ought to be punished, but he's so darned even-tempered that I don't think it would even occur to him to spank me. I'll admit that I'm kind of cautious about coming out with it outright. I'm afraid that he'll think that I'm kinky or that I'm not satisfied with him. I *am* satisfied with him. He's very considerate in bed. But sometimes I want more than consideration. I want excitement, and a good spanking. I want to feel my bottom stinging."

Ruth, a 33-year-old systems analyst from Orlando, Florida, told me that she would simply like to have sex more often. "Michael and I have been married for three years now, although we've known each other for almost five. When we first met, we were at it all the time. I couldn't keep Michael out of my panties for more than a few hours at a time. We used to make love in the car. We used to make love in the shower. We used to make love in the backyard, in a small corner where the neighbors couldn't see us. Now, for some reason, we hardly ever make love at all . . . maybe once a week, if we're lucky. I've asked Michael if there's anything wrong, but he says no. He still loves me; he's still very affectionate. But whenever I start to kiss him and cuddle him he always has something more important to do, or he says 'later.' I don't think that there's anybody else . . . he works at home most days and he wouldn't have the opportunity. But I'm becoming so frustrated. I'd like to make love at least four or five times a week. Lately I've been masturbating every day just to keep myself from feeling so tense. I go to the bathroom at the office and take this huge dildo with me. I sit on the seat and push it up and down inside me and tug my clitoris at the same time. I close my eyes and try to pretend that Michael's in the john with me. It brings me off, but it's not the same. I just don't know what to do."

Alexandra, 36, a hairdresser from Boston, Massachusetts, has always been aroused by fantasies of bondage. "Ever since I can remember, I've had all kinds of bondage fantasies. They usually take place in this beautiful house, which is furnished very richly with gold chairs and tapestries and paintings, and it's always filled with flowers. Everybody else in the house is properly dressed, but I have to walk around dressed in nothing but very high heels, with a tight black leather collar around my neck so that I have to keep my head up straight, and a black leather costume made of nothing but studded black leather straps. My breasts are bare and my nipples are pierced with gold rings, which have keys dangling from them. One strap passes between my legs and is pulled up very tight so that it cuts right into my pussy and makes it bulge out on either side. I have to wear leather wristbands and they're chained together so that my movements are very restricted. In most of my fantasies the people in the house are having a formal party and I have to walk around serving the drinks and the food. After the party I have to change into a very tight basque that leaves my breasts bare, and I have to put on a black blindfold. They handcuff me with my hands behind my back and make me kneel in the center of the floor. Then every man in the room takes it in turns to open his pants in front of me, and have me suck his cock. I have to do it in a very elegant way, just touching the tip of their cocks with my tongue, and then licking them all the way up from their balls to the head of their cocks, then slowly and gently sucking them, then taking them into my mouth as far as they will go, so that they're actually fucking my mouth. If I do it wrong, or if one of the men doesn't reach a climax, they snap a small leather whip between my legs, or across my breasts. Sometimes I have to suck two men at once, and then my whole mouth is filled up with jostling cocks. They're right with each other to see who can push most cock in. Some of the men like to shoot their come right down my throat: others like to shoot it all over my face and my breasts and my basque. I've had this fantasy over and over, and it always turns me on. Sometimes I think about it when Jack (her lover) is making love to me. The problem is that Jack is a very regular guy and sex for him is something which you keep for Saturday night. He doesn't even think about touching me until we've both taken a shower and put on our nightclothes and turned out the light. I love him dearly, but I keep thinking to myself: is this all our love life ever going to be, straight Saturday-night sex while I keep having all of these fantasies about bondage?"

Joanna a 24-year-old flight attendant from Atlanta, Georgia, was aroused and intrigued by descriptions of "wet sex" that I mentioned in *Single, Wild, Sexy . . . Safe,* my previous book for single women. Wet sex or "water sports" or "golden rain" is a term used to describe lovemaking which involves urination.

When I edited *Penthouse Forum* magazine, I was surprised at the number of couples who responded to our discussion of wet sex in the letters columns (which, incidentally, and despite of popular conjecture, are genuine letters and *not* invented by the magazine's editorial staff). It appeared that many women found great sexual release in openly urinating in front of their partners, especially at the moment of orgasm, and that they also enjoyed touching and stimulating their lovers' penises while they urinated—even to the extent of having their lovers urinate over their faces or their breasts or between their legs. Again, the erotic excitement seemed to stem from doing something "forbidden" and "dirty" (although fresh, healthy urine is completely sterile), but some of the arousal for women came from urinating someplace else apart from the bathroom, and in some other position apart from sitting down.

Joanna said, "I thought your wet sex interviews were very arousing and disturbing. I guess they challenged something inside me, as a woman. Men can stand up to take a piss, and they can pretty well do it wherever they want, whereas women have to crouch down and make a damp patch on the ground. The morning after I read your book I went into the shower, naked, and before I switched on the water I pissed standing up. I put my hand between my legs and I felt it coming out of me. Of course it went all down my legs and wet my feet, but I didn't care. I felt a really strange kind of relief, like I was allowing myself to do it in a different way because I was grown-up and a woman and I could do it any way I wanted.

"I did it two or three times more. Once I stood in the middle of the kitchen and just wet myself, right through my panties, so that it all ran down my legs. Another time I lay back on the sun-lounger in my roof garden, totally naked, and I stretched open my pussy with my fingers, and I pissed straight up in the air. It was warm and glittery and I loved it. It's fantastic. You don't even believe how far it goes. Of course I pissed all over myself, but it didn't matter. I was so excited that I massaged piss all over my nipples and thighs and between my legs and masturbated myself. Why not? I felt like I was free.

"How I can ever say anything to Gerry (her boyfriend) I simply don't know. I don't know what I can tell him. I'd *like* to tell him, for sure. What I'd really like to do now is to play with his cock while he's pissing, but I'm far too embarrassed to say anything. I just couldn't."

Although their difficulties might seem unrelated, all of these women are suffering from the same problem in their relationships. Whatever anybody says about men and their insatiable lusts, the fact is that the majority of men in marriages or long-term relationships become very complacent about sex, and fail to understand that they need to *work* at keeping their love lives exciting.

Because most men can be sexually satisfied very quickly, they forget that their partners might need a whole lot more; and they also fail to understand that their own pleasure could be multiplied several hundred-fold if they were more skillful and more adventurous—and if they made an effort to put their partners first.

Most of the time, it's not their fault. They simply don't know what degree of stimulation a woman needs, because nobody has ever told them—not even the women in their lives. Even the most sensitive and experienced of lovers can't *guess* how this partner is feeling, not unless she gives him some clear response.

So how can you turn your ordinary, less-than-considerate lover into an all-night, every-night mover? The secret—as we've hinted at earlier in this book—is *show-and-tell,* but mostly show. And a little flirtatious trick that most women are very good at already, which is what I call *negative encouragement.*

Let's see how both of these factors can work. Jeanette was complaining that her partner Garth was obviously interested in trying sexual variations, but didn't understand that when she said no she really meant "persuade me." Of course the sexual politics of what a woman really means when she says no to a man are highly complicated and are still the subject of ongoing legal and moral debate. But in Jeannette's case, she was aroused enough to want to have anal intercourse, but she wanted Garth to take the responsibility for it. She suspected that it might hurt (and indeed it might, because anally she was a virgin). If it did hurt, and if she didn't enjoy it, she didn't want him to say "What are you complaining about? It was you who wanted to try it."

She wanted some decisiveness. She wanted some masculine dominance. But at the same time she wanted to be wooed into anal sex, rather than forced. When she said no to Garth she really meant yes but she meant "yes, if you can seduce me into doing it . . . yes, if you can do it to me strongly but gently . . . yes, if you can take charge, once in a while, without being aggressive or selfish or far too quick."

I suggested to Jeanette that she should encourage Garth to be more decisive about sexual variations by putting him in a position in which he almost had no choice to be anything *but* decisive. This necessitated taking at least one decisive step of her own—but it wasn't a step that in any way detracted from his feeling of virility or his sexual standing in their relationship, which was very important to both of them.

First of all, though, I recommended that she prepare herself for anal intercourse by getting used to the feeling of having a large phallic object inserted in her rectum. Although anal intercourse is a sexual variation that has been common in almost all civilizations since the beginning of recorded history, the fact remains that a woman's rectum was not designed for the insertion of a man's erect penis.

Your natural reaction when an object is pushed against your anal sphincter is to contract it tight to prevent the object from entering. In order to enjoy anal intercourse without pain or discomfort, you have to teach yourself the reverse response—to open your anus wide so that your lover's penis can slide inside your rectum without hurting you.

A generous amount of lubricant such as KY is essential, and will make anal intercourse much easier and much more exciting. Unlike 20 years ago, when I first published *How to Drive Your Man Wild in Bed,* you can now buy lubricant products that are specially formulated for anal intercourse, and which have cinnamon or fruit fragrances.

However, I reassured Jeanette that she didn't have to worry about anal intercourse being dirty. Although the rectum does contain virulent bacteria (which is why you should always take great care not to enjoy anal stimulation immediately followed by vaginal stimulation without your lover thoroughly washing his penis or fingers or any sex toys you might have been using in between) it contains little or no fecal matter until you are ready to go to the toilet. If you are planning on an evening of intercourse, of course, it makes sense to go to the bathroom before you start making love.

Not only can you buy special anal lubricants these

days, you can buy a wide range of sex toys that are specifically designed for safe and exciting anal stimulation. You could use any of these by yourself in one of your Sex Glow sessions, and if you video-record it and show it to your lover, that could be one way of letting him know that you'd like to try some anal games.

One of the most popular new anal vibrators is the Spiral of Lust, which is soft and flexible, with a twisted thread so that you can actually "screw" it into your anus. Then there are a wide range of so-called butt plugs, which are short fat vibrating bungs in very soft plastic which can be pushed into your anus quite firmly without any danger of them being lost inside. One of the more sophisticated "butt plugs" has a hand-operated pump which you can inflate when it is inside your rectum. There are all kinds of other designs, the most effective of which is the Anal Placater, which has a thin flexible shaft with knobs on it, and a heart-shaped head that wriggles wildly inside your rectum when you switch on the vibrator.

You could of course use a standard vibrator, but some of them are too big for comfort, especially if you haven't taken a penis into your bottom before.

Jeanette chose a specially designed kit which included a basic plastic vibrator with three different latex sleeves that could be fitted over the top of it. One sleeve was covered with rows of soft spikes; the next had a ridged base and then a long thin finger on the end; the third was a penis replica with a protuberant head and exaggerated veins.

"At first I felt very self-conscious about using the vibrator. I never masturbated when I was younger, and the idea of touching myself didn't come too easily to me. But one evening when Garth was held up at the office, I took a shower at about seven o'clock and then I went to bed completely naked and told myself that this was the evening I was going to try it.

"I sprayed myself with my favorite fragrance, Giorgio, and then I opened a fresh tube of lubricant which I had bought from the drugstore. I took the vibrator out of my nightstand and chose the sleeve which looked like a man's cock. I squeezed out a large handful of lubricant and massaged it between my legs. It was probably too much, bit it was very chilly and slippery and it felt good. I massaged it around my clitoris and into my vagina, slipping my fingers in and out. Then I took the plunge and slipped one finger into my asshole, and lubricated it as much as I could. In fact it was so slippery that I managed to slip two fingers inside.

"I slicked up the vibrator with lubricant, and fitted the sleeve over it. It was thinner than a real cock, much thinner than Garth's, but I was pleased about that because it didn't seem so frightening. I rubbed the head of it against my clitoris, and in between my lips, until I was used to the feel of it. Then I slid it inside my vagina, and pushed it in and out a few times. I closed my eyes and it felt good. I loved the way the knobby head of it rubbed against the inside of my vagina, and when I squeezed my muscles tight I could feel the big thick veins. It was only plastic, but it felt like a real hard cock, and of course I could push it in as deep as I wanted it to go, and keep it up me for as long as I wanted.

"I was really aroused, and I started to play with my clitoris and slide the vibrator in and out of my vagina, and I almost forgot what I was supposed to be doing. I hadn't even switched on the vibrator motor yet, and I was close to having an orgasm. When I'm making love, I always like it if Garth pinches my clitoris and tugs it out a little way. I pulled my clitoris out then, and switched on the vibrator, and touched the head of the vibrator up against my clitoris, so that my poor stretched-out clitoris was literally buzzing!

"I was very turned-on, very excited, very wet. The juice was pouring out my vagina and down between the cheeks of my bottom. I buzzed my clitoris some more, and nudged the vibrator in between my lips. Then I lifted up both legs and opened them really wide, and pressed the head of the vibrator against my asshole. I remembered what you'd told me to do . . . to push *against* it, so that my asshole would open. And that's what I did. I slid the vibrator slowly into my asshole, and it didn't hurt at all. I looked down between my legs and I could see it gradually disappearing into my bottom, and it felt absolutely fantastic. It was like I was being fucked in places where I didn't even know that woman could be fucked. I felt nerves tingling where I didn't even know I had nerves. I pushed the vibrator right in, as far as it would go, and then I pulled it out again, and used the head of it to tingle my asshole, all around the entrance, and then pushed it slowly in again. My asshole was shiny with lubricant and juice, and a little bit red, too, but I remembered to keep on pushing against the vibrator rather than pinching my muscles in, and it went in and out of me beautifully.

"I'd always had fantasies about having a cock up my ass, but when I felt that vibrator the first time . . . I didn't have any idea how good it was.

"I practiced for maybe an hour, sliding that vibrator in and out of my ass, and tugging my clitoris at the same time, and then, without any warning at all, I just orgasmed—is that the right word? I suddenly felt a warm, tight feeling in my bottom and my asshole clenched so tight that I had to push the vibrator further up to stop myself from squeezing it right out. My hips started to buck up and down and my nipples were sticking out and there was nothing I could do to stop myself.

"I didn't want Garth to make love to me that night. I was too sore and too tired! But the next night I was ve-e-ery seductive. I wore my black lace cat suit. It has patterns of bows and butterflies on it, but apart from that it's totally sheer, and it has an open crotch, so that you can make love without even taking it off. I'd worn it only once before, on Garth's birthday, more for fun than anything else, but it had really turned him on then, it had made a special occasion into a *very* special occasion, and I thought this was the time to wear it again.

"I was wearing it when Garth came home. He was pretty tired—he'd had a long day, full of meetings. But he was still impressed. He said, 'What's this, I'm another year older?' But I told him I'd been relaxing, that was all, and I'd felt like wearing something casual. He kissed me really strong and deep, and he cupped my breasts through the lace. He has a way of rolling my nipples between finger and thumb which I love, and it felt especially good through lace. He reached down and cupped my bottom cheeks, too, and let his fingertips trail over my open crotch, just touching my pubic hair, and he must have felt that it was wet, because I *was* wet, I was really excited already.

"I poured him a vodka martini made just the way he likes it, and we sat on the couch together in the breakfast area listening to the TV news. He had his arm around me and he was very affectionate, but he wasn't coming on to me, which is what used to upset me. I *knew* he loved me. I *knew* that I turned him on. But he didn't seem to have the courage to show me how he felt, by taking charge of the whole situation and just fucking me. It was like he was always worried about committing himself; worried that *I* might not want to do it, even though *he* did. He said, 'You're feeling sexy this evening, aren't you?" and I said, 'You've noticed?' I didn't want to bring him down or anything, but here I was, sitting snuggled up to him in a black lace crotchless cat suit, and he had just noticed that I was feeling sexy? Anyway, as you suggested, I said that my friend Diana had given me a present, which was the vibrator.

"He didn't like the look of it at first. Well, no, to tell you the truth, I think he did really. I think he was quite excited but he didn't want to show it. He switched it on so that it buzzed, and I asked him if he wanted me to show him how it worked. I took it from him, and I buzzed it around my breasts and my nipples. I took my right breast out of my cat suit, and touched the tip of the vibrator against my nipple, so that Garth could see it crinkling and rising up. Actually vibrators feel wonderful when you massage your breasts with them, really sexy.

"I opened my legs a little and squeezed the vibrator between my thighs. He said, 'What does that feel like?" I mean, he was starting to get *very* turned-on, just watching me do it, and I said, 'It's terrific, you ought to try it for yourself.' I opened the buttons of his jeans and took out his cock. It wasn't fully hard, but it was growing bigger all the time, and it had that wonderful smell that a man's cock had after he's been working all day, kind of funky but very exciting. I ran the vibrator up and down the shaft of his cock and his cock swelled right up in front of my eyes until it was literally straining. The head of it was shining and purple and I leaned forward and sucked it for just a moment. It was so big that it practically filled my whole mouth, and it tasted of all those beautiful masculine tastes.

"I massaged the head of his cock with the vibrator for a while, but then I ran it down between my legs, right between my lips. I kissed him and ran my finger through his hair, and then right in front of him I opened my legs and pushed the vibrator into my vagina. Garth couldn't believe it. I lifted one leg and hooked it over his shoulder. I spread the other leg wide apart. My vagina was wide open, and he could watch me push this vibrator in and out of it, right in front of him. I was so juicy that the vibrator was shining, and juice was dripping over my fingers. I had never been that juicy before.

"Garth stripped off his shirt and his pants and tried to climb on top of me, but I wouldn't let him. I said, 'This vibrator's fantastic . . . what more could I want?' And I deliberately turned over, face down on the couch, and kept the vibrator up inside of my vagina. All right, I did give Garth a pretty strong hint . . . I lifted my fanny so that he couldn't really fail to see what he was supposed to do.

"He tried to take out the vibrator one more time, but I wouldn't let him, and I kept moaning, 'It's so good, it's so good. . . ,' and it *was* so good.

"Garth leaned over me and squeezed my breasts, which were hanging exposed out of the front of my cat suit. But then he parted the cheeks of my bottom with his fingers, and touched my anus; and of course my anus was slippery with love juice and lubricant, and I deliberately *pushed* against his fingertip so that my anus actually opened, you know, like a little mouth, I could feel it open.

"Garth knelt up behind me and placed the head of his cock between my bottom cheeks. I knew that this was the moment, and I did everything I could to relax but to push against him, push against him, so that my asshole was wide open when he tried to slide his cock in. If I hadn't, I don't think he would have gotten it in at all, not without hurting me.

"But when he did, when that big purple head plunged into my asshole, that was much, much better than any vibrator. That was warm, stiff flesh, that was real cock, buried in my bottom. I reached between my legs and I could feel my anus stretched wide open, and this huge hard cock right inside it, and pushing deeper still, deeper and deeper, right into my rectum, right into my bowels, right into my body, right into my soul, that's what it felt like.

"I was still buzzing that vibrator inside of my vagina, and I was able to twist it and turn it so that it buzzed and massaged Garth's cock, right through the skin between my asshole and my vagina. He was really turned-on, really excited. he was gripping my hips and he was ramming himself into me, again and again. I could feel his big hairy balls banging against my hand. I took out the vibrator and let it drop onto the floor.

"Suddenly he pulled me tight against him, so that his whole cock was completely buried inside my bottom, and for a second he was stock-still. I squeezed my bottom muscles like I was massaging his cock. That hurt a little bit, but it was a good hurt.

"All of a sudden I felt his cock twitching, and he really groaned. He was pumping his come into my ass and there was nothing he could do to stop himself. After a moment or two he took himself out of me, and I felt his come sliding out of my asshole and down the backs of my thighs. Garth turned me over and we held each other tight for a long, long time. He really *held* me, you know—protectively and lovingly, in a way which he hadn't done for quite a long while.

"He asked me if I'd enjoyed it, as if *he'd* instigated it, you know? I was pleased about that, because we'd tried something that I'd always wanted to try, but Garth felt as if he was the one who had thought of it. It did our sex life a whole lot of good, because once he'd tried anal sex his interest in sex really revived, and he wanted to try all kinds of things, especially oral sex, and he got really good at that, really skillful, and of course I love it, it's the best.

"I love anal sex, too, but I have to be in the right mood for it and very turned-on. It's very deep, very physical, if you know what I mean. If I'm not in the right mood for it, I find it uncomfortable. But if I do, it's amazing. I can have an orgasm just from having my bottom fucked, without even touching my clitoris.

"I'll tell you one time I really liked. Garth was sitting watching TV, and he said, 'Come here, sit on my lap.' He pulled me toward him with one hand, and he opened his jeans with the other, so that his cock stuck out. It was incredibly big and hard. He unfastened my shorts and pulled my shorts and my panties halfway down my thighs. Then he lowered me down on his lap so that his cock went into my cunt. He lifted me up and down a few times, until I started to get wet. Then he took out his cock out of my cunt, and massaged my anus with cunt juice. I knew what he was going to do and I said, 'Garth, no . . .' but he said, 'Come on, sweetheart, we can always stop it if you don't like it.' He pushed his cock into my asshole and I sat right down on it, with my full weight. It felt huge, and my muscles started twitching. But after a few seconds I relaxed, and I just sat on his lap watching TV with him, with his cock right up inside me, while he reached around me and slid his hands into my T-shirt and played with my breasts.

"I guess we must have sat like that for almost 20 minutes. It felt so good I didn't want to get up. We didn't come, either of us, but it was such a beautiful experience."

Jeanette's diplomatic use of her "friend's" vibrator was a way of *showing* and *guiding* Garth into making love the way she wanted. Most of us find it difficult to talk about sex with our partners with complete openness and frankness—especially concerning sexual variations. It's not easy to sit down cold and say, "Why don't you persuade me to have anal sex?" or "Why don't you go down on me more often?" and there is always the risk of an oversensitive partner feeling that you are being critical rather than simply making a suggestion. But showing and guiding—especially if you do it in the heat of sexual excitement—can overcome any risk of resentment while giving you all the sexual fulfillment you're seeking.

Let's take a look at the ways in which Hedda, Ruth, Alexandra, and Joanna managed to show and guide their partners into giving them the erotic excitement they wanted.

EIGHT

More Ways to Have It Your Way

Today's woman tends to be far more knowledgeable about sex and her own physical and emotional responses than today's man. One of the reasons for this is that women are much more willing to talk about sex between themselves, and to share their experiences and their problems. Most women feel much less competitive about sex than men, and are not as embarrassed about seeking help and advice.

Mark, a handsome 26-year-old engineer from Berkeley, California, told me, "I had trouble keeping a full erection during sex. I worried about it so much that, after a time, I could scarcely get an erection at all. I didn't know who to turn to. My girlfriend began to think that I didn't love her anymore; but who could I ask? Sure, I have plenty of friends, but what was I supposed to say to them, 'Hey, Jack, I'm having a serious problem in keeping it up. What do you think I should do?' Men just don't admit things like that to each other, do they?"

Whereas Julie, a pretty 31-year-old illustrator from Los Angeles, California, said, "I had a couple of bad sexual experiences with men, and even when I met Rick I had trouble reaching an orgasm. I kept having this feeling that I should hold myself back, that I shouldn't commit myself. I talked to a couple of friends about it, particularly an older friend, Marie, and she did everything she could to tell me how to relax, how to let myself go. She convinced me that an orgasm wasn't necessarily a commitment: it was part of expressing myself, like laughing or crying or singing."

Another reason why women are so much more knowledgeable is that women's mass-market magazines regularly carry explicit features about sex. Even though these articles sometimes convey the false impression that every woman's life should be a carnival of multiple orgasms and thrilling affairs with muscled Romeos, many of them provide detailed and sensible information about sex of a kind which is not available to men, unless they buy a sexually explicit magazine such as *Playboy* or *Penthouse.*

During the course of researching this book, I was pleased to see that a well-known women's magazine suggested to its readers that women who suffer headaches after orgasm should try taking a large dose of vitamin E after sex. This kind of practical, unabashed advice is far less available to men, even though their partners expect them to be knowledgeable and skillful and completely "in charge" of their sexual relationship.

Even today, many men are vague about sexual anatomy and sexual technique, and their ideas about lovemaking are based either on hearsay or dirty jokes or pornographic videos. What is completely missing in their sexual technique is any kind of understanding of women's sexual needs (which are very powerful, but different from a man's, as we have clearly seen), and any appreciation of how a woman can be made to feel sexually ecstatic—as one writer put it, "like a whore and a queen, all in one."

Most common complaints from women? "He's much too quick when he makes love." "He hardly ever speaks during sex . . I like flattery, I like to hear him whisper filthy suggestive things in my ear, even though he doesn't actually do them." "He doesn't seem to realize that I want a climax, too." "He can't understand that women like different, kinky sex, just as much as men do. I'm not a virgin bride. I'm a woman who wants to have some real excitement." "He keeps wanting to do kinky things, and I wouldn't mind if I did, but I wish he'd arouse me first."

Hedda, the 32-year-old fitness instructor we met in the previous chapter, had difficulty in persuading her husband to try a little mild spanking. A desire for spanking is an extremely common sexual taste, well within the parameters of "normal" sexual behavior. Its erotic appeal lies in the feeling of helplessness that the spankee feels during the act of spanking, and in the exposure of her bare buttocks to the spanker.

The principal reason why Hedda couldn't provoke her partner to spank her was because he was not a sexually dominant character—in fact, quite the reverse. While she had been very young and vulnerable when she met her first husband, who *did* spank her, she was now extremely physically fit (because of her work as an aerobics instructor) and also very confident (because of her long association with a much older man). Dave had been attracted to her because he preferred his women to dominate him, rather than the other way around.

I suggested to Hedda that she could encourage Dave to give her the kind of sexual pleasure she wanted by treating it first simply as a game. This technique works very well for all kinds of sexual problems, because it takes the gravity and the sense of commitment out of whatever sexual variation you want your partner to try. If you are lighthearted and playful about it, you can withdraw from it at any time you like (or at any time you sense that your partner really isn't enjoying it) with much less embarrassment and emotion than if you attempt to do it in a serious manner. All of us have inhibitions about sex—all of us have some secret desires that we're embarrassed to reveal even to our closest partners—and that's where game playing comes in.

Once you have introduced your partner to a new sexual variation in the form of a game, you'll be surprised how easily it will become a frequent part of your lovemaking repertoire. The most important thing to remember is to show him how sexually excited you are by what he's doing. He'll enjoy it and because you're enjoying it, and because he feels a sense of achievement.

When you're playing sexual games, you can use plenty of that *negative encouragement* we discussed earlier—saying provocative things such as, "Oh, don't do that . . . I'm sure you're too big for me" and "That's too sexy, I can't stand it," and putting him in a position where he virtually has no alternative but to do what you want him to do. For instance, many women who have complained to me that their partners gave them little or no oral sex were quickly able to solve their problem by frequently giving their partners oral stimulation in the time-honored "69" position, with their bare vulvas directly in front of their partners' face. The number of men who failed to respond to this silent and obvious invitation to give them cunnilingus was precisely nil.

Even though Dave was not sexually dominant, he *was* very sexually responsive, and so Hedda was counting on her own erotic excitement to rouse him into action.

"We were having supper together—southern fried chicken and potatoes and corn. I threw a corn kernel at him and hit him on the cheek. Then I threw another one and hit him on the nose. He wasn't angry, he's a very easygoing guy. He said, 'Come on, stop it, what are you doing?' but I threw one at him and hit him again. He threw one back, but he missed. This time, I threw a potato at him and it landed right in the center of his plate, right splash in the middle of his gravy.

"We were both laughing, but this time he stood up and came after me. He nearly caught me but I dodged around the table. We ran all the way around the table and then I ran through to the bedroom, jumping across the bed to get away from him. He said, 'Look at what you've done, I'm all over gravy!' I tried to run around the bed again but he caught me. We were laughing and fighting and rolling all over the bed. Then we dropped off the side of the bed onto the floor. The great thing was that I didn't feel like I was coming onto him, I mean not sexually, even though I was.

"I tried to crawl away across the floor but he caught my ankle and said, 'you're bad, do you know that?' I said, in this little-girlie voice 'Oh yes, and what are you going to do about it? You're not going to spank me, are you?' He turned me over onto my back and sat astride me and said, 'I just might do that.'

"I said, '*Please* don't spank me . . . I'll do anything. I won't be naughty again. I promise I'll be good. But please don't spank me.'

"I thought I'd persuaded him to do it, but he said, 'All right, then. So long as you promise to be good,' and he let me up. That was when I picked up one of the pillows and whacked him on the side of the head with it. He picked up another pillow and whacked me back. We had this furious pillow fight, and then he said, 'Enough, already! What's the matter with you?"

"He sat down on the edge of the bed, and pulled me across his lap, facedown. I wriggled and fought and tried to get up, but not *too* hard. As a matter of fact the whole situation was beginning to turn me on. He said, 'That's it!' and lifted up my skirt, and it was then he saw that I wasn't wearing any panties . . . I'd left them off on purpose. I said, 'Don't spank me, don't spank me, don't spank me!' He was still laughing, but he gave me a slap on my bottom.

"I said, 'Don't! Don't' but what I meant was 'Do it again!' because it was lovely. He smacked me again, and there's nothing like it. I said, 'Ohhh . . .' and I opened my legs a little. He smacked me again, and again, and I felt this warm, sexy feeling all across my bare bottom.

"Just like you suggested, I showed him how excited I was. I climbed off his lap and knelt down beside him and pulled open his pants. He couldn't believe it when I took out his cock. He was only half-hard at first, but I took his whole cock into my mouth and started to suck it. I kept my skirt lifted up and I fingered myself at the same time. His cock swelled up so big that he almost choked me.

"I pushed him back onto the bed and climbed on top of him. I said, 'I won't be naughty again, I promise. I'll do anything.' Now he wasn't laughing . . . he was seriously turned-on. I took hold of his cock and put it up between my legs. then I slowly sat on him. I said, 'Feel my bottom, how hot you've made it.' He reached around and cupped my bottom in both hands. I rose up and down on top of him, and he loved it, and I loved it, too.

There's no feeling in the world that's better than riding up and down on your lover's cock.

"He rolled me over so that he was lying on top of me, then he rolled me over again so that I was lying facedown on the bed. He said, 'Your bottom's sure rosy, isn't it? All covered in bright red slap marks.' He opened my thighs a little way and then he pushed his cock into my pussy from behind, and made love to me very, very slowly, plunging deeper and deeper all the time.

"I reached down between my legs and fingered myself. I have a way of rolling and tugging my clitoris that always help me come to a climax. Dave kept on pushing himself into me deeper and deeper, and I could feel that wonderful feeling rising up inside of me, that feeling when you know for sure that you're going to have a climax and it's going to be a good one.

"I was almost there when Dave suddenly gasped out, 'I can't stop myself.' He pushed quicker and quicker, but at the last moment he took his cock out of me and shot his sperm all over my bottom. I could feel it spattering onto me, all warm and wet. Then he massaged it into my bottom cheeks, saying, 'Something to cool down that rosy-red rash.' He was still doing it when my own climax rose up inside of me and it was so huge and overwhelming that I almost fainted.

"We lay on the bed for a long time afterward just kissing and playing with each other's hair and looking into each other's eyes. Dave said, 'Did that paddling really turn you on?' I said, 'Sure, it did . . . you were so *masterful!*' I said it playfully, and then I started to tickle him. He just hates to be tickled. We rolled across the bed again, and this time he said, 'If you don't stop, I'm going to spank you for real!'

"I stopped, because I'd had enough for one evening. But after that, all I had to do was tickle him or tease him or provoke him when I felt like a spanking, and he did it, and because he knew how much it turned me on, it turned him on, too."

Many people derive sexual pleasure from spanking and flagellation, ranging from the kind of harmless bottom smacking that aroused Hedda to birchings, canings, and whippings. There is a vast and complex body of erotic literature and illustrations concerning "fladge," as it is often known. Some of it involves nothing more than a man putting a woman over his knee and spanking her bare bottom. These stories and drawings always make much of the "red glow" that suffuses the victims' "lily-white buttocks," so this is obviously a source of considerable erotic arousal, particularly for men, who like some visual evidence of the sexual effect they are having on a woman.

Other flagellation literature is far more sadistic. One of its more legendary proponents, the illustrator John Coutts, drew the *Adventures of Sweet Gwendoline* in the 1940s, in cartoon strips depicting women bound up in ropes, buckles, and straps, being regularly whipped by a high-heeled dominatrix. There are even drawings of teams of naked women with bits between their teeth and harnesses buckled tight between their legs, being whipped like prancing horses into pulling carriages. There are countless scenes of whipping and caning in that erotic classic *The Story of O,* and you can tell from the obsessive detail with which each instrument of torture is described that serious flagellation is a complex fetish.

With her hands pinioned behind her back, O is shown "the riding-crop, black, long and slender, made of fine bamboo sheathed in leather, an article such as one finds in the display windows of expensive saddle-makers' shops; the leather whip, which was long, with six lashes each ending in a knot; there was a third whip whose numerous light cords were several times knotted and stiff, quite as if soaked in water, as O was able to verify when they stroked her belly with those cords and, opening her thighs, exposed her hidden parts, let the damp, cold ends trail against the tender membranes."

Spanking is harmless erotic fun, but real whipping and caning is a serious and potentially dangerous sexual fetish, and although you can happily fantasize about it, you should never submit to it or agree to do it. There is no harm whatsoever in sexual fantasies, no matter how sadistic and lurid you may think they are (such as the dog-licking incident in Anais Nin's story). But you should be extremely cautious about trying to make them come true. In particular, you should never involve yourself in bondage or flagellation with a man you don't know well or trust implicitly.

Hedda was completely in control of her taste for a little mild spanking, and it became a spicy and exciting addition to her love life. She always made sure, however, that Dave never really hurt her, or that the game became too serious. "If I thought that Dave was in a bad mood, or really angry with me about something, I wouldn't even think of provoking him into spanking me."

And Dave himself? "I found it difficult to begin with, because I hate to cause Hedda any physical pain. But I know it excites her, and I know that I'm doing it because I'm sadistic, I'm doing it to turn her on, and that turns me on, too."

Ruth, the 33-year-old systems analyst, simply wanted to have sex more often, without always feeling that she was making the advances. This problem comes under the heading of "mismatched sex drives." In many relationships—especially in lengthy marriages or long-term sexual partnerships—one partner comfortably "settles down" without feeling the need for frequent sex, while the other partner remains sexually "hot" and consequently very frustrated.

If the woman is the more sexually-active partner, the problem is much more difficult to solve, because she needs an erect penis at the very least. A woman with a low sex drive can "just lie there" while her partner satisfies himself, but a woman with a high sex drive can't coax a disinterested partner into active penetration.

Ideally, this is a problem that you should discuss with your partner. Of course it takes much of the spontaneity and the excitement out of sex if he needs to be reminded to make love to you. But in many cases, men simply get out of the habit of making love regularly, particularly when they reach middle age, or when they're working very hard on their careers, and that habit *can* be restored if you work at it.

The first thing to remember is that a woman who wants frequent sex ought to be enticing. She ought to look sexy, dress sexy and behave sexy. I'm sure that you don't need much help in these areas, but it might be worth your reminding yourself to do something sexy every single day. Such as? Wake him up in the morning by kissing him, and caressing his cock and balls. Such as? Greeting him when he returns home in the evening with no bra and a partially unbuttoned blouse. Such as? Telling him about a sexy memory you had, sometime during the day ("remember the time we made love on the beach?") Such as? Asking to borrow his razor and his shaving gel, so that you can shave your pubic hair. Such as? Climbing into the tub with him, and touching him everywhere he likes to be touched.

You see, many of the women who complain that their lovers don't make love to them often enough are women who have also forgotten what *they* have to do keep a sexual relationship sparky. Sometimes it's time to be whorish; sometimes it's time to be brash. When he's decorating the spare bedroom, take off all of your clothes and go in and kiss him. You don't have to worry about the paint: you can always take a shower afterward. When he's lying in bed reading, sit on top of him naked and kiss him and tease him a little.

Undress in front of him—not like a stripper, but romantically and absentmindedly, taking off everything except your sweater and padding around with your bare bottom showing; or taking off your bra and blouse and fixing your hair while you're topless. Don't ever forget that *all men love to look* and you can give your lover dozens of daily opportunities to see something sexy—opportunities that will enhance his feelings toward you and give him erotic mental images that will stay with him all day.

Accidentally-on-purpose bend over to pick up a hair roller, so that he can see you in the dressing-room mirror. That fleeting image of your bare bottom and your exposed vulva will make more of an impression than you know. Accidentally-on-purpose leave the bathroom door open, so that he can glimpse you during some of your more intimate moments.

I'm not suggesting for a moment that you sacrifice your real privacy, because everybody needs moments when they need to be alone. But consider orchestrating a few moments when your partner glimpses you, such as when a Peeping Tom glimpses a woman through a half-lowered bedroom blind. Look through a good-quality men's magazine and see if you can re-create any of the poses in it—those seemingly casual instances when you lean forward in your bathrobe and expose a bare breast, or when you sit reading on the couch with your legs drawn up, exposing a curve of bare thigh.

All sexual relationships need constant care and attention, and quite a lot of nerve, too, if they're going to stay fresh and exciting. I suggested it to Ruth that she use her own regular masturbation as a starting point for improving her sex life with Michael. She was unhappy that she had to masturbate so frequently in order to satisfy herself, but she enjoyed masturbation, she was quick and good at it, and she knew exactly how to bring herself to a very high state of sexual arousal—which is another essential for improving your sex life with a partner whose sex drive is comparatively low.

There are few better ways to elicit a positive sexual response from your partner than by showing him just how aroused he makes you feel.

Of course, some women ask me, *Why should I?* They always thought that it was the man's job to arouse the woman. They always thought that it was the man's job to spice up their sex life, and to introduce new variations and suggest new ways of making love. But no sexual relationship ever improved through one partner failing to keep it interesting, and the other partner sitting back and resenting it. If your lover isn't making love to you as often as you want him to, and in all the ways that you want to make love, then it's up to you to take some positive action. After all, *you* will benefit just as much as your lover—if not more so.

A word of caution, though: while it's critical for you to show your lover that he turns you on, *don't* be too eager to please. One of the most common mistakes that women make when they are trying to improve their sexual relationships is to "fake" much more erotic excitement than they are actually feeling. They pant, they gasp, they twist their hips, they close their eyes, they murmur "mmmmmhhhhh . . . mmmhhhh . . ."—they scream, even.

Every time I read a story about a woman who has regularly been disturbing her neighbors by making too much noise during sex, I can't resist a smile. Of course there are times when you feel so aroused that you have to cry out during sex. Screaming and moaning can be great aphrodisiacs—just like dirty language. But the reality is that profound sexual arousal is an internal sensation, and any woman who is still shouting and yelling at the top of her voice as she approaches her climax is an inexperienced exhibitionist who may never have felt the real volcano of a satisfying orgasm.

Some men find screaming and moaning quite exciting. More seem to find it distracting. "I had a relationship with a girl who always screamed at the top of her voice when she climaxed," said Ted, a 33-year-old research chemist from Tucson, Arizona. "The first time she did it, I felt like the greatest lover since Casanova. After the fiftieth time, it began to drive me crazy. I never had any proof of it, of course, but I began to suspect that she wasn't having a climax at all; and that maybe she never had. She thought that if she made this horrendous noise, that was as good as an orgasm."

Women who fake their sexual excitement in an effort to make their lovers feel more virile are not doing themselves any favors—not, in the long term, are they doing their lovers any favors, either. You should never give your lover the impression that he can turn you on at the flick of a switch (or the flick of a clitoris). You should never be reticent about showing him how aroused you are, because one of the things that makes sex so exciting for the man in your life is knowing that he has excited you, too. But his sexual skills will never improve if you make him feel that he is better in bed than he really is. You know how you like to be aroused, and for how long; make sure you find a way of letting *him* know how to do it, too.

Ruth set out to improve her sex life with her husband Michael by mutual masturbation. As sex writer Louise Short put it, "'Mutual masturbation as the prelude to the sexual act can stimulate more response in a woman than she ever expected to feel and more gratification in the man. Even if she has achieved an orgasm before actual coitus she may find herself relaxed and ready to experience yet another orgasm during coitus. The man, for his part, can enjoy a languorous sensuality through pre-coital stimulation by his partner which he only imagined before."

Ms. Short seems to assume that mutual masturbation must inevitably be followed by intercourse—which of course is not necessarily the case—but she does mention one married woman who enjoys mutual masturbation with her husband because "during this foreplay they are free to give gentle instructions and they have thus revealed more of their personal sexuality than unadorned coitus ever allowed for."

And she discusses the interesting sex life of one woman who told her, "All my husband and I ever do is mutually masturbate. It is an infallible method of contraception and we enjoy it heartily." This couple had been married for 12 years. For some reason, both of them felt a psychological resistance to intercourse, and Ms. Short says that "analysts could have a field day with them."

However, "by their unity and their even-tempered love for each other, they embody the truth that in bed, between consenting human beings, nothing is ever wrong except failing to try something that might bring them closer together and give them mutual joy."

It was in this spirit that Ruth began her program of masturbation. "I started at bedtimes, because it was easier to reach Michael's cock when he was wearing pajamas or a bathrobe, and we were both in a very relaxed mood. We were in bed together and he was reading a report for work the following morning. I simply slipped my hand into the waistband of his pajamas and started to caress his pubic hair and down between his legs . . . very gently, very casually. I gently ran my fingernails around his balls, and then began to squeeze and manipulate his cock.

"I did it in such an offhanded way that he almost didn't notice that I was doing it. I didn't start wildly rubbing his cock or anything like that. He smiled at me and kissed me on top of the head and said, 'What are *you* doing?' but all I said was 'Enjoying myself, what are *you* doing?' He said, 'Working, unfortunately.'

"He didn't stop me, though. I kept on stroking and touching and squeezing his cock until it started to rise. It grew bigger and harder and stuck up through the opening in his pajamas, but I still didn't rub it hard. I circled my fingernails around the head of it, and tickled the little opening, and then ran my fingernails all the way down the length of it, down to his balls. I kept on doing that, circling and touching and tickling, and all the time his cock grew harder and harder.

"Like you suggested, I waited until his cock began to ooze out a little juice before I started to touch myself. Then I reached inside my nightshirt and started to play with my nipples, fingering them and touching them in the same way that I like to touch them when I masturbate, very lightly, scarcely touching them at all. I took my hand out of my nightshirt, and collected the juice from Michael's cock onto my fingertip, and then reached back inside my nightshirt and smeared it on my nipples, like a lubricant.

"Of course Michael was beginning to pay more than a little attention to what I was doing. He said, 'Honey, this is great, but I have so much work to do.' I kissed him and said, 'Okay . . . don't let me disturb you.'

"I didn't stop, though. I kept on stroking his cock, and now I reached down between my legs and started to play with myself, just fingering my clitoris. Michael was very turned-on by now, even though he didn't want to be; and he dropped his report on the bed. But I said, 'Don't, you don't have to, this is terrific, just the way it is.' I pulled down the sheet and lifted up my nightshirt and started to rub myself, right in front of him. "This was what took the most nerve, because I'd never done it right in front of him before. I masturbated myself the way I always do when I'm at work, except I didn't have my dildo with me. I slipped my pinkie into my vagina and tugged my clitoris with my thumb and my index finger. At the same time I kept on rubbing Michael's cock, but now I was doing it harder, because I had all of his attention.

"He kissed me and tried to climb on top of me so

that he could make love to me, but I said, 'No . . . not yet. Not this time. Let's just do this.' I took his hand and put it between my legs and said, 'Look, if you stroke me like this, it feels fantastic.' He started to do it. He pulled me too hard at first, so I said, 'That's it, but gently,' and it didn't take him long before he was doing it just right, and it felt *great* for the first time ever, Michael was masturbating me, instead of having to do it myself.

"I kept rubbing him and rubbing him, but he was very slow in coming. I don't know what it was, maybe the stress. But I didn't concentrate on him so much . . . I concentrated on what he was doing to me, like you said I should. He had never turned me on so quickly. I was incredibly juicy and Michael's fingers were all wet. He tugged my clitoris faster and faster, and then I felt that tight sensation between my legs which always means that I'm going to come soon . . . and before I knew it, I was tightening and tightening and then suddenly I was washed away.

"A second afterward, Michael climaxed, too. His sperm shot all over my hand and across my nightshirt. I kept on squeezing him and massaging him until he was soft, but even then I didn't want to let him go.

" 'You gave me the climax of the century,' I told him; and he was smiling like a kid who's just won a prize. Mind you, I was smiling too. I couldn't keep the smile off my face for the rest of the evening.

"That night, in the middle of the night, he woke me up by putting his arm around me and gently playing with my clitoris. It was very dark and we were both very tired, but we made love, full glorious intercourse, slowly and sexily, and it was great. I lay back feeling his cock sliding in and out of me, feeling his warmth, hearing his breathing, and it was just wonderful.

"Our lovemaking didn't change overnight. Michael isn't a very spontaneous person, and sometimes I think he felt like making love but wasn't sure if I wanted to, so he didn't try. But I kept on masturbating him regularly . . . and not just in bed, either. Once I took out his cock when he was making a long-distance call to his employer, and masturbated myself too. He made love to me for hours after that, literally hours, until I was tired out. He came twice, too, which he'd never done before, leastways not with me.

"These days he makes love to me much more often, and he is almost always the one who initiates our lovemaking, too, right from the beginning. But that doesn't stop me from masturbating whenever I feel like it!"

What makes this pleasuring technique so effective is that—unlike an attempt to have what Ms. Louise Frost calls "unadorned coitus"—it can be started very gently and casually, and if your partner really doesn't feel like sex, it needn't go any farther than a little mild petting.

If it *does* go farther, it can very smoothly and easily lead into full lovemaking—and lovemaking in a way that will leave your partner feeling he has done his manly duty and satisfied you to the very best of his sexual abilities (if not better.)

I always encourage couples with mismatched sex drives to do their best to keep up frequent lovemaking—even if that lovemaking amounts to nothing more than an intimate kiss or a lingering embrace or a few minutes of sexual massage. Even very passionate couples can get out of the habit of making love frequently, especially if they are experiencing external pressures in their relationship such as financial or career problems, sometimes sports and hobbies absorb too much energy. If some couples put into their sexual relationships only a tenth of the amount of dedication they put into their other activities such as jogging and aerobics, they would discover to their pleasure that every night can be a wild and exciting night, even in a relationship they thought had become routine.

Now let's take a look at a different problem altogether: that of Alexandra, the 36-year-old hair stylist from Boston, Massachusetts, who was aroused by fantasies of bondage and body piercing, although her boyfriend Jack was "a very straight guy," and she didn't believe that he would be willing to try anything so bizarre.

Bondage is a complex and fascinating sexual variation, and almost everybody who is aroused by it has very individual tastes. Some women are highly stimulated by the idea of being tied to a bed with scarves or cords while their lover "has his way" with them however he chooses. Once they are helpless, the woman can be subjected to tickling, stroking, brushing, and sexual exploration, often to the very brink of orgasm before the pleasure is deliberately withheld. Many bondage enthusiasts add to the "victims' " helplessness by blindfolding them. Other stimulation used during bondage can include penetration with dildos or vibrators, oil massage, talcum powder massage, or mildly sadistic "punishments" such as gentle spanking or the attachment of clips or clothespins to nipples and vaginal lips.

Other women are excited by more complicated bondage, either in chairs or standing up, in positions that expose them sexually. Here's a description by the celebrated bondage artist John Coutts of how to tie up a naked woman in a plain straight-backed chair: "Tie her wrists to each of the back legs, just below the seat, then pull her forward till her bottom rests right at the edge . . . then put the cord under the chair back top & over her shoulders, under her arms, cross over, back & then bring forward to go back between her thighs— & then make the ends fast to her wrists where they're tired to the chair leg. To keep her knees separated don't just tie her ankles outside the chair leg but draw them together behind the front legs of the chair first & then tie each ankle to its respective leg. You will find that she cannot move at all & everything (i.e., her vulva) will be displayed."

Coutts supplies more than a dozen line drawings of "how to tie up naked women," including a step-by-step diagram of how to find a woman with her arms behind her back and her legs apart, which could be described as *Practical Bondage.*

Most people derive some erotic pleasure from fantasies, of domination and submission, but devotees of bondage take their fantasies a good deal further. Any form of bodily decoration or restraint is in some form a sexual display—earrings, tattoos, tight belts, lacings, neck bands, garters, and ankle chains. Many devotees of bondage make permanent commitments to their sexual preferences by piercing their bodies and inserting rings or studs which can be used in their bondage games.

After ears and noses, the most common piercing is nipple piercing, both male and female. Some men say that they had little or no sexual sensitivity in their nipples before piercing; and some women with pierced nipples have told me that they are capable of reaching orgasm just by having their nipple rings tugged or rotated.

The *Kama Sutra* describes *apadravyas* or "penis-enhancers" who perforated the male organ "as for earrings" and inserted various hard objects in order to give them more sexual excitement. Sometimes the object would increase friction or stimulation during intercourse; sometimes the insertion alone was enough to give the enthusiast all the erotic excitement he craved. These days, men who have had their penises pierced will occasionally remove the "sleeper" ring so that they can experience the operation all over again.

There are scores of varieties of rings and studs designed for the piercing of the penis and the vagina. Probably the best known for men is the Prince Albert, or "dressing-ring," a large ring about the diameter of a nickel which enters the head of the penis just above the urethra (the canal where the sperm and urine are expelled) and exits just behind it. This ring was originally supposed to have been designed for Victorian gentlemen who wore tight breeches, so they could firmly fasten their penises down their right or left leg. But it is also supposed to enhance erotic arousal during intercourse. An unusual variation on the Prince Albert is for a man to have his navel pierced with a prominent stud, so that the penis can be lifted up vertically and attached to the belly button.

Men also have themselves pierced with dydoes, which are studs about three-quarters of an inch long with a small sphere on either end. These are pierced through the thick rim of the head of the penis, so that one end of the ball rests in the groove just behind the head, and the other end protrudes on the edge of the rim. Dydoes are usually worn in groups of five or six or even more, all the way around the penis, and sometimes in conjunction with another dydo that is pierced horizontally right across the tip of the penis, called an ampallang. During intercourse, this collection of dydoes has the effect of making the head of the penis knobbly with metal spheres, and increasing a woman's stimulation.

Both men and women have themselves pierced with guiches, which are, large rings that go right through the perineum, which is the fleshy area that separates the testicles (or vagina) and anus. Gentle tugging on the guiche during orgasm is supposed to prolong your climax.

Women body piercers can have gold or diamond studs inserted in their vaginal lips, but rings are very popular, too, so that decorative jewelry can be hung from them, or so that a small padlock can be fastened across their vaginas (the key to which is kept by their bondage partner). I have seen men, too, with padlocks pierced through the ends of their penises.

Another permanent commitment to bondage is to have one's body tattooed in intimate places. I was recently shown a wildly extravagant tattoo of a rose, which appeared to be blossoming from a girl's anus, and bursting its petals all across the cheeks of her bottom. Another tattoo depicted Cleopatra-type asps, sliding across a girl's thighs and showing venomous interest in her bald-shaven vulva.

A sensible word about piercing and tattooing, particularly to younger people. It *is* erotic, it *is* different, and it can be very arousing. But it has two distinctive characteristics, apart from being arousing. It is permanent, and however much it excites you now, think about living with it for the rest of your life. It is also very compelling. The more holes you pierce in your body, the more holes you feel you want. The more tattoos you have, the more you need. It is the very act of permanent self-disfigurment that is exciting.

When I use the word "disfigurement," I don't mean that all piercing and tattooing is ugly or dangerous. The choice is up to you. But it is worth thinking long and hard before you do anything to your body that you might regret later. Over the past 20 years, I have received several letters from desperate women who have asked for help with tattoo removal, and have experienced problems after overenthusiastic piercing. "In Frank, I met the kind of man that I'd always wanted. When he saw the studs in my pussy lips, he couldn't take it, he didn't want to know me anymore. He knew I wasn't a virgin, that's what he said—he knew that I'd once belonged to somebody else—but he didn't want it shoved in his face every time he made love to me."

A staggering variety of bondage paraphernalia is available for sale through mail-order sex catalogs—so that almost every taste can be accommodated. At the milder end of the scale, there are various "strap suits" for women, which are body harnesses of studded black leather, usually leaving the breasts exposed. The "'Cruella" strap suit is an arrangement of belts that surround the breasts and leave the wearer's vulva completely exposed, while the "Domina" bikini has an open crotch but a metal chain that runs between the vaginal lips. The "Ring Binder" features metal rings to surround the nipples and a tight leather strap to divide the vaginal lips. The "Ram Raider" is a leather-and-steel-ring girdle that has an integrated latex dildo which is buckled firmly into place inside the vagina.

Even in less extreme catalogs you can now find penis gags, which are leather bits of latex penis inside them, so that a large plastic penis is forced into your mouth when your lover buckles it around your head, and Arab straps, which are studded black leather harnesses for your lover's penis and testicles, some with "ball-dividers."

There are endless varieties of leather and latex leggings, stockings, G-strings, and skirts, and many different versions of "orgasm pants." These are designed both for men and for women, and have lifelike latex dildos built into them for vaginal and/or anal penetration, some of them equipped with vibrators.

More extreme outlets sell items such as neck cuffs ("these can be very severe when secured"); sheath arm binders, which are leather sheaths in which both arms are buckled behind the "victim's" back; ankle cuffs; "overnighters," which buckle a woman's wrists against her thighs, making it impossible for her to resist having her thighs spread apart; and discipline helmets—"made of the finest, most form-fitting kidskin leather available—they are made to fit very tightly around the head and neck when completely strapped and laced—it laces up the back and has four straps attached—one strap cinches the neck, allowing for no empty space or light—the second strap goes around the mouth and when tightened and buckled pulls the gag (which is attached to the inside of the mask) firmly into position, cutting off all sound—the third strap is around the eyes—the fourth strap secures the entire helmet, going around the chin to the top of the head, pulled tight, the jaws are drawn into the built-in gag—when the helmet is completely secured your partner will not be able to utter a sound, besides being rendered totally helpless."

Some of this bondage gear is extremely specialized and very expensive—and, apart from that, it has to be treated with great respect.

I talked to Alexandra about bondage to decide whether she was genuinely interested in sadomasochistic sex or if her fantasies were nothing more than that—fantasies.

Many women have erotic daydreams about finding themselves helpless at the hands of a rampant lover, but real bondage is quite different. Even serious bondage enthusiasts are very cautious about their sexual practices. One of the more knowledgeable of them emphasized that "bondage is for pleasure, not for pain."

He went on to say, "The things you read about something being tied in an outlandish position for overnight are written only for fantasizing and reading enjoyment. Yes! It *is* part of the game to tell your slave, 'you're going to be gagged and blindfolded for hours or even overnight.' This is part of the excitement. But a human being cannot withstand severe bondage for any length of time.

"If you are going to use a gag, never leave the room. Always check to make sure the subject is breathing normally. If there is the slightest irregularity, take it off, saying, "I'm going to take this off for a couple of minutes so that you can answer some questions." You can put it back on again after a short while. But take it off again at a shorter interval of time.

"If you're going to use a mask, do so with extreme care. Some people might not think that they have claustrophobia but learn fast that they do when a mask blocks out all their senses."

The more she learned about bondage, the more Alexandra realized that she was much more excited by the idea of it than she was about the possibility of actually doing it. All the same, she did want Jack to behave more assertively, and for that reason I suggested that she simply try to play out the fantasy that turned her on so much, to see how Jack responded. I could give her no guarantees that he would react in the way that she wanted him to, but she agreed that there was no harm in trying. The worst that could happen was that she could have a little fun.

"When he came home that first evening, I was all dressed up like a French maid—well, a very sexy French maid. I wore a lace cap and a black lace basque and black stockings, and black spike-heel stilettos. The basque covered my breasts but I didn't wear any panties. I was very nervous before he came home. He's such a straight guy, I thought he was going to be offended, or think that I was drunk or something. But in fact he was kind of bemused, you know. Kind of turned-on, but not at all sure what was happening.

"He said, 'What are you dressed like that for?' and I said, 'I wanted to be your maid tonight . . . I wanted to give you a good time, so that you can put your feet up and relax and enjoy yourself.' He said, 'Well, this is something. You can do this anytime you like.'

"I was so nervous! I felt so naked and exposed, but at the same time that was what my fantasy was all about, feeling naked and exposed. I said, 'What would you like? A drink first, or a blow job?' He said, 'What?' He couldn't believe what he was hearing. I said, 'Come here,' and I knelt down on the floor in front of him in my basque and my stockings and I opened his pants. He said, 'You can't do that, I haven't taken my shower yet.' I said, 'I'll be your shower,' and I reached inside his shorts and took out his cock.

"Just the way you suggested, I said to myself, 'this is me, this me living out my fantasy . . . I'm a slave, I'm a servant, anything he wants me to do, I'm going to do.' His cock was soft but I took it into my mouth and started to suck it, and it stiffened up so fast you wouldn't even believe it.

"He said, 'No, not now,' but I took his cock out of my mouth and licked the tip of it, and said, 'You don't really want me to stop, do you?' and he smiled at me and shook his head. I held on to his thighs and I took his cock back into my mouth and I licked it and sucked it and squashed it up against the roof of my mouth. I started to masturbate him, too, with my hand, and he let out such a moan you wouldn't believe it.

"His pants were halfway down his thighs by now. I gripped his ass in my left hand and forced him into fucking my mouth. I bared my teeth a little so that they caught the tip of his cock when it went in and out.

"Then I gripped his ball bag in both hands, and dug my fingernails into it, and pulled it hard, and rubbed his cock hard. He was crying out and his leg muscles were hard like rocks. He suddenly came, without any warning at all, and come was flying everywhere, all over my cheeks, all over my lips, stuck in my eyelashes, dripping down my neck. Jack knelt down, too, and kissed me, and we both fell sideways on the floor and kissed and licked each other and it was like a whole new love had lit up between us.

"Jack made love to me again that evening, when we went to bed. I held onto the bedposts and pretended that I was handcuffed to them, while he made love to me. But then I felt like clutching his beautiful muscly bottom and scratching his back and pulling him into me harder and harder, and you can't do things like that when you're handcuffed, can you?"

What Alexandra discovered was that she was highly aroused by images of bondage and slavery and sadomasochistic sex, but that on the whole she actually preferred her relationship with Jack as it was, stable and sharing and secure. She did manage to inject more excitement into her love life by dressing sexily and "breaking the rules" a little—giving Jack oral sex as soon as he came home, walking around the house naked and semi-naked, and by trying to talk to him much more freely about sex. But once she had gotten him out of the routine of straight, once-a-week intercourse, she found that she was content for her fantasies to remain fantasies, and to leave the world of bondage to the true enthusiasts.

However, she did titillate Jack by greeting him one evening wearing nothing but jeans and nipple jewelry—a string of pearls suspended from nipple to nipple with slipknot nooses—"the tightening of the nooses will send lascivious thrills through your nipples." And when she undressed for him that evening, he discovered that she was also wearing a clitoral clip—a vaginal decoration with two dangling gold chains and sparkling semiprecious gemstones on the end. "No piercing required," Alexandra told me.

In many relationships, frustration and a lack of sexual communication leads to one or other partner having exaggerated fantasies about sex. But the first place to look for fulfillment is not in your fantasy but in your relationship. It may help to include some elements of your fantasy in your everyday sex life, as Alexandra found out. But what she needed most of all was affection and attention, and much more frequent lovemaking.

It's interesting to note that because she was so much of a "slave," she used her teeth to titillate Jack's penis during oral sex, and dug her fingernails into his scrotum to make him ejaculate. In other words, she wasn't a masochist at all, but quite sexually dominant.

Joanna, the 24-year-old flight attendant from Atlanta, Georgia, was shy about introducing "wet sex" into her relationship with her boyfriend Gerry. Erotic urination excited her, it gave her a sense of freedom and release, and this was a feeling she wanted to share with the man she loved. However, she worried that he might not understand how she felt; and that he might even find her sexual behavior disgusting.

I suggested that she was underestimating the intense interest that most men have in the female private parts, and forgetting that men have a very much more open attitude toward urination. Because of the differences in their anatomy, men can (and do) urinate openly, in front of each other, in the street, in the woods, wherever—whereas women almost always do it in private, with the door locked, and even if they do chatter from cubicle to cubicle in public washrooms, they don't see each other urinating, and in fact they don't even see themselves urinating.

Kathy, a 42-year-old feminist activist from New York told me, "I first did it when I was going through counseling because of the problems I was having with my first husband. He was very repressive and always made me feel as if I was some kind of inferior species. After two-and-a-half years, I began to believe that I *was* inferior. I would never interrupt him when he was speaking; I would always have his meals ready for when he came home. If he wanted to have sex with me I would have sex. He was a lousy lover: he never once cared if I was enjoying myself in bed, so long as he got his rocks off. I began to feel like the lowest of the low, as I had no human rights, no identity, no pride, nothing.

"My counselor was a woman. She wasn't especially feminist in her attitudes, but she did believe in women's sexual rights. She said I had as much right to sexual satisfaction as my husband did; and that I should make sure that I got it. She gave me a whole range of exercises to boost my sexual pride, including masturbation and even flirting with other men! But the exercise which gave me the greatest sense of sexual release was when she told me that next time I took a shower, I should urinate standing up. Just stand there, and let it go, and put my hand down between my legs to feel it coming out.

"Some of my friends thought the whole idea was disgusting. But when I actually did it, it wasn't disgusting at all. There was something very erotic about it; and also something very proud about it, that I didn't have to crouch down if I didn't want to. I just stood in the shower with my legs slightly apart and let it all pour through my fingers. I suppose it's an act of defiance, in a way—a refusal to let yourself be limited by anything at all, and especially by your sex."

Apart from the sexual politics of it, many couples find an occasional bout of wet sex to be highly exciting. In normal sex, ejaculation or orgasm is very brief, whereas urination is a very much more bombastic and longer-lasting way of displaying your sexual feelings. Many women enjoy it because it allows them to give a visual display of their erotic excitement. Then, of course, there is the excitement of doing something "dirty" and "forbidden."

As we've discussed, the fresh urine of a healthy person is completely sterile, and there is no harm in using it for any kind of love play, or even in drinking a small quantity. Like all sexual variations, wet sex can become a problem if a person's interest in it becomes obsessive, or if they are unable to achieve satisfaction without it, but a great many couples try it now and again in their lovemaking and find it thrilling and liberating.

I advised Joanna that if she wanted to introduce a little wet sex into her relationship with her boyfriend Gerry that she ought to incorporate it with another strong form of stimulation so that he would immediately associate the passing of urine with obvious sexual enjoyment. She should try to make it seem as if her urination was not so much an act of sexual self-assertion as a response to the pleasure he was giving her. In other words, she should try urinating during intercourse or when she was giving him oral sex, so that he would think that he had excited her so much that she was unable to contain herself.

This may sound like a betrayal of the principles of honest and open sex—not to mention a betrayal of the principles of women's sexual equality. But there are times in every relationship when you have to make compromises in order to show your partner what you feel and what you need. If your partner is more likely to try some new sexual variation because you make him feel that *he* initiated it and that you are doing it because *he* wants you to, then there's no harm in that. Next time you'll probably find that he *does* initiate it.

Joanna chose to introduce Gerry to the pleasures of wet sex during intercourse, because they often made love on the sun-lounger in Joanna's roof garden, where copious wetness wouldn't matter. "It was a beautiful warm afternoon. I'd been drinking white wine spritzers, mostly club soda, and I made sure that I hadn't been to the bathroom since early morning. I was wearing my pink swimsuit and Gerry was wearing his Bermuda shorts. He started kissing me and getting all affectionate, and he sat on the edge of the sun-lounger and kissed my lips and my neck, and caressed my breasts through my swimsuit.

"He pulled my swimsuit to one side so that my right breast was bare, and he licked and kissed my nipple. I love it when he sucks my nipple right into his mouth and quickly flicks it with his tongue, that's beautiful. It was so beautiful I almost wet myself then and there, because I was bursting to go to the bathroom anyway.

"He began to touch me between the legs, inside my knees and my thighs and then up to my cunt. He stroked me through my swimsuit, these long, gentle strokes, and I really was terrified that I wouldn't be able to stop myself.

"He pulled the crotch of my swimsuit over to the side, so that my cunt was exposed. My swimsuit was quite tight, so that my cunt bulged out. It's mostly shaved, but I always keep a little plume of hair just above it—just to remind Gerry that I'm a natural blonde! Gerry played with my clitoris with his fingertip, and then he opened my cunt lips with both hands and leaned forward and ran his tongue all the way down it, right from my clitoris all the way down to my asshole, and then he licked it again and again.

"I reached over and took hold of his cock, which was standing up hard and straight inside his shorts. I thought that if he went on licking me, I was going to have to let go, right in his face, and I didn't want to do that the very first time. So I burrowed my hand inside the leg of his shorts and found his cock and started to rub it hard. It felt gorgeous-silky-skinned and hard as a rock. I always call it his joystick—you know, what with working for the airline and everything.

"I tugged down his shorts and said, 'Fuck me, come on, Gerry, I need you to fuck me. I need you so bad.'

"He climbed onto the sun-lounger and pushed the head of his cock into my cunt. Just the head, nothing more. I tried to squeeze my cunt so that I could suck more of him in, but of course I couldn't. He was holding himself up with one arm, so that he could fondle my breasts and play with my nipples. He was taking it so slow and I wanted to go so desperately!

"At last, though, he leaned forward, and his whole

long cock slid into me, all the way in, so that I could feel his balls dangling against my bottom. He pressed his weight on my stomach, and it was all I could do not to let go. He started to fuck me harder and faster. It was hot and he was sweating. His muscles were tense and he was all wet with perspiration. He fucked me harder and harder, his cock was flying in and out of me and it felt like the warmest most tingling feeling in the world was rising up between my legs.

"I reached down and held my cunt lips wide apart, so that he could fuck me deeper and deeper. Every time he pushed in, he pressed my bladder and gave me this pain that was partly a pain and partly a fantastic pleasure.

"He was panting, and he was gritting his teeth. I could feel his balls and they were tight like walnuts. It was then that I started to piss. I said, 'Ooohhhh. . . .' and just let myself go, and this hot stream came jetting out of me, splashing all over his pubic hair, gushing all over his balls, and all over our thighs.

"You don't have any idea how much it turned him on. He said, 'You beauty, you're pissing.' and he started to fuck me even harder. I never thought his cock could go up me that far. He put his hands down and massaged my thighs and my bottom with wet hands, and I did the same to him, massaging piss all over his back and his sides and even his nipples.

"He climaxed—this huge, rippling climax that seemed to tear right through him. He sat up, all wet, and there was thick white rope of sperm which connected the end of his cock to my open cunt. I reached down and slowly rubbed it between my cunt lips, around and around.

"I said, 'Now I'll need washing, won't I?' and I took hold of his cock and pointed it between my legs. I don't think he understood what I meant at first, but then he said, 'Me?' and I said 'Go on, I dare you.'

"It took him a moment, because his cock was still hard. But then he managed a short, sharp gush, and then another one, and then a long hot stream. I was holding the shaft of his cock and I could actually feel it running through him. I aimed his cock so that it splashed all over my clitoris, and at the same time I rubbed my clitoris with my fingers. I never knew that *anything* could feel like that. It was wet, warm, splashy, sexy, exciting, everything . . . and the best feeling of all was the feeling that I had persuaded Gerry to do it and he hadn't been angry or upset or disgusted or anything.

"We took a shower together afterward, and then we went to bed and made love very slowly and very dryly. But we've done it again two or three times more; and these days, if I'm sitting on the toilet taking a pee before my bath, he'll sometimes come in and kiss me and reach down between my legs and play with me while I'm pissing. These days we feel like there's nothing we don't share. We feel like there's no embarrassment between us at all. We can do anything; we can talk about anything. When you have a relationship like that with a man—or with *anybody,* I guess—it's something very special."

There are many different sexual variations that can help to drive you and your man even wilder in bed. In fact, there are as many different sexual variations as there are different people, because everybody is aroused by a different combination of sights, sounds, feelings, and fantasies.

Driving your man even wilder in bed begins with sexual confidence and sexual self-knowledge—your own Sexual Glow—and from there it goes on to showing and guiding your man what you want and what you feel—using your Sexual Glow to illuminate your love life. He cannot possibly know everything that excites you and everything you want to try . . . any more than *you* can guess what variations (or what special combination of variations) *he* would like to try.

But by increasing the temperature of your sex life—by making love more frequently and more inventively—you will create an atmosphere in which both you and your partner will feel much more free to experiment with new variations.

Many women seem surprised that I am such a strong advocate of improving your existing relationship rather than enlivening your sex life by seeking casual affairs on the side. In my experience, however, even the most stale sexual relationships can be easily improved, and although casual affairs may offer temporary excitement (apart from being very flattering), they rarely do anything to turn people into better lovers. Good sex comes from imagination, caring, and constant responsiveness. Good sexual relationships require thought and work and self-improvement.

The excitement of a new lover always wears off; but the excitement you can have by being a really good lover never leaves you.

All the same, let's take a look at two couples who added spice to their sex lives by sharing their beds with another partner.

NINE

Three's Company

Twenty years' experience of talking to men and women about their sex lives has shown me quite clearly that, for most couples, "swinging" or "swapping" with other couples is ultimately very destructive. A few people are able to carry on an "open" relationship without jealousy or recrimination, but usually this relationship—even if it was intensely sexual—was emotionally superficial, and the partners' self-interest came before their interest in each other.

They were often highly aroused by the idea or even the sight of their partner having sex with somebody else, because their own stimulation was more important to them than the closeness of their marriage or their long-term relationship.

Many women have fantasies about making love to other men apart from their relationship and the security that goes with it. Apart from that, there is always the danger of contracting AIDS or other sexually communicated diseases.

Occasionally, however, a situation arises when the introduction of a third person into a marriage or a long-term sexual relationship can be highly invigorating. They bring in new ideas, new excitement, and a revived feeling in both partners that they are still as sexually attractive as they were when they first met each other.

I can't emphasize often enough the importance in a sexual relationship of *feeling* sexy, of having that Sexual Glow, and of making your partner feel sexy, too. I have observed some couples for days on end, who never exchange a kiss or a hug or an intimate look of sexual affection. They believe that they are still in love with each other, and they always express surprise if I suggest otherwise. But they have gotten out of the habit of *showing* it, and showing that you still find your partner sexually attractive is the first requirement in any thrilling relationship.

Quite a few wives have said to me, "Why should I keep on showing him that I find him attractive when he never even bothers to bring me a bunch of flowers?"

The simple answer is that, in a sexual relationship, two wrongs *never* make a right. It's absolutely critical that you keep up the habit of displaying your affection, even at times when you feel that you're not getting very much affection in return. The day that you both start saying to yourselves, "Why should I bother?" is the day that your relationship will start becoming an arrangement rather than an affair.

Every now and then, a third person can enter a stale relationship and help both partners to rediscover each other. Threesomes that are arranged deliberately seldom seem to work out well; they can even become disastrous. But when someone comes along whom you and your partner both like equally well, the results can be remarkable.

There's no question that the risks involved aren't extremely high. One or other of you could easily fall in love with your new sex partner. One or other of you might suffer such pangs of guilt or jealousy that you feel unable to continue your existing relationship. You might *all* end up falling out—I've seen that happen, too. But if you are both mature and thoughtful about a threesome, and if you are both aware of what the consequences may be before you enter into it, then you can experience some intense and unusual sexual excitements, and the experience can be very positive.

Here's Verna, 33, who was married to 37-year-old

Steve for six years before she realized that "my marriage was flat as a pancake."

Steve was part owner of a van rental company in Pennsylvania, and worked very long hours. "I guess we'd just grown apart, sexually, because Steve came home late every single evening, and he was always too tired to make love. I loved him, there wasn't any question about that, but I began to feel frustrated and irritable, and of course I always took it out on Steve, which made matters worse instead of better.

"One day Steve came home and said that he'd hired a new assistant. She came from Pittsburgh and had recently gotten divorced, so she was single and lonesome and looking for friends. I suggested he bring her home for supper one evening. He hemmed and hawed about it, and then said okay. He didn't seem very willing at first, but I had lost my job at the market just after Christmas when they laid off 29 staff, and I was pretty lonesome, too. I had to spend all day in the apartment with nobody to talk to: I was dying to make some new friends.

"When Laura showed up my first reaction was pretty negative. I thought she was showy. But the more she talked, the more I grew to like her, and by the end of the evening she and I were getting along so well that Steve could hardly get a word in edgewise. She was small and dark-haired and very pretty. Her mother was Puerto Rican. She was very vivacious, too. She laughed a whole lot and she was one of those women who make you feel better just by talking to them.

"I could see that Steve liked her, too. She wore this low-cut ruffled blouse and whenever she leaned over to help herself to anything, I could see him giving sideways looks down her cleavage.

"When she was gone, we both agreed that she was great fun, and that we both liked her. When we went to bed that night, Steve was really passionate. He undressed me himself, which is something he hadn't done for years, and he made love to me just the way he used to. Afterward I said, 'We should have Laura around here more often, if she turns you on that much.' He said, 'All right, she's sexy, what's wrong in that?' I said, 'Nothing, I agree with you. I think she *is* sexy.'

"Steve had to spend three days at a convention in New Jersey, so while he was gone I invited Laura over to keep me company. We had a great time. We went shopping, and then we went home and opened a bottle of wine. I hadn't laughed so much for longer than I could remember.

"I told Laura that she was very beautiful, and that Steve liked her, too. She said that Steve was very attractive, and that I was lucky to have him for a husband. I said that our marriage was going through a flat state, and that we hardly ever made love. She said that was crazy, her husband had wanted to make love to her every night, and he used to hit her if she ever refused. 'He used to make me walk around the house with no panties on, so that he could put his hand up my skirt whenever he felt like it. He used to treat me like an animal that was made for his pleasure. He used to call me Animal sometimes and make me crawl around on my hands and knees so that he could fuck me from behind.'

"She said he was always fooling around with other women, and that she had come home two or three times and found him in bed with somebody else. When she complained about it, all he said was, you're welcome to join in . . . nobody's stopping you. Once when she was drunk and very angry she actually took him up on his offer, took off her clothes and climbed into bed.

"Of course I thought this was incredibly sexy and interesting. I asked her what they had done together, the three of them. She said that she had kissed this other woman, and fondled her breasts, and then gone down on her while she had given her husband oral sex. I said, my God, I could never have sex with another woman. But Laura said, 'You'd be surprised, it's so different from the way you think it is. For instance, have you kissed another woman . . . I mean kissed her properly?'

"I said of course not. But Laura was sitting right next to me on the couch and she put her arms around me and kissed me. Very slowly, she didn't force me. I could smell her perfume and I could taste her lipstick.

"She ran her hands through my hair, and then she

opened her mouth a little way and slid her tongue into my mouth. She was the first person I'd kissed like that since Steve and I were married, and she was definitely the first woman I'd ever kissed like that.

"I didn't know what to think. but she kept on kissing me, again and again, and soon I found I was kissing her back, and sliding my tongue into *her* mouth, too. I was very excited, I wanted to do it more and more and never stop.

"She unbuttoned my blouse and felt my breasts through my bra. I kept thinking, this is wrong, I'm not a lesbian. But Laura must have guessed what I was thinking, because she said, 'Just because you enjoy sex with another woman that doesn't make you gay, does it? Gay is what you are inside; sex is what you do on the outside.'

"She was wearing this loose white sweater. She pulled it off over her head, and then she took off her bra. I hadn't realized how big her breasts were until she did that. They were enormous, but they were very firm, and a beautiful shape, and very wide nipples. She held them up in her hands and said, 'Go ahead, touch them,' and so I did, and they felt wonderful. They were so warm and heavy and soft-skinned.

"She unfastened my bra, and took it off, so that I was bare-breasted too. She held me close so that our breasts squashed against each other. She kissed me again, and then she kissed my neck and my shoulders and all around my breasts. She held one breast in both hands and licked at the nipple with the tip of her tongue, so quickly that it was like watching one of those humming-birds. Then she went to the other breast. Nobody had ever licked my nipples like that before, ever, and began to feel that I was going to have an orgasm without Laura even touching me anyplace else.

"But she said, 'Come on, let me show you,' and she stood me up, and unzipped my jeans. I felt a little frightened, then, but she kissed me again and said, 'See how much you like it . . . if you don't like it, we can always stop.'

"I think that persuaded me more than anything, because men never say that to you . . . they just *assume* that you're going to like it, and too bad if you don't. She pulled my jeans right off, and then she took down my panties. She sat me back down on the couch and then she quickly took off her own jeans. Underneath she was wearing white see-through nylon panties and I could see that she didn't have any pubic hair at all, just bare pussy. She didn't take off her panties at first, but she kissed me and kissed my breasts, and then she ran her tongue all the way across my bare stomach and down the sides of my thighs. Then she licked me all the way up the insides of my thighs from my knees to my pussy. I could feel her long hair tickling my thighs. Then I felt her fingers opening up my pussy lips. Then I felt her tongue tip on my clitoris, only the tiniest, quickest flicker—one of those feelings that almost drives you crazy because it's so delicious that you have to have more of it, but when you try to have more of it you lose it altogether.

"I buried my hands in her beautiful long hair and stroked her ears and her cheeks and I closed my eyes and let her carry me away. She was so skillful with her tongue, I didn't care whether she was a man or a woman or an alien from another planet. All I could feel was this warm wet tongue flicking my clitoris, and then slowly licking down to my pee hole (urethra). She licked all around that, and even stuck the tip of her tongue a little way into it. Then she continued on down and licked all around my vagina. I shuddered, but she said 'Ssh,' and she reached up with one hand and started to massage my left breast and gently twist my nipple around and around.

"She kissed my pussy, with her tongue slipping right inside my vagina, and licking the walls of it. She could kiss and lick so beautifully, I couldn't believe it. She licked all around my asshole, and pushed her tongue into that, too. Then her tongue went back to my clitoris, and now she started turning me on for real.

"Nobody, but nobody, had licked me like that before. I was so wet that I was leaving a damp patch on the couch. But still Laura wouldn't stop. She went on licking me faster and faster, until it seemed like the whole room went dark. She told me that I screamed when I had an orgasm, but I didn't hear myself. I can remember bucking up and down, and I remember her tongue still flicking at me long after my orgasm was over, so that I kept twitching and twitching. I opened my eyes and I looked down and I was just in time to see her sticking two fingers into my vagina, and then taking them out again and licking them.

" 'Tastes delicious,' she said. Then she said, 'Here,' and took off her panties, and climbed on top of me, so that her bare pussy was right in front of my face. I looked at it for a long time—more out of curiosity than anything else. You don't often get the chance to look at another woman's pussy so close. Her pussy lips were quite dark because she was so dark-skinned, but inside it was bright pink, and it was shining with juice, just like mine was.

"She said, 'You can touch, if you like.' But she didn't make me feel that I *had* to, like men do when they suggest that you take hold of their cocks.

"She looked back at me and smiled, and it was such a beautiful smile. Her breasts were hanging down and when she moved her nipples brushed against my stomach.

"I reached up, very cautiously, and I ran my fingertip down between her legs, from her asshole to her clitoris. She said, 'That's nice,' and it *was* nice, it was all wet and warm and plump, like some kind of split-open fruit. I couldn't believe that I was doing it, touching another woman this way, but I was so excited that I guess I blocked out all my inhibitions.

"I opened her pussy with both hands. A big fat drop of clear juice dripped out it and fell onto my chest. I opened it wider and looked inside. It was such a beautiful color, all shiny pink, and it was such a beautiful shape. I felt as if she'd told me a wonderful secret.

"She didn't encourage me, she didn't say anything, but I lifted my head and kissed her pussy with my lips. I licked my lips and tasted her juice and it was such a strange flavor . . . like fruit juice and salt and very thin honey. I licked her pussy again, and then again, and then again. I couldn't get enough of it. I got so excited I pressed my whole face into her bare wet pussy, with my nose right inside her vagina. I had juice all over my chin and even my eyelashes were sticking together.

"I licked her and licked her. Her clitoris was standing out, swelling bigger and harder. She began to shake and pant and sweat. Her breasts were swinging and I reached underneath her and took hold of them, one big breast in each hand, and squeezed them and dug my fingernails into them and pulled at her nipples. All the time I kept licking her clitoris and all around her vagina.

"I didn't think for a moment that what I was doing was wrong or unnatural. I didn't love her; I wasn't in love with her; but we were two people enjoying each other's bodies and enjoying all the excitement of sex, and if we happened to be two women instead of a man and a woman, what difference did it make? I loved licking her, it was so different and so exciting. I dipped my finger into her vagina to wet it and then I screwed it slowly into her bottom. Steve used to do that to me, when we first made love together, and I used to love it, but he hadn't done it for three or four years. I just wanted to know what effect it would have on Laura. I was licking her clitoris, and right in front of me, only about an inch away, was my finger buried in her anus, right up to the knuckle, and every time she squeezed it, every time her anus puckered up, I could see it in every detail. What amazed me was that she didn't have a single hair, not even around her asshole. Her pussy was completely smooth and bare. It was like she was 'nakeder than naked.'

"She climaxed, and when she climaxed she was very wet. It poured out of her vagina almost like she was pissing, although she wasn't. I took almost a mouthful of it, and swallowed it, and didn't taste of anything but sugary water. But Laura leaned forward and she shook and she shook and she didn't stop shaking for almost a minute. I lay back on the couch and I felt really strange, like 'I've just had sex with a woman!' but Laura turned herself around and hugged me and held me close and kissed me.

"She reached down between her legs and smothered her hand with wet juice. She massaged my breasts with it, pulling my nipples until they were stiff, and then sucking them, too. She sat on my chest with her legs wide apart and took hold of each of my breasts and pressed them right into her wet vagina, flicking my nipples against her clitoris. Both of my breasts were covered in juice, and she massaged them like she was using massage oil.

"I guess we could have gone on making love for hours. I loved the feel of her body, the softness of her skin, the way her breasts squashed in my fingers. I loved the taste of her juice, and I loved her gentleness. She licked me like a butterfly; she kissed me like an angel. We spent almost a half-hour in each other's arms, not saying very much. Then she sat up, and opened up my legs, opened them really wide, and dipped her head down and licked and sucked my pussy. She said, 'I want a good taste in my mouth to take home.' "

Many women enjoy sexual stimulation with partners of the same sex—and this is not to say that they are necessarily lesbian. Many men enjoy sexual stimulation with other men, particularly group or mutual masturbation, and this doesn't necessarily mean that they are gay.

Remember: there is nothing wrong with any sex act which two (or more) people mutually enjoy, and which involves no physical or emotional risk.

Verna wasn't a lesbian, but it did take another woman to help her understand the lightness and the delicacy and the skill that it takes for one person to arouse another. She had accepted Steve's infrequent and uninspired lovemaking for too long, and it was critical for her to educate him as soon as possible, so that he would give her the kind of loving she both needed and deserved.

Incidentally, I have advocated for years that lovers ought to taste their own love juices, so that they are familiar with the tastes and the consistencies of the fluids that they expect their partners to enjoy. Men should masturbate and swallow their own sperm; women should lick their own vaginal juices. The smells and the tastes that are produced by sexual secretions are enormously powerful aphrodisiacs; and even people who have expressed extreme reluctance to try oral sex become "oral sex addicts," and find that they can't get enough of those particularly pungent fragrances and flavors. Some companies have tried to produce sprays and lotions that simulate the odors produced by human sexual organs, such as SHR Natural Feel Secretion which is supposed to "feel and smell like a rampant bippy." Other companies produce male pheromone sprays which allegedly smell like sweaty testicles and rampant penises, and are supposed to bring women running.

Smells *do* have a very strong sexual effect. Norman Mailer mentions in his biography of Marilyn Monroe that she upset the assistant at a fashionable clothes store because she wore no underwear and she smelled of recent intercourse. One famous financier refused to let his Titian-haired wife bathe for days on end because he was sexually excited by the smell of "ripe redhead."

In fact, the sexual effect of smells is so strong that I once recommended to men who want to arouse their girlfriends that they should masturbate into their shorts a couple of hours before their date—literally "creaming their jeans"—and that women should masturbate before a date, making sure that they insert the fingers of both hands into their vagina and anus, and then trail their fingertips right under their partners' noses.

Hygiene of course is essential in sex: but you will be amazed by the effect that a waft of vaginal secretions has on a man. I talked to one young wife who inserted nine cherry tomatoes into her vagina and then served them (unwashed) to her husband. His verdict? "These are the best-tasting tomatoes I ever ate—where d'you get 'em?" Maybe you ought to try it. Or maybe you ought to try the sexual come-on that always arouses Tim, 37, from Darien, Connecticut: "My wife Sue wears her G-string panties all week, and when I go to work on Monday I always find them, unwashed, in my briefcase. They're black or white nylon, lace pattern, so they're small enough to crush up into your fist. I can sit through executive meetings breathing in the smell of the nylon that was next to my wife's vagina for the past seven days; and the elastic that was pulled up tight between the cheeks of her bottom. Ripe, strong and exciting. I could never wait to get home."

Women who use their imagination rarely find that

their sexual relationships flag. There's nothing wrong in being risqué now and again. One wife packed sexually suggestive audiotapes in her husbands luggage when he went abroad on business meetings, so that he could sit in executive-class listening to all of the erotic things that she was going to do to him when he got home.

Another took highly explicit Polaroids of herself in sexy underwear, and concealed them in her husband's luggage.

It isn't necessary to have a partner who travels away from home to try little erotic tricks like this. One man found a vibrator and a pair of crotchless panties under his pillow when he went to bed, and a perfumed note from his wife saying, "How about it? Love, F."

How did Verna use her newly awakened skills in her relationship with Steve? She liked Laura so much that she decided that she wanted to show him how creative and sensitive lovemaking could be, and that the best way of doing it would be for all three of them to go to bed together.

"A few days after Steve came back from Jersey, I invited Laura to have dinner with us. Steve didn't mind at all because he liked Laura as much as I did. Halfway through the evening, I arranged for a friend of mine to telephone to say that he was Laura's landlord and that a pipe had burst in her apartment. Of course Steve immediately suggested that Laura stay the night.

"We had a wonderful dinner together with lots of wine. I don't think Steve suspected that anything had happened between us, but the atmosphere was quite electric because Laura and I were both very excited about what we were going to do. When I carried the plates into the kitchen she kissed me and squeezed my breasts through my dress. I touched her breasts, too. She was wearing a very low-cut bodysuit and I was very daring and slipped my hand into it, and into her bra, so that I could stroke her nipples.

"After dinner we sat around for a long while, drinking wine and talking and listening to music. Laura sat very close to Steve and kept touching his hand when she was talking and leaning across him whenever she wanted more wine so that her breast brushed against his arm. I could see that he was very attracted to her, and the strange thing was that instead of feeling jealous, which I always used to do whenever a pretty girl started coming on to Steve, I actually felt more excited, because I knew that *I* could have sex with Laura, too.

"When it came to bedtime, we let Laura use the bathroom first and I lent her one of my nightshirts. I went through to our bedroom to undress, and Laura said good night to Steve by giving him a kiss. It was quite a kiss, too, by the sound of it! But that's what we'd planned.

"Steve and I got into bed and Steve was already turned-on. His cock was sticking out and he was all ready to get on top of me and fuck me without any foreplay at all. But it was then that Laura knocked on the bedroom door and asked if she could borrow some nail-polish remover. When she came into the bedroom she sat on the edge of the bed (which we'd prearranged between us) and started talking about how wonderful our evening together had been. So I said, 'It doesn't have to end yet, does it?' and I pulled the sheet aside and said, 'Why don't you join us?'

"That was the critical moment and my heart was pounding like crazy. I don't think Steve could believe what was happening. I said, 'You don't mind, do you, darling?' and he just looked at me with his eyes as wide as saucers and shook his head.

"Laura went around the bed and climbed in next to Steve. She cuddled up close to him and said, 'This is cozy, isn't it?' I think he nearly climaxed on the spot. I cuddled up to Steve on the other side, and kissed him and ruffled his hair. Laura started kissing him, too; and then she leaned across him and kissed me. We gave him a demonstration of really erotic tongue-kissing right in front of his face . . . licking and sucking each other's lips, and sticking our tongues in and out of each other's mouths.

"I reached down and cupped Steve's balls in my hand. They were wrinkled and tight, and his cock was hard like the bedpost and running with juice. I didn't dare to rub his cock because I knew that he would shoot out much too soon, before we'd had any fun.

"I drew down the sheet, and showed Steve's hard-on

to Laura. She gently ran her fingers down it, and between us we both fondled his balls. We were all so excited that we could hardly breathe!

"Laura knelt up and pulled her nightshirt over her head. Her breasts swung bare and Steve didn't need any coaxing to take them into his hands and squeeze them and caress them and kiss her nipples. I took my nightgown off, too, and I climbed over Steve and put my arms around Laura. I loved the feeling of her naked body, her breasts pressing against mine. We kissed and touched each other everywhere, and all the time Steve was kissing and stroking both of us. He touched one of my nipples with his juicy cock, and then he touched one of Laura's nipples, and then he held our breasts and slowly rubbed our nipples together. I never had such a feeling in my nipples before, they were actually tingling.

"Laura wriggled down the bed until she was kneeling between my thighs. She parted my legs wide and said to Steve, 'Hold her open for me.' Steve knelt beside me, kissed me, kissed my breasts, and then he reached down and opened my pussy lips with his fingers. Laura said, 'Wider,' and he stretched them apart so that you could see everything. Then Laura leaned forward and flicked my clitoris with the very tip of her tongue, and gently licked my open vagina. She said to Steve, 'Why don't you try it?' so they changed places. Laura held me open while Steve licked me . . . and he licked me like he'd never licked me before. Laura was leaning over me so that her breasts kept swinging and brushing against mine, and I lifted my head a little and opened my mouth and took a mouthful of stiff nipple.

"Steve went on licking and licking and before I knew what was happening I was having an orgasm. He had never made me feel so good before. I held him tight and kissed him and I really felt that something fantastic had happened between us.

"I reached into the nightstand and took out a condom. Steve and I hardly ever used one, except for anal sex, but it wasn't fair to expect Laura to make love without him wearing one. Steve lay on his back on the bed while I held his cock up straight. Laura unwrapped the condom, held it between her lips, and rolled it onto Steve's cock with her mouth, I'd heard about that, but I'd never seen a woman doing it before. She was so good, she did it in one smooth movement, and then she gave him a long suck before she lifted her head up again.

"I sat up, and straddled Steve's hips, and Laura took hold of his cock and guided it up inside my vagina. All the time she was stroking and caressing my pussy lips and my clitoris and prodding my bottom with her finger. Steve started to push up into me. He was very excited now and all he wanted to do was to fuck me very hard and quick. But Laura gripped his balls in her hand and made him slow down. She dug her fingernails into his balls until he said 'ouch!'—even though it turned him on—and she massaged his cock every time it came sliding out of me.

"Then it was her turn. She lay on her back on the bed and lifted her legs so that Steve could put his cock into her from the side. I opened up her bare pussy and helped Steve to slide into her. It was incredible to watch, my husband's hard cock up inside another woman's vagina, sliding in and out. She started to flick her clitoris with her fingers, but I leaned over and started to flick it with my tongue.

"I ran my tongue down to her vagina, and all around Steve's cock, so that I was licking the two of them where they joined. Laura started to make gasping noises, and I licked her clitoris even quicker. I held Steve's balls in one hand, rolling them between my fingers, and with the other hand I played with Laura's left nipple.

"They both came almost together. Laura was shaking and shaking and I thought she was never going to stop. Steve was gripping my hair. I took Steve's cock out of Laura's vagina, and his condom was filled up with sperm. I drew it off him, and slowly massaged him with his own sperm. His cock started to stiffen up again, especially when Laura joined in, and soon it was stiff enough for me to sit on, and have a long, slow fuck, while Steve and Laura kissed each other and Steve played with Laura's breasts. He didn't climax a second time, but it was a beautiful relaxed way of ending the evening.

"We didn't all sleep together—our bed wasn't big enough, and besides it was too hot! We never had a threesome again, either. Laura met one of Steve's friends and started dating, and the last I heard they were thinking of getting married. We still think about that threesome—sometimes I think about it privately, without telling Steve about it. Other times we talk about it to turn each other on.

"But it marked a turning point in our sex lives because we were both shown that we were sexually attractive to other people, and we were both shown that there are dozens of different ways of having a wild time in bed.

Dr. Gilbert D. Bartell, an anthropologist who studied group sex practice in and around Chicago, Illinois, published a three-year study about group sex, and found that the decision to participate in group sex usually came from the man rather than the woman. Although women are much more aware of their sexual status than they were 20 years ago, Western society is still dualistic with the man considered to be the dominant partner in premarital and marital relationships.

Dr. Bartell decided that men involve themselves in group sex in order to act out their sexual fantasies, whereas women use it to fulfill a social-romantic need and to reinforce their feelings of sexual attractiveness.

He claimed that there were several emotional and psychological dangers in group sex, particularly if the man failed to live up to his own sexual self-delusions, and if the woman found that her phsyical appearance did not match up to other women (at least in her own opinion) and that she did not attract as many other males. In some group sex situations, one partner can be more popular than the other, which can introduce a very destructive element of jealousy into the relationship.

On the whole, my experience is that those couples who actively seek to participate in threesomes and other forms of group sex have recognized that their sexual relationship is already seriously lacking, and thus there is very little harm in their looking for new erotic thrills with other people—*provided*, of course, that both partners are equally enthusiastic about group sex, and *provided* that both of them are fully aware that the effects of group sex on an ailing relationship can be unpredictable. It can bring about the end of a relationship just as dramatically as it can revive it.

Always remember that in real group sex (unlike fantasy group sex) the people with whom you will be making love will be real people, with lives and problems and tastes of their own. A woman who is thinking about group sex should ask herself not so much if she fancies the idea of making love with a different man, but whether she can tolerate her partner making love to another woman.

She should also ask herself if she is prepared to take the risk of meeting another man whom she prefers to her existing partner, and if she is prepared to take the risk of her partner meeting another woman whom he prefers to her.

Contrary to many expert predictions of the 1970s, greater sexual knowledge and greater sexual equality between men and women has not led to a widespread breakdown in one-on-one relationships. Percentagewise, the evidence is that there is *less* group sex today than there was 20 years ago. This is not only because of the threat of AIDS, but because couples are finding it easier to talk to each other about their sexual feelings, and willing to work to improve their love lives.

Men are becoming more sensitive to the needs of their women, and women are becoming much more confident abut their ability to satisfy their men (and themselves, too.)

The result is that, 20 years later, you have both the will and the means to drive your man not just wild in bed, but even wilder. Start today!

TEN

Thirty-three Ways to Drive Your Man Even Wilder Tonight

1. Greet him at the door "wearing" bra and panties made of nothing but body paint.
2. Tell him to close his eyes because you have a surprise for him . . . then take out his penis and slip it into your mouth.
3. Wear your shortest skirt, and make it obvious during the evening that you're not wearing any panties.
4. Climb into the tub or shower with him and give him the intimate soaping of his life.
5. Produce a new ladies' razor and a can of shaving gel and say that you were thinking of shaving off your pubic hair . . . but you're sure that he could do it better.
6. Rent or buy a sex video and tell him you want to watch it together.
7. Buy a vibrator and ask him to try it on you.
8. Buy *two* vibrators and ask him to try them on you.
9. Buy *three* vibrators and try one on him while he tries two on you.
10. Lie on the bed waiting for him when he comes out

of the bathroom, wearing nothing but black stockings and a garter belt and a black blindfold.

11. Put a blindfold on him, then tie his wrists with scarves or cords so that he can't escape . . . then give him the longest, slowest sessions of oral sex that he's ever had.
12. Touch him and masturbate him at every possible opportunity . . . when he's reading, when he's watching TV, anytime . . . tell him that you're hungry for his hard-on.
13. Take him to bed and whisper dirty nothings in his ear. *Really* dirty.
14. When he makes love to you, take his penis out before he ejaculates, and finish him off with your hand, so that he ejaculates over your breasts.
15. Give him oral sex, and make a point of aiming his ejaculation over your face.
16. Smear massage oil in your cleavage, so that he can slide his penis between your breasts and make love to you that way.
17. Flavor your nipples with strawberry or mint (or whatever his favorite flavor happens to be) and ask him to taste them.
18. Dangle clip or screw on earrings from your nipples.
19. Clip pendant earrings to your vaginal lips.
20. Insert a flower stem in your anus (not a rose, of course, too thorny!) so that your bottom is decorated with petals.
21. Buy yourself a leather strap suit (or make your own out of thin black leather belts or dog leashes).
22. Tell him he's been neglecting you in bed lately and that you're going to have to punish him with a slipper or a belt on his bare behind (but don't get *too* carried away!).
23. Make a sexy video of yourself during the day and watch it with him in bed.
24. Lubricate your back passage liberally, and then cup your hand over your vagina and refuse to let him make love to you any other way.
25. Buy a strap-on dildo (they're only a little more expensive than hand-held) . . . strap it on, and use it to penetrate him from behind, while you use your

hand to pleasure his penis . . . you'll be amazed how many men enjoy being "taken" by a woman.

26. Show him exactly how he can best stimulate your clitoris with his fingers . . . make him practice until he gets it right.
27. Don't allow him to penetrate you until you've reached your first orgasm.
28. After he's made love to you, give his genitals a luxurious and lascivious tongue bath. You'll be surprised how often this leads to second helpings!
29. Wake him up in the middle of the night by sucking his penis.
30. Leave this book beside the bed, with a bookmark stuck into your favorite page.
31. Tell him your favorite fantasy . . . the one you've never told anybody before.
32. Pack something sexy in his briefcase every day . . . panties, or a picture, or a sexy lettering telling him what you're going to do to him when he gets home.
33. When he gets home . . . do it.